Sir Joh
actors
made h
and ha
perforn
has spa
roles a
the pla
for wh
severa
STAG
TIME

John Gielgud

EARLY STAGES

First published in Great Britain in 1939 by Macmillan and Co. Ltd.

This edition first published by Hodder and Stoughton Ltd. in 1987

Sceptre edition 1990

Sceptre is an imprint of Hodder and Stoughton Paperbacks, a division of Hodder and Stoughton Ltd.

British Library C.I.P.

Gielgud, John, *1904–*
Early stages. – 2nd rev. ed.
1. Gielgud, John 2. Actor – Great Britain – Biography I. Title
792'.028'0924 PN2598.G45

ISBN 0-340-53039-1

Printed and bound in Great Britain for Hodder and Stoughton Paperbacks, a division of Hodder and Stoughton Ltd., Mill Road, Dunton Green, Sevenoaks, Kent TN13 2YA. (Editorial Office: 47 Bedford Square, London WC1B 3DP) by Richard Clay Ltd., Bungay, Suffolk.

CONTENTS

Richard II, Old Vic, 1929
Lino-cut by Pauline Logan

My experiences convinced me that the actor must imagine first and observe afterwards. It is no good observing life and bringing the result to the stage without a definite idea. The idea must come first, the realism afterwards.

ELLEN TERRY
The Story of my Life

An actor hearing an author read a play in which he is to impersonate a character ought never to be told in advance the part which is to be assigned to him, as otherwise he only pays languid attention to everything that is not his part, and the ideas of the author escape him. He forgets too often that he is not himself the keyboard but that he forms part of the general harmony.

SARAH BERNHARDT
The Art of the Theatre

FOREWORD TO THE REVISED EDITION

This book was first published by Macmillan as long ago as 1939. It was republished by the Falcon Press in 1948, but has been out of print for many years. Since then I have written three further books, *Stage Directions*, *Distinguished Company*, and *An Actor and his Time* and a biography of me by Ronald Hayman was published in 1971. A further biography by Gyles Brandreth, *A Celebration* was published three years ago, in 1984.

This new edition of *Early Stages* is ostensibly the same as the 1939 edition except for a few minor cuts and revisions. The impetus which originally gave me the idea of writing this book was my wish to describe the Terry family (my relations on my mother's side) while the impact of their remarkable personalities was still comparatively fresh in my memory, though none of them were still alive by 1936, the year in which I started work on the book. These passages, I hope, may still stand as something of my own individual record of their remarkable charm and talents.

In this new edition I have added four short excerpts of mine which I wrote for another book: Hallam Fordham's 'Photobiography' of me, published by John Lehmann in 1952 and now out of print. The first of these excerpts I have included as a Preface—and the others as a Coda. These bring my story another thirteen years forward and seem to me to follow smoothly on the original narrative.

1987 JOHN GIELGUD

ACKNOWLEDGEMENTS

I am greatly indebted to Phyllis Hartnoll and Alan Dent who gave me such invaluable help with the first edition of this book. I am also grateful to Alan Dent for compiling the index.

PREFACE

The expression 'Let's go to a show' is currently used nowadays to refer to all forms of entertainment including the living theatre. This expression would have horrified my relations, the players of a former generation, who always spoke of the theatre as their 'work', and of the 'play' or the 'piece' in which they were appearing. They also liked to mention that they had been offered (or had accepted) an 'engagement'. Yet it is the 'show' that has always appealed to me in the theatre, and I have never been able to look at a play from a purely literary point of view, or care very greatly for its intellectual or philosophical contribution, unless its theatrical effectiveness has appealed to me first.

I was born into the purple of the Terry family (though my parents were neither of them at any time upon the stage), so it was natural, I suppose, that the theatre should have attracted me at an early age. It appealed to my eyes first, soon it caught at my heart, and lastly its magic reached my ear. Colour, romance, and passion—suspense, action, splendour and emotional self-indulgence—all these I longed for and revelled in from my youngest days of theatregoing. The writing of a play meant little to me, and the art of acting I took for granted.

Consequently it was many years before I began to understand anything of the selective control and technical skill needed by an actor. I thought acting was an imitation of life, that emotion had only to be felt in order to be expressed upon the stage. The art of diction, timing, rapport with other actors, pace, clarity, style, the means of reproducing a part continually over a number of performances—of all this I was entirely ignorant. I found it very hard, as a beginner, to concentrate on my own small part and work at it doggedly in order to perfect it. I was often more interested in the other characters than in the rôle I played myself. As soon as I began to think how *I* must walk and speak and act I was paralysed by self-consciousness and affectation.

I did not know then that my real ambition was not to act but to direct. I think I began to suspect it a little when I worked with Komisarjevsky, after I had been an actor for three or four fumbling years. It was his influence that set my feet, for the first time, on the right track in my attitude towards my work. Acting in Chekhov under his direction, I began to realize how a part should be lived from within, and how certain significant characteristics from that life should be selected in order to illuminate the character in the particular situations demanded by the author. From him I learnt, too, the essence of musical form with which all good acting and direction must be concerned—the pace and rhythm, tune and shape of scenes and speeches, as well as the art and force of pause, crescendo, and climax.

Ambitious as I was from the first to see my name outside a West End theatre, I was, as it turned out later, fortunate in being considered, as a young actor, to be highbrow and precociously unreliable. I was not sufficiently handsome to be immediately eligible for the juvenile leads who decorated many of the fashionable plays of the twenties, swinging their tennis racquets in open-necked shirts and immaculate white flannels. My only experiment of this kind (in the immortal *Charley's Aunt*) was a conspicuous failure, and I was not to attempt a similar part (Inigo Jollifant in *The Good Companions*) until nine years later, when I was a comparatively seasoned veteran and had played both Hamlet and King Lear.

J. B. Fagan, Nigel Playfair, Barry Jackson and Komisarjevsky were the first to show an interest in my early amateurish efforts at self-expression. They developed my taste by engaging me to act in fine plays with many gifted players. I was observant and industrious, though also vain and affected.

It was a good time for experimental work, done modestly and cheaply. Classical revivals were out of fashion. The actor managers' reign was over. The London theatre was recovering slowly from the confusion of the 1914–18 war. Noël Coward was writing his first play. Basil Dean's productions at the St. Martin's were the most ambitious contribution to the new era. The other West End theatres were mostly filled with light comedies, farces and melodramas, many of them, even in those far-off days, imported from America.

Barrie, Galsworthy and Pinero were almost at the end of their long and successful careers, though Maugham and Shaw were still to write several of their best plays.

The most popular stars of the period were probably Gerald du Maurier, Henry Ainley, Marie Tempest, Gladys Cooper and Matheson Lang, the last-named (with his costume and melodramas) carrying on the romantic tradition of Fred Terry and Martin Harvey, both of whom only appeared occasionally in London but still toured the provinces successfully. Ellen Terry had made her last professional appearance at the Lyric as the Nurse in Doris Keane's *Romeo and Juliet* in 1919, and Bernhardt and Duse were about to make their farewell visits to London under the banner of C. B. Cochran (who also presented the Guitrys—with Yvonne Printemps, and Reinhardt's great spectacles *The Miracle* and *Sumurûn* at Olympia and the Coliseum). Karsavina was still appearing with the Russian Ballet of Diaghilev at the old Alhambra. Sybil Thorndike was acting in Grand Guignol, and was not to play *Saint Joan* until 1924.

Players still took curtain calls after every act of a play (even if they had just performed a death scene), and understudies seemed to appear with great frequency in leading parts, especially at matinées. This was lucky for the understudies (and I have always boasted that I never understudied a leading part in my young days without getting an opportunity to play it), but it was less agreeable for the public: I well remember my baffled rage as a boy, when, after three or four hours' queueing for the pit during my holidays from school, the slip fluttering from the programme told of the absence of the star whom I most desired to see.

As a beginner my career was uneven and seemed to lead in no particularly definite direction. I was tall, mannered, highly strung. I spoke and moved jerkily, my emotions were sincere but undisciplined, I had some gift for character, some feeling for poetry, some idea of timing in comedy, yet my sense of humour was strictly limited by a youthful self-importance and terror of being ridiculed. I longed for encouragement and popularity, and count myself fortunate now (though at the time I resented it bitterly) that I had candid friends who laughed at my obsession with myself and the theatre, and made fun of my mannerisms and vanities at a time when a crowd of sycophantic admirers might have encouraged me to a fatal indulgence in my worst faults. Several times in these early years I seemed to be bound for a certain success in London—each time some chance intervened to disappoint me and I was forced to make another start on a slightly less ambitious scale. When I finally decided to go to the Old Vic in 1929 I had already been a leading man (of a sort) in the West End for three years, but the haphazard mixture of parts which had come my way made me feel that I was chosen at random and that no manager or director cared particularly whether or not he engaged me, and it depressed me, even then, to be drawn out of a hat, as it were, from a crowd of other competing players, for a juvenile part of no particular quality, even though the living this offered me was a fairly good one. The special performances in which I had appeared for the Sunday societies, my work at Barnes with Komisarjevsky and at the Regent with Playfair, had given me greater artistic satisfaction than my run of over a year in Basil Dean's *Constant Nymph* with a star cast in the West End, and I vaguely felt that in Shakespeare I might somehow satisfy some of my ambitions, and develop such latent abilities as I believed were lurking in me, if only I could find a way of expressing them successfully.

CHAPTER ONE

1904–12

Shortly before I was born my parents moved into a new house.

Mother, with her usual care as a housewife, insisted on sitting in the hall to watch the furniture being unloaded from the vans. Somebody suggested that the cradle ought to be brought in first, as it was obvious that it might be needed at any moment. I suppose this was my first attempt at working up an entrance, as we say on the stage.

The new house was tall and thin and semi-detached. The square in which it stood was most confusingly numbered and the houses all looked alike, so we were grateful for the one original feature ours possessed. We used to shout to the cabdrivers who tried to take us the wrong way, 'No, no. Number 7. In the Main road. The house with the blue window-boxes'.

There was stained-glass in the hall, and an enormous basement below, to which we sometimes penetrated, clattering down the wooden stairs to stir the Christmas puddings in the kitchen or watch Mother sorting large piles of linen in the servants' hall.

Our nurseries were upstairs on the third floor, with a gate on the landing and wire-netting to prevent us from tumbling over the banisters—one of my recurring nightmares when I was little.

The house was very draughty, and there was never enough hot water for baths, but I loved every inch of it, and, perhaps because *The Cherry Orchard* had in the meantime become one of my favourite plays, I felt quite a Chekhovian regret when I came to leave it for ever, some twenty-five years later. (It has since been converted into flats.)

I have two elder brothers, and one sister, three years younger than myself. I can remember seeing her in one of those wooden pens where very young children are put just before they can walk, and solemnly shaking hands with her over the top. I can also dimly recall my nurse washing herself as she got up in the night nursery, before we were supposed to be awake, and wondering at her many petticoats and the elaborate way she did her hair. She used to wear filigree silver belts, lace blouses with ribs in the neck and a watch on a silver bow. I remember the pain of having appendicitis, and being operated on in the day nursery in a great hurry, and walking to my first kindergarten school with my father. He used to madden me by crossing the streets at exactly the same kerbstone every morning. I did not greatly care for the kindergarten, it appears. On the first day I sat down in the middle of the room and burst into tears. 'But, darling, this isn't school. It is only play', someone said, at which I cried all the more and proclaimed loudly, 'I want to go to a real school, like my brothers'.

Our name is Lithuanian—not Scottish, as many people imagine. It lends itself to an amazing variety of mispronunciations and strange spellings. (Mother once had a letter addressed to Mrs Gradgrind.) Everyone told me I ought to change it when I first went on the stage but I was very obstinate on the subject. My father's grandfather, another John Gielgud, who had fought with the Polish cavalry, left his native country after the insurrection of 1831, when his brother, General Anthony Gielgud, was killed and the family estates were confiscated. Father's parents were both Polish, but my grandfather was born in England. He worked at the War Office for some years, and was Foreign Correspondent to a number of newspapers.

I feel that I ought to apologize for this rather scrappy information about my Polish ancestors. I have never been able to follow the various ramifications of father's family, and my mother's theatrical relations, the Terrys, always had the stronger hold upon my interest. I gather that the Gielguds were patriots, with more enthusiasm than competence; but I was very much interested to hear that my father's grandmother had been a very well-known Polish actress, Madame Aszperger. I believe that a bust of her still stands in the foyer of the Opera House at Lvov. My father, when he was a little boy, was sometimes sent to stay with her in her flat, which was over the theatre, and on one occasion, when he had been naughty, she took him out of bed and put him into one of the boxes to watch the performance. I was not surprised to hear that this treatment restored him to good behaviour immediately.

Father's parents were not well-off, but they were charming and cultured and knew many of the artistic and literary celebrities of the day. Among these were the Arthur Lewises and their four daughters, of whom my mother was the eldest. Arthur Lewis was a rich man who loved entertaining. He was one of the directors of Lewis and Allenby, a well-known and fashionable haberdasher's shop in Conduit Street. He was also an enthusiastic amateur painter and often exhibited at the Royal Academy. He owned a beautiful house on Campden Hill, called Moray Lodge, where he gave parties and organized a mildly Bohemian Glee Club called 'the Moray Minstrels'. At Moray Lodge you could wander in the garden, sniff the hay, and perhaps meet a cow which the Lewises kept for fresh milk for the children. Such was the blessed rusticity of Kensington in the eighties. You might also see Arthur Lewis at his easel, and his wife and daughters, wearing bustles, playing lawn-tennis or sitting under the trees. There were horses and grooms, dog-carts and a conservatory, and a Highland cottage called *Divach* near Inverness, where the family went for summer holidays.

At Moray Lodge, and in Scotland too, there were parties, picnics, governesses, children, distinguished visitors, and all the leisured comfort of late Victorian family life, made more exciting in this particular family by a (strictly proper) link with the arts and the theatre, for Kate Terry, the eldest sister of the family to which Ellen, Marion, and Fred belonged, had married Arthur Lewis in 1867.

Her four daughters, though they adored their father, were all proud to use their mother's name as well, and the two who did not marry, and the third, who kept her maiden name for the stage, called themselves Terry-Lewis. Grandmother Kate had made the name of Terry famous long before Ellen first appeared. In the short time that she was on the stage she was the rage of London and Manchester, leading lady to Henry Neville, Ophelia to Fechter. She played Juliet, Beatrice, Cordelia, Portia and other Shakespearean heroines, besides the heroines of many plays by authors of her own day. As a child she had been praised by no less a person than Charles Dickens, in a letter that is still treasured by the family, for her performance as Prince Arthur in *King John* with the Charles Keans, and had appeared in most of their famous Shakespearean productions at the Princess's Theatre in Oxford Street. While little Ellen was making her début in the children's parts, acting Mamilius and Puck, Kate was playing leading parts as Ariel and Cordelia. The sisters must have studied together a great deal during these early years, and Kate's salary paid for the education of most of her younger brothers and sisters.

When she married Arthur Lewis, Grandmother was still in her early twenties, but in 1867 she decided to leave the stage. Her farewell performances as Juliet, first in Manchester, then in London at the Adelphi, were great nights in theatrical history. After her wedding she was strong-minded enough to put the thought of acting completely from her, in order to concentrate on the duties of a wife and mother. Kate Terry retired, but many years later in the 1890s, when her youngest daughter, Mabel Terry-Lewis, was to make her début as an actress, her return to the stage was announced. The play was *The Master* and it was produced under the management of John Hare. It was not a success, and I believe my grandmother had a very poor part, but Bernard Shaw, in one of his brilliant notices in the *Saturday Review*, describes her performance vividly. He writes of her coming on as a modest, middle-aged lady, determined to show the audience that she was only there to encourage and help her daughter's first appearance. Then suddenly she seemed unable to help herself, twenty years fell from her in a flash, and she was revealed as the accomplished actress who had forgotten nothing of the mysteries of her craft.

Kate Terry was something of a martinet where her household and children were concerned. The interview between her and my father, when he called at Moray Lodge to ask the hand of her eldest daughter, was an alarming occasion, slightly mitigated by the gentle charm of Arthur Lewis. But all was well in the end, and stately approval was given to the marriage. This was in 1893. Not many years afterwards Arthur Lewis lost his money and had to give up his beautiful houses. He died while I was a child, to the great regret of everyone who loved him, and, by the time I was aware of my grandmother, she was a gay but slightly formidable old lady with a beautiful voice, a fine expressive face, and the Terry nose and mouth. She lived at the far end of the Cromwell Road, which I detested for its dreariness as we walked along it to visit her. Fortunately, we were sure of finding considerable amusement and fascinating company when we arrived. Grandmother's house was small and slightly sinister. There were masses of pictures on the walls, photographs and sculpture everywhere, and an ostrich egg hung in a net in the library window. Grandmother demanded that her many possessions should be scrupulously dusted and kept in order, and the servants were always giving notice. On the ground floor, the sitting-room had sliding doors which led into the dining-room, and when I saw the set for the fourth act of *The Seagull* at the New Theatre in 1935, that room suddenly came back to me, with Grandmother playing Miss Milligan and laughing good-naturedly at the gossip of a very loud-voiced old American lady who was her paying guest. I have always regretted that I was too young to talk much about the theatre to Kate Terry. What thrilling stories she might have told me of the Charles Kean days, with their processions and tableaux and flying ballets and sumptuous archaeological scenic effects. I cannot remember now what I did talk to Grandmother about, but she used to take me to many of my early theatres.

The first play I ever saw was *Peter Pan*, when I was seven. My parents caused me agonies by arriving late. Even now, I cannot bear to miss the beginning of a play. I still love to see the curtain glow as the footlights come up, and to hear the first notes of the orchestra—always provided there is an orchestra. Once, during the First World War, when I was about thirteen years old, my brother came home on leave, and we had a big party at the Gobelins Restaurant, which was fashionable then, for lunch and a matinée of *The Bing Boys on Broadway*. I dismayed the party by making a scene when I saw from the clock that we were twenty minutes late for the performance. When I went to the theatre with Grandmother we nearly always sat in a box, and I would see the principals specially bowing to her when they took their calls. The management would send us tea in the interval, and often we would go round behind and meet the leading actors in their dressing-rooms. Grandmother was a wonderful audience. She laughed and cried whole-heartedly in the theatre, and I naturally did the same. Even today I still weep so easily at a play that I am sometimes ashamed of myself. The Terrys all have the same weakness, on and off the stage. 'Weak lachrymal glands, my dear', said a famous specialist to my mother, who was particularly afflicted in this way. This capacity for crying easily is sometimes useful to me as an actor, and the sight of real tears always impresses those in an audience who are sitting close enough to see them. But on some nights the tears refuse to come, and then I feel I am not giving my best at that particular performance. Fortunately, however, the effect is more important than the tears themselves, which actually convince the actor more than the audience. I remember being much impressed by hearing my cousin, Phyllis Neilson-Terry, say one night, standing in the wings before she went on for an emotional scene, 'Shall I give them real tears to-night?' Although the impulse may be a natural one, crying on the stage is quite a technical feat. One learns to cry with one's eyes, but not, as in real life, to choke or run at the nose. Ellen Terry says in her book 'My real tears on the stage astonished some people, and have been the envy of others, but they have often been a hindrance to me. I have had to *work* to restrain them.'

Sometimes Grandmother would take me to see Fred, Marion and Ellen act. How excited I used to be when I was taken to a theatre where one of them was appearing! I saw Marion in a play called *Wonderful James*. She played the wife of a penniless adventurer who posed as a wealthy man, and in the first act they came together to some business-office. Marion swept in, very dignified, in a grey velvet cloak with ospreys in her hat. Biscuits and port were brought and she went on talking grandly, furtively dropping biscuits into her hand-bag all the time. Later in the play she had a very funny scene in which she sat working a sewing-machine, with an overall over her smart dress, murmuring sadly, 'Nothing in the larder but half a chicken and a bit of tinned tongue!' I saw her play Mrs Higgins in Shaw's *Pygmalion* with Mrs Patrick Campbell, in *Reparation* at the St. James's with Henry Ainley, and, last of all, at the Globe in Somerset Maugham's *Our Betters*. In private life she was regal and kind, with a low voice and very beautiful diction. She had a most charming figure when she was younger, and waltzed with infinite grace. She always spoke of a job as 'an engagement' and told me two things I have never forgotten: 'Never say your salary is so-and-so; let them make you an offer first and then tell them, if necessary, what you had in your last engagement', and 'You must never say it is a bad audience. It is your business to make it a good one.' She was an odd woman in many ways. She had an amazing gift for enslaving people, friends or servants, making them happy to fetch and carry for her, in spite of the fact that she was rather autocratic and exacting in her demands; and she was extremely secretive about her personal life and the state of her finances. On one occasion, I believe, she walked out of Moray Lodge in a rage because Arthur Lewis had looked at her pass-book.

It is sad that Marion has been so soon forgotten. Many people of her time thought her a better actress than her more famous sister. This generation seems scarcely to have heard of her, but there is little doubt that she shared with Mrs Kendal the distinction of being one of the finest comédiennes of her time. Also, like Dame Madge, she was equally good in emotional or sentimental parts. She seldom appeared in Shakespeare but she played occasionally for Ellen at the Lyceum when the latter was ill, and acted some of her parts in provincial tours. My father remembered a wonderful performance she once gave of Rosalind at Stratford-on-Avon. In *Lady Windermere's Fan* she created a precedent by playing an adventuress, a daring departure from her usual run of parts, and it was one of her greatest successes. Years later, something of the same kind was to happen when Lilian Braithwaite played in *The Vortex.* It is always interesting for an audience to see an actress of sympathetic parts playing a 'woman with a past'. As Mrs Erlynne, Marion, with her brown hair powdered with bronze dust, made an enormous success and delighted Wilde, the author of the play, as well as the public. She played with Wyndham and Alexander, created many of the leading parts in the plays of W. S. Gilbert, and was the original Susan Throssel in Barrie's *Quality Street*, in which she appeared with Seymour Hicks and Ellaline Terriss.

When I saw her towards the end of her career in *Reparation* she had only two short scenes, but her performance was immensely distinguished, and Henry Ainley, with his usual courtesy, would bring her out at the end of the play and kiss her hand before the audience. I remember another example of Ainley's tact and fine manners. The occasion was a not very successful opening performance of *Much Ado about Nothing* in which he had played Benedick, very finely I thought, to Madge Titheradge's Beatrice. When the play was over, he stepped forward, and bowing towards the stage box where Ellen Terry was sitting, half hidden by the curtains, he said, 'We have had the honour of playing before the greatest Beatrice of all time'.

Like Ellen and Fred, Marion had great difficulty with her memory in later years, and her devoted nieces would spend hours helping her to memorize her lines. She was very reluctant to admit her weakness in this direction, and developed a brilliant technique for covering her lapses or mistakes, gazing majestically at the other actors until the prompter came to her rescue.

Florence Terry, another sister, died at an early age. I never knew her. Edith Craig has told me that Florence had had little recognition from biographers, though her talent was also considerable. She played Nerissa to Ellen's Portia, both at the Lyceum and on tour, and the sisters loved acting together in their charming scenes. Florence and Marion were very devoted and were often photographed together.

Though Kate and Marion Terry were sisters, they were actresses too, and I had an amusing glimpse of this when I went one evening in 1919, with my mother this time, to the first night of *Romeo and Juliet* at the Lyric Theatre, when Ellen Terry played the Nurse to Doris Keane's Juliet. Kate and Marion were standing together in the foyer as we passed. They chatted together, and people going in bowed to them, thinking no doubt that the scene was a pretty expression of family affection. But no! It was the Terry blood and not the Terry charm which was at work. They were to enter the auditorium of a theatre. I did not understand why they parted, Kate to enter the stalls by one door and Marion by another. Kate must have hurried, for she entered the right-hand door first. As I walked down the opposite passage to the stalls with my mother I could hear the applause, and we saw Grandmother smiling and bowing as we went to our seats. Then Marion entered, close behind us, and received an ovation from the audience. But I made the mistake of saying to her proudly in the interval, 'Grandmother had a wonderful reception'. Aunt Marion's voice was very gentle as she answered, 'Did she, darling? I expect they thought it was me.'

Fred Terry and his lovely wife, Julia Neilson, were my idols of course. I saw them first together on the stage in *Sweet Nell of Old Drury* and I remember how Julia saw us and threw a dazzling smile in the direction of our box. On another afternoon I was taken down to the Boro' Theatre, Stratford, now, alas, no more, to see *The Scarlet Pimpernel*. After the play I went round to the stage-door. It was a dark foggy evening. Uncle Fred came out on to the step in all the glory of his white satin and lace, and pressed a sovereign into my hand, like some dandified deity from Olympus.

By this time I was deep in dressing up, charades and acting games of all kinds. I was about eight or nine years old. I was not yet stage-struck in the sense of wanting to go on the stage, and I am not conscious of any moment when I suddenly sat up and said 'I am going to be an actor'. But I see now that my Terry instinct to act was pretty strong from the beginning, though I did not recognize it at the time. I was supposed to be delicate when I was a child, and I enjoyed and exaggerated my illnesses, with the special food and added attentions. My mother used to read aloud to me. Scott rather bored me, and I used to be horribly embarrassed by the passages which she rendered in a rather good Scotch accent. But Dickens I loved. We would both be quite overcome with emotion in the sentimental scenes, and by the time we had killed Dora or Sydney Carton we would both be choking and 'too full of woe to speak'!

When I was recovering from some disease or other (jaundice or chicken-pox, I forget which) I developed a passion for painting backcloths and designs in pastel for my toy theatre. The colours, in spite of liberal applications of 'Fixatif', which smelt like pear-drops, would blow about all over the room and make chalky smears everywhere. I used to prop my cardboard scenery on the mantelpiece and get up in the middle of the night and turn on the light to look at it. (Already I had the stage illusion that everything looks twice as good by artificial light.) I was furious next morning because the doctor seemed too busy to congratulate me when I drew his attention to my efforts. I was very fond of an audience. I found that I could play the Merry Widow Waltz by ear, and was deeply hurt when, after a triumphant rendering of it for my nurse's benefit she said drily, 'Your bass is wrong, and it isn't written in that key', and sat down and played it correctly herself.

My eldest brother Lewis was a scholar at Eton, and there were three of us upstairs in the nursery, my sister Eleanor, my brother Val and myself. We began our stage enterprises with a model theatre—an inspiring affair of cream and gold with a red velvet curtain, given me as a birthday present by Mother. We all made up plays and took turns in performing them, standing behind the theatre and moving the leaden figures about with our hands which were plainly seen by the audience. Cardboard figures with wires were too flimsy and difficult to manage, we decided, and in the strangely unquestioning manner of children we accepted the giant's hands moving about in every scene, and simply ignored their existence. Val was responsible for most of the plots and dialogue, and I used to paint the scenery. I had a very strong feeling for space and colour on the stage from the first, and the fascination of scenery, costume and pictorial illusion has never left me. As a child I had no real talent in this direction or I should certainly have become a scenic designer and not an actor at all, but in those early days it was the scenery first and the play afterwards so far as I was concerned.

We were very mercenary in the management of our theatre. Val and I were partners in management, in the manner of Uncle Fred. My sister was 'Lady Jones', a fabulously rich patron of the theatre who financed our brave productions. As a family the Terrys have not a great sense of humour (Ellen always excepted), and we played the theatre game all day long with dreadful seriousness. 'Lady Jones' financed us in a series of alarming plays dealing with our grand Terry relations. In one of these we put Grandmother Kate Terry on the stage, and most of our aunts as well. There was a ship scene, with Grandmother in the throes of seasickness shouting for her deaf maid. We thought this Family Play extremely funny, but unlike our more serious performances—mystery plays, costume melodramas and society triangles, to which we tried to inveigle an audience of parents or servants—it could only be performed in guilty secret.

On the top floor of the house was an attic in which Val and I laid down an intricate model railway system. Here also were Val's toy soldiers. He must have had nearly a thousand of them, and amused himself ceaselessly with battles and manœuvres. We came to a working agreement by which Val helped me with my theatre on condition that I took part in his campaigns upstairs. I fancy that he got the best of the bargain, for he entered into my form of make-believe with enthusiasm, while I was rather bored by his. The most practical use his soldiers had, so far as I could see, was to serve as puppets in my theatre. I used to steal them when he was not looking and convert them to my own use by judicious applications of gold paint. I also used the passengers of a toy station that I had been given. Two ladies in motor veils and red Edwardian dresses did duty for almost every female character and I spent hours transforming them with plasticine into Elizabethans, a sticky and unconvincing process. I used also to invent opportunities for firework displays, and compile scenarios which involved magic thunderstorms or naval reviews with showers of electric sparklers and magnesium flares. Where the requirements of my theatre were concerned I was quite shameless. I robbed the canary of its seed and sand for a convincing 'set' representing a stormy desert, and stole the miniature grand piano out of Eleanor's doll's house for a drawing-room scene.

Not only did we play the soldier game and the theatre game continually, but we kept wonderful notebooks in which we recorded every detail of both games with a wealth of lavish journalistic style. My mother has preserved one of the volumes in which some of our magnificent productions are recorded. The title-page announces grandiloquently, 'The New Mars Theatre, in Trafalgar Square, W.1. Erected between April 1912 and March 1913. A list of plays produced between 1913 and 1919. Under the joint management of V. H. and A. J. Gielgud.'[1] It should be noticed that 'Lady Jones', though she certainly did her duty as the principal and frequently the only member of our audience, receives no kind of recognition. The plays have imposing titles: *Lady Fawcett's Ruby*—this has a pleasing ring of Pinero or Wilde—*Kill That Spy*, a war play, of course—and *Plots in the Harem*, probably inspired by *Kismet* and *Chu-Chin-Chow*. The volume is embellished by a photograph of the Mars Theatre, with Val, Eleanor and myself posed in front of it. Val is sitting stiffly in a chair, wearing a straw hat. I am on the ground in less formal headgear, and Eleanor has the uneasy air and ingratiating smile of someone who is there on sufferance—which she probably was.

When we became older, Val was given the nursery for his study and I was allowed to instal my paints, books, gramophone and records, and of course the theatre, in the attic. This was to be my own special room until I left home to take a flat for myself. I spent hours up there designing and constructing stage scenery, years after we had outgrown the theatre game. We no longer fought campaigns or made up plays, and I built my sets more solidly with bricks and plasticine, and balanced electric bulbs hanging at the end of wires above the stage, on piles of books, boxes and magazines. Sometimes in the middle of the night, jumping out of bed and creeping upstairs to look again at some marvel I had created earlier in the day, I would trip over the wires in the dark, and everything would collapse with a loud crash and wake the entire household. I felt sure that I was destined to be a stage designer if only I

[1] I was christened Arthur John.

could manage to draw correctly, but my father kept telling me that I would first have to study architecture, and, with my utter incapacity for maths, this prospect filled me with dismay.

One afternoon Uncle Fred had treated me to a terrific luncheon at the Eccentric Club. The lunch had been delicious, but not an unqualified success so far as I was concerned. Over the soup I had rashly enthused over my second cousin, Gordon Craig, the son of Ellen Terry. Fred was somewhat sceptical and I did not then know that he had recently suffered an expensive failure with *Sword and Song*, a play which Craig had decorated (very beautifully) for him. Later, as I ate my pudding, I remarked how much I had admired Moscovitch's[1] performance in *The Great Lover*. Fred went quite red in the face and told me with some wealth of language what he thought of an actor who made love to a woman on the stage leering up at her suggestively as he kissed her hand. I did not dare to say that this behaviour had seemed to me quite in the spirit of the character in the play. I felt it was time to change the subject, and wondered if I could persuade Uncle Fred to appreciate my talents as a stage designer. I succeeded in taking him home with me, and dragged him up the many flights of stairs to my workroom. Proudly I showed him two of my latest efforts, a sand-strewn desert, and a street for *Twelfth Night* (both inspired by *Chu-Chin-Chow*). The street went up to the back of the stage in rows of uneven steps, with arches and perspectives, shutters, balconies and so on. Uncle Fred gazed in silence, then solemnly shook his head. 'Much too expensive for touring', he said reflectively. 'Too many rostrums, my boy.'

The nicest room in our South Kensington house was the large white drawing-room on the ground floor, which was seldom used except for parties and celebrations. There was a grand piano (on which father's playing sounded much finer than on the upright in the nursery), gold wallpaper and a large painted Chinese screen which I still possess. I was deeply embarrassed when Father pointed out to me that one of the ladies painted on it was 'in the family way'. I think I had never heard that pregnant phrase before. The screen hid the door from the people sitting in the main part of the room, and kept out some of the draught as well. On Christmas

[1] Maurice Moscovitch had previously had a great success at the Royal Court, under Fagan's direction and management, as Shylock—a vivid performance which I well remember.

Day my various Terry relatives used to come to lunch or tea, and then my stage-struck heart would beat and I was in a state of unmitigated rapture. First, Grandmother, stout and jolly, with a special armchair at table and special pickings from the turkey (the Terry appetite was as unfailing as the Terry charm). Then my mother's three sisters, Janet, Lucy and Mabel. Next to appear would be Marion, making a superb entrance with her gracious smile and beautiful sweeping carriage. After lunch we would hear someone else arriving with a jolly laugh and jingling of coins, and Fred's head and shoulders would loom up over the screen, with Julia behind him in lovely clothes, her arms laden with beautiful and expensive presents.

All of a sudden there would be a hush in the room. An old lady had come in and was finding her way from one group to another, settling at last in a low chair. It was Ellen Terry, bowed and mysterious, under the shadow of a big black straw hat, covered in scarves and shawls, with a large bag holding two or three pairs of spectacles, like a godmother in a fairy tale. She wore a black and grey gown, very cleverly draped on her slim body, too long in front (as she always wore her stage dresses), and bunched up over one arm with wonderful instinctive grace. When her hat and shawls had been taken from her, there were coral combs in her short grey hair and coral beads round her neck. With her lovely turned-up nose and wide mouth, and that husky voice—a 'veiled voice' somebody called it once—and her enchanting smile, no wonder everyone adored her. We children, of course, found her far the most thrilling and lovable of all our exciting aunts and uncles. Even though she was vague and we felt she was not quite sure where she was or who we were, her magic was irresistible. 'Who is this? Who? Jack? Oh, of course, I remember. Well, do you read your Shakespeare? My Ted[1] has written a wonderful book on the theatre. I'll send it to you.' So she did. I have it still—her own copy, scribbled all over with notes and comments. 'You know, I fell down this morning in Charing-Cross Road and I was laughing so much that I could hardly move when the policeman came to help me up. Hullo, old Kate. Hullo, Polly.[2] Who's this? Fred? Where's my bag? My other spectacles are in it. Oh, I have to go on somewhere. I can't remember. Oh yes, Edy Gwynne's. I must be off. I have a nice new flat in St.

[1] Gordon Craig.

[2] Marion Terry—a pet name.

Martin's Lane, near all the theatres and do you know, the other day who should come in but Jim' (James Carew, her husband). 'Imagine, he is living in the same building. Wasn't it sweet of him to come and see how I was getting along?' And so with much fluttering and kissing and bundling she was gone.

CHAPTER TWO

1913–19

Ellen Terry had said, 'Do you read your Shakespeare?' In those days I certainly did not. I read Henty, *The Jungle Books*, most of Harrison Ainsworth, all E. Nesbit, and Clement Scott's notices of the Lyceum productions, Ellen Terry's Memoirs and everything else about the theatre that I could find on the library bookshelves. Also I saved up to buy, or begged people to give me as presents, books with pictures by Beardsley, Kay Nielsen or Dulac. These artists inspired me at different times to make masses of indifferent drawings and stage designs. I was always talking about Gordon Craig too, but I am sure I did not really understand in those days what his books and drawings meant, and was chiefly impressed by the fact that he was my second cousin.

Val used to read history, especially anything about Napoleon and his campaigns, *Raffles*, *Arsène Lupin* and John Buchan. We both of us discovered Compton Mackenzie and Hugh Walpole about the same time, and devoured all their early books with terrific enthusiasm—but not Shakespeare.

The first Shakespeare play I ever saw was *As You Like It* at the Coronet Theatre, Notting Hill Gate, with Benson and Dorothy Green. This must have been in 1912 or 1913. Of course I only took in the plot and the scenery. There was solid ivy for Orlando to nail on to a very shaky canvas wall in the opening scene, a nd the terraces of Duke Frederick's garden were ingeniously transformed into forest glades by covering them with autumn leaves, which the actors had to plough through for the rest of the performance. The Doris Keane *Romeo and Juliet* of 1919 was the next Shakespeare play I went to see. I was much older by then and, as if I knew that this play was to be a very important one for me when I grew up, I remember the whole production very vividly. Edith Craig had arranged the thrilling fights. The ball was lovely too, staged very simply in tall curtains, with big Della Robbia swags hanging between the pillars and in a great circular wreath above the centre of the stage. Juliet was in silver lamé. This was not perhaps quite the correct thing, but it looked very grand to me, and Ellen Terry as the Nurse wore a big hat tied under her chin, and a gay yellow and black checked cloak in the street scene. When she forgot her lines she pretended to be deaf, and one of the other characters whispered them in her ear.

Leon Quartermaine, as Mercutio, made an enormous success on the first night. With his usual modesty, he left the theatre after his death scene, and was not to be found when the audience clamoured for him at the end. I thought he gave a beautiful performance, though Fred Terry, who had once been a fine Mercutio himself, disagreed with me. I always seemed to say the wrong thing to Uncle Fred. 'My dear fellow', he said, 'he jeers at Tybalt for being a lisping affected fantastico, but that is exactly the way he himself plays Mercutio!'

There was a very unfortunate arrangement in the bedroom scene in this production. The curtain rose to reveal Juliet lying asleep in a very narrow bed, with Romeo dressing himself on the other side of the room. It was not until he had buckled on his sword that Juliet awoke with a start and leapt out of bed with 'Wilt thou be gone? It is not yet near day'. People in the stalls were shaking their heads, and even I had an inkling that the scene had not begun in a very poetic atmosphere. During the interval I kept remarking in a loud voice, 'Isn't Aunt Nell wonderful?' and my relatives hushed me saying, 'You must never discuss actors aloud in the stalls on a first night', a warning which I have often tried to remember since. In the scene when the Nurse comes to waken Juliet, Ellen Terry played exquisitely, though the audience held its breath when she stumbled on the darkened stage, feeling her way up the steps to draw the curtains at the window. After the mourners had left the scene she stood by Juliet's bed, folded the girl's hands, and knelt down beside her body as the curtain fell. I shall never forget the absolute simplicity with which she did this.

I suppose it was not a great performance of the Nurse. There was too much of Ellen Terry's own sweetness and personal charm, but now and again there were superb hints of character. 'He that can lay hold of her shall have the chinks' was one, and 'No, truly, sir, not a penny' was another. And in the scene with Romeo and Friar Laurence how perfectly she conveyed the tiredness of the poor old lady, yawning very discreetly when she said, 'O Lord, I could have stayed here all the night, to hear good counsel'. Like all great players she listened beautifully, making the scenes alive for the other characters by the unselfish way she 'gave' to them.

The 'cords' scene, as I remember, was cut altogether. Perhaps Ellen Terry could not learn it, and even without that scene the evening was far too long. In the last act, poor Basil Sydney began to beat on the tomb doors, and the stage hands, supposing the signal had been given to 'strike', began to lift the front cloth, displaying large scurrying boots and bright lights. The curtain hastily descended, but the atmosphere was ruined and the play ended tamely. It was embarrassing to feel that Mercutio and the Nurse had stolen the success of the evening, but Ellen Terry brought Romeo and Juliet before the curtain, linked her arms in theirs, and said with infinite tact and charm, 'I do so hope you will love these young people as much as I do'.

When it was all over we went round behind, and there was a tiny room with masses of flowers, and Aunt Nell, tucked up on a sofa, tired out but still adorably greeting crowds of people, none of whom, I am sure, she recognized at all.

I am a born Cockney, and as soon as I was given a latch-key and allowed to go out alone I used to walk about the London streets all day long, discovering Chelsea and the City churches and Chiswick Mall and Hampton Court. As children we all felt more at home in London than anywhere else. At any rate, we never looked forward half so much to our Easter and summer holidays as we did to the weeks at Christmas, when we stayed at home in London and theatres were the order of the day. For one thing, our parents had no outdoor hobbies. They were rather unusual in not liking games or sports of any kind. They did not play cards or go racing or swim or ride, and so we were never forced to learn to play games ourselves, nor were we ridiculed at home when we were bad at them, as most children are when they are little. When we were older we still invented our own games, which we found easier to excel in, and went on playing these until we were almost grown-up. We could none of us ride or swim, and we were dreadfully bad at cricket and football. I was conceited too, and hating to make a fool of myself. I tried to avoid learning anything that did not come easily to me. We used to go to the seaside at Easter and to the country in August—furnished houses at Littlehampton and Selsey, at Beaconsfield, Chipstead, Berkhamsted and Uckfield. I expect we were extremely lazy, and that other children found us very maddening and superior. Of course, we were also self-conscious about our shortcomings, and hated being shown up. We therefore avoided making friends so far as we could until we went to school. There we had a pretty bad time at first, and no doubt we richly deserved it.

Mother was inclined to spoil me, particularly as I was supposed to be delicate and 'artistic', and Father was a somewhat distant figure who had to be met at the station every evening when we were in the country and accompanied on long walks at week-ends, or to museums, picture galleries and concerts on Sundays when we were in London. He was very alarming when he was angry and very charming at other times. I owe to him such grounding as I possess in music, painting and history, and he never tried to crush my mania for the theatre, which he loved himself but within more modest bounds.

He deplored the extravagance which seemed to be natural to all his children, though I cannot imagine whence we all inherited it, for my mother was ever a most economical and unostentatious person. Father gave us all allowances and latch-keys at an early age, but frowned severely on taxis, theatre seats and expensive restaurants. He always travelled by bus himself (as he did almost until his death, at the age of 88), went to the theatre in the pit, and chose the hard seats above the organ at the Albert Hall, because you could hear there better than anywhere else. After a while Val and I began to look forward to concerts with real enthusiasm, though Eleanor never cared for them very much. All the same, our parents decided for some reason or other that she was to be the musician of the family, and she endured several years' training with various teachers. She has never touched a piano since, while I, who played quite well by ear (which made me lazy in learning from music), was not forced to study as I should have been, and gave up my music lessons as soon as I went to school.

My education began at Hillside, a preparatory school at Godalming, and continued at Westminster School in London. My brothers were both at Hillside before me, and both were head boys.

Lewis left for Eton with a scholarship, and afterwards took a Demyship at Magdalen, Oxford. Val and I were rather dejected by his brilliant success, as our parents were constantly reminding us that they hoped we should follow his example at the earliest opportunity.

Val was head boy at Hillside when I arrived there, and I was Gielgud Minor. I took in my surroundings with my usual passion for detail. I believe I could still draw an accurate plan of the house, and the big playing field, with the corrugated iron gymnasium in a corner of it, the cricket pavilion, and the six poplar trees which used to rustle and toss in stormy weather. When Lewis was at the front during the First World War he wrote a poem about some poplar trees, and I was much impressed when it was published in the old green *Westminster Gazette* which Father used to bring home from the City every evening. I always imagined the trees of the poem were those of Hillside, but Mother has assured me since that Lewis was thinking of the poplar trees in France.

Hillside was a ramshackle house, built on a very steep incline. Changing rooms and classrooms had been added to the original structure, and to reach them we had to toil up and down endless flights of wooden stairs, round unexpected corners, and through dark stone passages. The most terrifying corridor led, round several winding turns, to the squash court and the school lavatories. I disliked walking here alone on murky winter afternoons, when the light came fitfully through the corrugated iron roof, casting enormous and appalling shadows, and the cisterns dripped and gurgled in the distance but, it was alarming to meet someone unexpectedly, or to hear footsteps close behind me—worst of all if some humorist jumped out on me as I passed.

In the library I could read the papers. I would rush through my breakfast and dash there to snatch the *Daily Sketch* on the morning following the Theatrical Garden Party, when the centre page would be filled with photographs of the stars—(I can see one now—Nelson Keys as Katharine of Aragon and Arthur Playfair as Henry VIII in a skit on the Tree production in *The Grand Giggle*). On these I would gaze enraptured. The library was a favourite retreat of mine. The only alarming feature of the room was the window seat, which had cupboards running all round it underneath, making a sort of tunnel in which I was sometimes imprisoned by my enemies. Here I would lie, bent double, and half suffocated, while my captors sat on the window seat above me, drumming with their boots on the cupboard doors which barred all chances of escape.

I took pleasure in the poetic melancholy of the winter, which I had never spent in the country before—the foggy, mysterious playing-field, with the high goal-posts wreathed in mist and the ground churned up and caked with frost, echoing to the dull thud of the footballs and the squeal of the referee's whistle as we grunted and panted up and down in our red and black striped jerseys, with our breaths streaming out in white jets in front of us. I reached the extreme pitch of nostalgia on Sunday afternoons, when we walked, two and two, for five miles over the muddy fields, to Compton or Puttenham or the Hog's Back, trudging slowly home again in the twilight past the gates of Charterhouse, with the lights twinkling in the shadowy houses, trees and hedges looming up in the darkness along the steep lanes on either side of us, and church bells ringing sadly in the distance.

Food seems very important in my memories of Hillside—the noisy meals, which the masters carved, the joint which was 'roast on Monday, cold on Tuesday, and hashed on Wednesday',[1] and the rude jokes about the 'skivvies' who served us. Sunday morning with sausages, and the days when there were loathsome parsnips. Then there was 'fruit' in the matron's room in the afternoons, which we were allowed to order once a week ourselves out of our pocket-money—almonds and raisins and tangerines and brazil nuts in the winter, and baskets of raspberries and cherries in the summer. These we would take outdoors and eat slowly, luxuriously, lying out on our rugs under the trees, with grey felt hats pulled over our eyes, gossiping and whispering smutty jokes while we watched a cricket match through a long sunny afternoon. And at the beginning of term there would be a great smuggling of plum cakes and sweets and dates and figs, and 'feasts' in the dormitory after lights out.

I enjoyed my years at Hillside, although I cannot claim to have distinguished myself when I was there. My best school subjects were Divinity and English. I scrambled through Latin and Greek after a fashion, but mathematics defeated me altogether. I tried my hand at carpentry for a little while, and my mother probably cherished a hideous carved box which I proudly presented to her, though I omitted to explain that most of the work had been done

[1] As Lewis Dodd was to say later in *The Constant Nymph*.

by the Carpentry Master, who realized after many weeks of toil that I should never complete my work without some help from him.

I thought I sang rather well. At Sunday services my shrill treble would soar above the other voices during the hymns, as I stood with my head thrown back, hoping to be seen as well as heard.

My histrionic cravings found another more legitimate outlet. We were encouraged to act in the winter and spring terms, and it was then that I appeared for the first time before an audience. My performance of the Mock Turtle in *Alice* was duly tearful, and I sang 'Soup of the Evening, Beautiful Soup', with increasing volume and shrillness in every verse. I was a bland Humpty-Dumpty and an impassioned Shylock. Another term I played Mark Antony. I remember waiting for my entrance standing on an icy stone conservatory floor shivering in my toga. I warmed up, however, as soon as I began to act, and as my courage grew I must have played with all my might, for I succeeded in reducing the only titled parent to tears and was presented to her afterwards in the headmaster's drawing-room.

Another boy who was with me at Hillside was Ronald Mackenzie, afterwards the brilliant author of *Musical Chairs* and *The Maitlands*. I was not particularly friendly with him when we were at school, but, years afterwards, a line in *The Maitlands* brought Hillside vividly to my mind, when the backward son admitted that all he had learned at school was 'a little Latin and how to swing across the dormitory on the iron girders'. I must explain that at Hillside there were iron girders running across the dormitory which was called 'Cubicles' (though the wooden partitions which had given it its name had disappeared by my time). There were two rows of beds with red rugs on them, and newcomers each term were always initiated by the same ceremony. They had to cross the room, from one row of beds to the other, swinging hand-over-hand on these girders, an alarming ordeal frequently accompanied by the flicking of wet towels and the hurling of sponges.

My talent for games remained at zero, but I somehow managed to get into the Second XI at football. When a notice was put up at the end of the term assessing the merits of each individual member of the team, my name was at the bottom with the remark: 'Gielgud. An opportunist merely.' I have always tried to live up to this.

When I became head of the school, I was, as a matter of prestige I suppose, appointed scorer for the First XI at cricket. There were enviable privileges attached to this position. On the occasion of 'away' matches, I would be let off morning school and drive by brake to the opposing camp, where I ate an enormous tea and enjoyed the satisfaction of making entries in the scoring book in my small neat handwriting, of which I was inordinately vain.

The First World War began while I was on holiday from Hillside. I was going by train with my mother, Val and Eleanor, to a house my parents had taken at Crowborough for the summer, and I vaguely remember buying newspapers at some junction, and Mother's face as she read the news. Soon after this the headmaster's brother, in whose form I had been a pupil only a term before, was killed, and even in our small school the casualty lists used to be read out every few days.

Lewis went to France with a commission and was badly wounded. He was not expected to live, and my parents were rushed over to see him in hospital. Their reactions were unexpected. My father was very much knocked-out by the strain, and came home exhausted as soon as Lewis was off the danger-list, whereas Mother, whose nerves were usually her greatest weakness, rose to the occasion with amazing calm, and made herself so useful writing letters and doing jobs for the nurses and men that she was allowed, contrary to all precedent, to stay at Le Touquet for eleven weeks, which gave her enormous pride and satisfaction.

Our headmaster went to the front, leaving the school in charge of a Mr Taylor, who wore a W. G. Grace beard, and played in staff matches in a minute cricket cap which looked extremely odd in conjunction with his otherwise dignified appearance. He used to interview us, sitting in a very low creaking basket-chair and wearing ancient leather bedroom slippers, in a funny little study reeking of tobacco and Harris tweed. The walls were hung with scores of photographs of former pupils in little elaborately carved picture-frames, with pipe racks and University shields hanging on the wall above their heads. The later chapters of *Goodbye Mr Chips* reminded me of him forcibly.

On the whole, I was sorry to leave my preparatory school when the time came, and I even regretted the places I had always disliked most, the Charterhouse swimming bath (which I had always hated, with its dreary sort of watery echo), and the stone-cold passages of Hillside, with the steep steps leading from the long dreary corridor where we kept our play-boxes.

I looked at the landmarks on the journey between Godalming and Waterloo for the last time—Guildford station, Brooklands, Carter's seed ground, and the big building near Clapham Junction with the words 'Shakespeare Theatre' painted on it in enormous letters. The sight of that theatre had always cheered me as I went back to school, and I used to wonder excitedly what delights lay concealed behind that grim brick wall.

I had failed to get a scholarship at Eton as Lewis had done. My mother went down with me to Windsor for the examination, but I felt sure that it would be a wasted journey. I suppose I knew that I had not done enough work. I had a bad attack of conscience at the hotel, and sat up half the night searching the dictionary for words I thought I should be asked next day. I cribbed the only correct answer to my maths paper, but even so I was awarded only four marks out of a hundred!

A few months later I tried to get a scholarship at Rugby, where Val was, but failed again, to my secret satisfaction, as the atmosphere of the place sounded, from my brother's description, a great deal too uncomfortable for my luxurious tastes. In the end I went to Westminster.

I managed to win a non-resident scholarship, but I was extremely idle. Drawing was still my obsession, and I spent hours in the Abbey, trying to copy the banners and fanvaulting in a pastel drawing of Henry VII Chapel. But I think that even my love of the Abbey was very much mixed up with my love of the theatre. Only the other day I found a black-edged card which I had persuaded a friendly verger to give me when the wreaths were thrown away after an anniversary commemoration of Irving's death. On it was written, 'Rosemary for remembrance. E.T.'

When I first went to Westminster I was a boarder. Our nights were frequently disturbed by air raids. When the alarm sounded, we would put overcoats on over our pyjamas, and go down through the cloisters into the Norman Undercroft, one of the oldest vaults in the Abbey. There all the canons and deans would be collected, with their wives and families and servants. The three beautiful daughters of Canon Carnegie, in evening dresses and cloaks, sat on a bench with a white bulldog at their feet, looking for all the world like a conversation-piece by Sargent. One night the buttresses of the Abbey were covered with snow. They sparkled in the brilliant moonlight, while the bursting shells overhead and the searchlights swinging to and fro made an extraordinary picture in the sky. But air raids soon lost their exciting novelty, and some of us would seek an added thrill by creeping out of the Undercroft to see if one of the statues in the cloisters really turned over the pages of its book at midnight, as legend said it did.

We were allowed home for week-ends, and this seemed to prevent my settling down at school. At last I begged my parents to make me a day boy, using the raids and my subsequent loss of sleep as an excuse. My stratagem was successful, and I was allowed to go home in the evenings, work at my preparation in the library, and then go to bed. My father was not so fortunate. He was a Special Constable, and had to patrol the Chelsea Embankment, near Lot's Road Power House. When there was a bad raid he used to say that the spectacle over the river was so magnificent that it quite made up for his long hours of dreariness, but I imagine those nights must have been something of an ordeal for him after a long day's work in the City, and a great strain for my mother, who used to sit up half the night waiting for him, with a spirit lamp and sandwiches, trying to read, and listening for the 'all clear' signal which would herald his return.

How we loathed our clothes at Westminster!—the top-hats, which looked like sealskin after a few days, and the hideous all-round stiff collars which we had to wear. Ivor Montagu, who was in the same house as I was, brought special food to school, which he used to carry, for convenience' sake, in his hat. He was considerably discomfited, though the rest of us thought it a great joke, when somebody knocked it off in Dean's Yard with a snowball. On O.T.C. days we looked better (and felt more comfortable) in our uniforms, though our puttees were always a sore trial. On wet Saturday afternoons I used to climb, top-hat and all, to the galleries of theatres, undaunted by the sniggers which my appearance usually provoked. My father had taken me for the first time to see the Russian Ballet at the Alhambra, and I saved all my pocket-money (which I suppose I called an 'allowance' by now) to go again and again, enchanted by the brilliant décors and passionate dancing. Arnold Haskell, the ballet critic, was at Westminster. He became one of my greatest friends of those days, and we used to stand in queues for hours together. That first production of

Boutique Fantasque, the exquisite blue back-cloth and the little sofas in *Carnaval*, *Thamar's* enchanted tower and the glories of Bakst's rococo palaces in *The Sleeping Princess*, these were early ecstasies—though my youthful admiration was also extended quite indiscriminately to *The Bing Boys*, *Yes*, *Uncle*, and finally *The Beggar's Opera*.

I was still a boy, but I was lucky to have been born just in time to touch the fringe of the great century of the theatre. I saw Sarah Bernhardt in a one-act play in which she appeared as a wounded *poilu* of eighteen, dying on the battlefield. She looked unbelievably young and her voice rang through the theatre. Though her leg had been amputated, she stood up to take her call, leaning on the shoulder of one of the other actors. I saw Adeline Genée dance, and heard Albert Chevalier singing 'My old Dutch', and I saw Vesta Tilley once, and Marie Lloyd, too, in her last days.

In 1923 I stood in a packed audience at the Oxford Theatre to see Duse in *Ghosts*. It was the very last time she was to act in London. She seemed to me like some romantic Spanish empress, with her shawl draped wonderfully about her, and her fluttering hands. Her expression when she listened was marvellous, but I was not familiar with the play and could not follow it with any pleasure. There was certainly nothing Nordic about this Mrs Alving. What impressed me most was the tremendous reception the audience gave her, their breathless silence during the performance, and the air of majestic weariness with which Duse seemed to accept it all. There was something poignant and ascetic about her when she was old and ill, quite different from the indomitable gallantry of the crippled Bernhardt, and the ageless beauty and fun that Ellen Terry still brought with her upon the stage.

Sometimes, when we were not at school or at the theatre, Val and I used to roller-skate at Holland Park Rink. I was fascinated by the little model stages, with scenes from all the current plays, which were grouped in dark booths in the promenade. I have always loved aquariums, grottoes and waxworks, because they remind me of the peepshow side of the theatre. The effigies in the Abbey used to fascinate me for the same reason.

I longed for a great ceremony to be performed while I was at Westminster. I am sure I pictured myself singing 'Vivat Rex' at a coronation. As a matter of fact we were privileged, as Westminster boys, to be present on several exciting occasions before I left the school. I saw the procession at each opening of Parliament, and I was much impressed by the beautiful voice and faultless diction of Mr Bonar Law in the House of Commons, where we were allowed to sit in one of the Stranger's Galleries. When the Unknown Soldier was buried, we stood, dressed in our O.T.C. uniforms, lining the path from the street to the door of the Abbey. It was extraordinary to stand there, with arms reversed and faces lowered, and to know that the greatest men of our time were passing within a few feet of us. We were in the Abbey, too, at the wedding of the Princess Royal, and had a very close glimpse of the Royal Family as they passed. This was the last time I saw Queen Alexandra, still slim and elegant, walking beside the more opulent figure of Queen Mary. She had always been one of my heroines. I was taken to the Mansion House when I was quite small to present a purse to her for the Treloar Hospital, and took away with me the memory of a lovely bowing lady, as well as a real signed picture of her which hung over my bed for many years afterwards.

It was about this time that I made my first shy hints that I wished to renounce the idea of going to Oxford and try my fortune on the stage. I made the suggestion that, if I did not succeed before I was twenty-five, I would follow my parents' wishes and work to become an architect. Mother and Father were not very enthusiastic. They had just arranged for me to specialize in History at Westminster with the idea of trying for a scholarship at Oxford, but I felt how useless it would be to waste another four to five years before I began training for the stage. If I were to become an actor I must start at once.

Finally, after a good deal of discussion, I was allowed to enter for a scholarship at the dramatic school of which Lady Benson was the principal.

Here I arrived one morning, trembling with nerves, to find Lady Benson and Helen Haye confronting me in a tiny office. I recited 'Bredon Hill' from the *Shropshire Lad*, which I had heard Henry Ainley (dressed in uniform, with jingling spurs), give magnificently a few weeks before at a charity concert at the Grafton Galleries. I thought I had shouted the roof off, and was overcome with emotion when I was told I had won the scholarship. I was free to leave Westminster, and begin to study acting.

CHAPTER THREE

1920–21

I stayed with Lady Benson for a year, and found her a delightful woman and a splendid teacher. She worked in a funny ramshackle little drill-hall only a few yards away from my grandmother's house in the detested Cromwell Road. There was a minute stage and auditorium, with a glass conservatory leading out into a yard. The place was pulled down many years ago, but I always think of it when I pass the corner where it stood.

The War had come to an end shortly before I left Westminster. The rumour that the Armistice had been signed spread round the classrooms early in the morning, and no one was paying much attention to work when eleven o'clock came at last and bells began to ring. We streamed into Little Dean's Yard, and up the steps to Big School, where the headmaster dismissed us for the day. Some of us joined the enormous crowd of people in Whitehall, and were swept along up the Mall to the steps of the Victoria Memorial, where we stood for hours, waving our limp top-hats and shouting for the King and Queen. Lewis was demobilized soon afterwards. He had been working at the War Office since his wounds invalided him out of the army, and now he was able to go back to Oxford for another year. I went to lunch with him at Magdalen. He had beautiful white-panelled rooms in New Buildings, and we fed the deer out of the windows. He showed me Addison's Walk and the sweep of the High, the Shelley Memorial and Tom Quad. At the time I was mad about *Sinister Street* and *Guy and Pauline* and *Zuleika Dobson*, and Oxford seemed to me, next to London, the most glamorous place I had ever seen. We punted up the Cherwell for a moonlight picnic, and floated down again late at night with Chinese lanterns, and I stayed awake for hours when I got back to the hotel, listening to the bells and clocks striking in the darkness. I thought myself very noble to have given up the chance of becoming an undergraduate. What if I should make a failure of the stage? I don't believe the possibility had ever occurred to me before.

Naomi Mitchison and Aldous Huxley were great friends of Lewis's while he was at Oxford. Aldous had been with him at Eton too, and often came to our house in London. He looked then very much as he did in later life, with his thick glasses and long stooping body. He, Lewis and Naomi used to speak very slowly and drawl the ends of their words affectedly. This was the real 'Oxford accent' so much ridiculed and imitated since that time.

Naomi Haldane, as she then was, had an extraordinary personality. She was incredibly shy and clumsy, wore amazing clothes of strange cut and shape, and knew everything there was to know about Greek and Roman history and the archaeology of Egypt and Byzantium. At the age of eleven she wrote a play about Ancient Greece, which was acted on the lawn of the Haldanes' house at Oxford. Lewis produced it and also appeared in the same programme as Dionysos in *The Frogs* of Aristophanes. He looked very handsome, dressed in a leopard-skin and blue and gold buskins, with a vine-wreath round his head. Aldous played Charon, and rowed him over the Styx in a little boat with rockers set down upon the grass. Naomi had written another play, very elaborate and ambitious, with an archaic setting and modern dialogue. Val and I were both invited to appear in it, and the Margaret Morris Theatre in King's Road, Chelsea, was hired for the performance. The cast included Julian Huxley, the scientist, and Helen Simpson, the authoress. I only remember that I played a young Greek officer who befriended a British prisoner of war who was in my charge, and that Nigel Playfair's two sons, Giles and Lyon, aged eight and six respectively, acted far better than anyone else.

I had already made several amateur appearances since my days at Hillside. Some years before, at Beaconsfield, Val, Eleanor and I had got up a play with some friends with whom we were staying for the summer holidays. The performance was given in a charming studio belonging to G. K. Chesterton, and the great man himself came to see it, and delighted us by laughing uproariously. Val had written the scenario, and we all invented the dialogue as we went along—quite in the Commedia dell' Arte tradition! Eleanor played a maid in a very large cap, and I was a sinister adventuress in a big hat and evening dress, smoking a cigarette through a long black holder. I had appeared in Shakespeare too; I was asked to play Orlando in some performances of *As You Like It* which were to be given in the garden of a rectory at St. Leonards, and later in the grounds of Battle Abbey. I was sixteen by now and very vain. I affected very light grey flannels braced much too high, silk socks, broad-brimmed black soft hats, and even, I blush to admit, an eye-glass upon occasion, and I wore my hair very long and washed it a great deal to make it look fluffy and romantic. For Orlando, I slipped off to a hairdresser in St. Leonards and asked the man to wave it—'For a play,' I added hastily. 'Certainly, sir,' he said. 'I suppose you'd be in the Variety Company that's opening on the Pier this week.' Undaunted, I strode on to the lawn at the first performance, drew my sword fiercely, and declaimed, 'Forbear, and eat no more!' but unfortunately I tripped over a large log and fell flat on my face. This was only the beginning of my troubles, for in the last act, when I pointed to the path where I was expecting Rosalind, with 'Ah, here comes my Ganymede'—no Ganymede was to be seen. I said the line again, with a little less confidence this time; still no one appeared. I looked helplessly round, to find the prompter, his hands to his mouth, whispering as loudly as he dared across the hundred yards that separated us, 'She's changed back into her girl's clothes a scene too soon!'

I had also replaced a student who was ill in a couple of performances at Rosina Filippi's school in Whitehead's Grove, near Sloane Square, in an adaptation of a novel by Rhoda Broughton, and as Mercutio in three scenes from *Romeo and Juliet*. Miss Filippi had a broad, motherly face, grey hair and a rich, jolly laugh. She walked with an ebony cane, and wore black taffeta that rustled a great deal and a gold watch on a long chain round her neck. She conducted rehearsals with much authority and humour, but I was rather put out at the actual performance, when she sat down at a piano at the side of the stage and played twiddly bits all through my delivery of the Queen Mab speech!

With such a wealth of amateur experience behind me, I naturally started at Lady Benson's full of hope and self-assurance, once the terror of the scholarship examination was safely passed. Grandmother must have been in the country, for I received the following letter from her which I proudly pasted into the new scrapbook which I had bought that morning:

DEAR OLD JACK,

I am delighted to hear of your intended real start in a profession you love, and wish you every success. You must not anticipate a bed of roses, for on the stage as in every other profession there are 'rubs and arrows' to contend with. 'Be kind and affable to all your co-mates, but if possible be intimate with none of them.' This is a quotation of my parents' advice to me and I pass it on as I have proved it to be very sound. Theatrical intimacy breeds jealousy of a petty kind which is very disturbing. I hope you may have many chances with your various studies and prove yourself worthy.

I am returning on Monday and shall, I hope, have an opportunity to have a good old talk with you.

Meanwhile my love and congratulations.

Your affectionate grandmother,

KATE LEWIS

There were about thirty students at Lady Benson's, and only four of them were men. This of course led to great competition amongst us, so Lady Benson used to split up the good parts (such as Hamlet or Sir Peter Teazle), so that none of us should be made to feel important or indispensable, and made each of us play the same part in different scenes. When there were too many male characters in a play the slim girls played the young men's parts and the fat ones would appear in 'character' as Crabtree or Moses. I loved the rehearsal classes, but was less keen on the fencing, dancing, and elocution which completed the curriculum. There was also a 'gesture' class once a week, which Lady Benson took herself. One of her exercises was to make us rush in and express different emotions with the same line of dialogue. It must have been distinctly comic to see twenty-five young women and four self-conscious young men rushing through a door one after the other, uttering with hate, fear, disgust or joy the remark 'Baby's burning'.

Still I had not taken Ellen Terry's advice and read my Shakespeare. I cheerfully rushed at the purple patches set for us by the elocution master, and, having a good memory and a quick eye, polished off St. Crispin and Clarence's dream, Wolsey's farewell and Othello's speech to the Senate, in a very short space of time. I rehearsed some of Benedick, which I found very difficult to understand; and, as a crowning glory, I was allowed to study half a dozen scenes of *Hamlet*. When the day of the performance came, however, and my costume arrived, I was so delighted with the long black cloak I had to wear that I spent most of the first scene draping it over my arm and looking over my shoulder to see if it were trailing on the floor to my satisfaction. Shakespeare seemed easy to learn, at any rate, and I liked it because it was full of tradition and effective 'business'. There were plenty of good parts and strong situations, and I could make myself weep when I said certain lines, and listen to my voice as it soared in interesting cadences from one register to another.

I suddenly became aware of my legs. This was a terrible moment, for, until I realized that I was handicapped by a strange way of standing and a still stranger way of walking, I really thought acting might be a comparatively simple matter. I was not embarrassed at using my hands and arms, in fact at first I used them a bit too freely, but the moment I tried to move my legs they refused to carry out the simplest instructions. Only a few days after my arrival at the school Lady Benson had burst out laughing in the middle of a rehearsal and pointed at me with dismay. 'Good heavens', she cried, 'you walk exactly like a cat with rickets!'

I became acutely self-conscious, knowing that my laziness and my dislike of games had prevented me from learning, when I was a boy, to move freely and naturally. I walked from the knees instead of from the hips, and bent my legs when I was standing still instead of holding them straight. I am sure if I had been forced to run and swim when I was a child I should not have developed these mannerisms so badly, but it was too late to think of that now. Such a discovery in my first term at Lady Benson's was extremely depressing. However, it dealt a severe blow to my conceit, which was a good thing. Vainly I pored over books on Irving, describing his dragging leg and odd movements—vainly I imagined myself triumphing, like Sarah Bernhardt, in a part where I was lying in bed, or sitting in an invalid chair. (I had just been to see Claude Rains as Dubedat in *The Doctor's Dilemma* at the Everyman Theatre.) It was no use. My 'rickets' were to remain my principal bugbear on the stage for many years to come.

Somebody told me that theatrical students were able to walk on (without payment) in the crowds at the Old Vic, and as soon as term was over at Lady Benson's, I rushed off to the Waterloo Road to try my luck. I was taken on without an audition—perhaps some kind person had recommended me. I only remember climbing the stairs to the old saloon bar at the back of the dress-circle to my first professional rehearsal. The room was rather like a shabby version of the old Café Royal—fly-blown mirrors, plush benches, gilded plaster figures, and dust everywhere. The play in rehearsal was *Henry V*, with Robert Atkins as producer and Rupert Harvey playing the part of the King, Andrew Leigh as Fluellen, Hay Petrie as the Boy, and Florence Buckton as Chorus, dressed in black top-boots and Elizabethan man's costume. Through the glass doors I could see the rounded backs of the dress-circle seats, and the gilt decorations on top of the proscenium. All around me actors were sitting, crouching, muttering their lines to themselves, hearing one another from tattered little green books, slipping in and out for drinks or newspapers. Lilian Baylis occasionally hovered in the distance, but I never spoke to her. Sometimes I would timidly offer to hold the book for one of the actors, and sometimes Atkins would call out to 'that boy in the brown suit' to 'take his hands out of his pockets', as I shifted from one foot to another while a long scene, in which I held a spear, was repeated over and over again.

The first night drew nearer and nearer, and at last we were dressing, making up—six of us supers in one of the top boxes next to the proscenium. There was no dressing-room space in those days at the Vic. The leading lady dressed in Miss Bayliss's office, and the rest of the women in the saloon bar. They could be seen during the performance scurrying round the back of the circle dressed as Court Ladies, and scurrying back again dressed as Nuns a few moments later. There was no call-boy of course, so we used to peep through the felt curtains of our box to see if our cue was getting near, taking care to open the side closest to the stage so that no one in the audience should notice us. One night somebody dragged the curtain roughly aside, and down it came, revealing us all, half naked, to the astonished and delighted gallery!

Well, even if my first engagement was neither luxurious nor profitable, I was in a real theatre at last, working in a professional company, playing Shakespeare, and it was with high hopes and a beating heart, my knees pressed firmly back (for by this time they were knocking together as well as bending in their usual fashion), that I walked for the first time on to a professional stage, looked out across the footlights towards the exits glimmering like beacons in the darkness, and boldly uttered the only line of my first speaking part, 'Here is the number of the slaughter'd French'.

I was enormously impressed by some of the acting at the Vic. Andrew Leigh as the Fool in *Lear*; Ernest Milton as Richard II and Shylock; Hay Petrie as Shallow and Verges; Russell Thorndike and Florence Buckton in Ase's death scene in *Peer Gynt*. The Ibsen play was amazingly well put on, though I am sure it cost little enough. Russell was fine, especially in the ironic passages—in the African scenes he looked like Mr Fogg in Jules Verne's *Around the World in Eighty Days*—and he had some immensely funny business. In one scene he took off his trousers meditatively during one of his speeches and put up a large white umbrella. Later on, when he was leaving Anitra, he suddenly turned over a large cushion, produced the trousers from underneath, where they were being carefully pressed, and gravely put them on again. No one was supposed to watch the dress rehearsal of the play, but I climbed into the gallery and sat there for hours, all through a long Sunday, crouching under a large dust-sheet and hardly daring to breathe, determined not to miss a moment of the performance.

It was lucky for me that the actors at the Old Vic were all so busy that they had little time to spare for giving advice to young beginners. Some of them have told me since that I was so dreadfully bad as a super that they would have liked to have warned me against becoming an actor. Fortunately, I was quite unconscious of the bad impression I had created, and was only a little dashed when I was given no line to speak either in *King Lear*, Halcott Glover's *Wat Tyler*, or *Peer Gynt*, in all of which I 'walked on' in quick succession. Term was beginning again at Lady Benson's, and I left the Vic. Certainly nobody pressed me to stay on; and it was nine years before I passed through the stage-door in the Waterloo Road again.

CHAPTER FOUR

1921–22

I am always embarrassed when people ask me how they should set about looking for an opening on the stage, for I gained my first engagement entirely through influence. I had just completed three terms at Lady Benson's. Grandmother had been to see one of the performances, but otherwise I imagined that the family were not particularly interested in the new recruit. But I was wrong—for out of the blue one morning came a letter from Phyllis Neilson-Terry. Again I rushed to paste into my book the second important document in my stage career. The letter offered me four pounds a week to play a few lines, understudy, and make myself generally useful on a tour of *The Wheel*, under Phyllis's management, in the autumn of 1921.

I had met Phyllis, of course, and admired her very much. I knew of her spectacular success at His Majesty's under Tree, when she had played Desdemona and Viola at seventeen. Later she had acted in *Priscilla Runs Away* at the Haymarket, as Trilby and Lady Teazle at His Majesty's, and as Juliet at the New under her father, Fred Terry's, management. Then she had married Cecil King and gone away to America. Grandmother had once taken me on the stage to meet her after a performance of *Drake*—the only time, by the way, I ever went to His Majesty's as a boy—and I was bewildered at my efforts to talk to her while such exciting things were going on all round us. White horses were being led away in one direction, the porch of St. Paul's Cathedral was being rolled off in another, there were cloths being raised and borders dropped. I stood gaping with wonder and bewilderment, and there was Phyllis towering over me, looking even taller than she really was in her magnificent robes and crown, smiling and telling me to feel the weight of the wonderful necklaces she wore. She came once or twice to our house at Christmas, but I hardly saw her again until she offered me my first engagement. Her reappearance in London, on her return from America, in *The Wheel*, by J. B. Fagan (which she presented herself), was a great success. Now she had booked a long tour of fourteen or fifteen weeks in the provinces, and I was to be in her company. It was not a big cast, and rehearsals were not very alarming, as most of the company knew the play already and there were only a few changes to be made. I appeared for two minutes right at the end of the last act with a few lines to speak, but found I was given plenty of other things to do, holding the book, checking the actors' entrances, giving cues, helping to work the effects, and so on. Cecil King, Phyllis's husband, was charming to me and joked a great deal with everyone, and there was no question of my being singled out for favouritism. If anyone resented the fact that I was only there because I had the luck to be Phyllis's second cousin they were far too nice to show it.

We opened at Bradford, a romantic city in my imagination because Irving died there. There was not much romance about it in reality. I had a back 'combined' room, where I stood the first afternoon, looking very glum, gazing out of the window at a vista of smoke-stacks, factory chimneys and grubby back gardens. On the table, with its thick plush cloth edged with bobbles, lay strewn the contents of the tuck-box packed by my thoughtful mother—tinned tongue, sardines and pots of jam. I was very homesick, but slightly embarrassed when the landlady, in a large hat with feathers, took pity on me and cheerfully bade me join her in the kitchen for a drink, introducing me to several of the 'turns' from the local music-hall. What a snob they must have thought me!

I was very inexperienced as a toper. After a few weeks, I began to go 'pub-crawling' with three or four men from the company, and one morning I ordered Guinness and Gin and Italian in quick succession (I had picked up the names of these drinks from the others), turned green and fainted dead away.

I found the assistant stage management work harder than I expected. I had to dress in my uniform and be made up some time before the curtain went up every night so as to see that everything was ready on the stage. The two men with whom I shared a dressing-room helped me as much as they could, but I was an absolute duffer with greasepaints for many weeks. After half an hour's work I used to look either as red as a Cherokee Indian or else yellow and streaky, and I used far too much grease and not enough powder, so that my face shone like a full moon. On Saturday nights I had to see the scenery out of the theatre, which was rather alarming—especially if the staff had got a little drunk by one in the morning—and I would drag myself wearily home to my digs as the last big waggon rumbled away to the station in the darkness. Then all day Monday there would be the business of unpacking and 'hanging' the play in the new theatre, rehearsing the lighting and the orchestra, arranging the cue-lights, the call-sheets, and the thousand and one other details on which the smooth running of a play depends.

It was good for me to find out from the very first something of the complicated routine of a theatrical production. Playing a small part eight times a week takes up little of the day, and on tour there was nothing to do but read or go for walks or to the cinema. So I was quite glad of a full night's work and two full days a week in the theatre, though, of course I grumbled when matinée days and understudy rehearsals interfered with my spare time. I had the usual kind of touring adventures. Once I arrived in Leeds with two other members of the company, with whom I had arranged to share that week, and the door of the digs was opened by a Chinese gentleman. 'My son', said the Yorkshire landlady, and then, as we looked startled—'You should see my girl—she's in hospital now, unfortunately, burnt herself badly. Fair as a lily she is.' The bath upstairs was full of coal, and strange sounds came from the basement. After an uncomfortable week, we rashly paid our bill on Saturday night, although our train did not leave until the following evening. So we were a little dismayed when we woke late on Sunday morning to find an empty house, and a little burnt porridge in a bowl in the sitting-room grate, apparently the only food available. The landlady had decamped, taking her Oriental family with her. We were firmly convinced that we had spent a week in an opium den!

Sheffield was deadly, Hanley, Preston and Leeds not much more cheerful, and the digs varied from extreme discomfort to comparative luxury ('Lav. in Pub opp.' as a theatrical paper once advertised laconically). At Aberdeen I was asleep in a strange kind of box bed let into the wall—the rooms were very tiny but spotlessly clean, and the porridge was delicious—when someone arrived from the theatre to tell me I had to play one of the leading parts that night, as the principal was ill. It was an important moment for me to appear for the first time in a big part under Phyllis's critical eye, but apparently I rose to the occasion. Everyone seemed agreeably surprised, and I was delighted at the congratulations I received. But Nemesis was to follow. Phyllis wrote to my parents of my success, and, as they were coming to visit me at Oxford a few weeks later, she most kindly suggested that I should play the part again for the performance at which they would be present. The principal was asked to stand down, and again I dressed and made up with a trembling hand. Alas! my acting was dreadful. Nothing that I had done well before seemed to be right a second time; half-way through the play I knew that I had failed. I was deeply ashamed when I had to go out to tea with Phyllis and my parents afterwards, and imagined that the chauffeur shot me a look of unutterable disdain as I stepped into the grand car belonging to the management.

I lived, for the week we were at Oxford, in theatrical lodgings in Paradise Square. It was strange to be playing there as an actor, and to wander round Magdalen, where I had lunched with Lewis, and Trinity, where I had stayed with Val. In two years' time my contemporaries from Westminster would be coming up to Oxford as undergraduates. I wondered how far I should have progressed in my profession in those two years and whether I should regret my choice. I shared my lodgings that week with a charming actor in Phyllis's company, and he talked to me very kindly about my work. He had guessed, when I had gone on as understudy, that I had some instinct for the stage, but he also realized that I needed to learn control and to gain some technical knowledge for my work. I told him I had studied with Lady Benson, but he urged me to spend at least another year at a dramatic school when the tour came to an end. He suggested the Royal Academy of Dramatic Art, in Gower Street, where he had been trained himself. I took his advice, and managed to win a scholarship there on my return to London.

The school was much larger than Lady Benson's, though the classes were similarly arranged. Kenneth Barnes was the Principal. Claude Rains and Helen Haye were two of the teachers—also Miss Elsie Chester, a formidable old actress with a crutch, which she was reputed to hurl at people when she was displeased with their behaviour. The old house in Gower Street has been quite rebuilt since my time. In those days there used to be a labyrinth of stone steps leading to a basement canteen, presided over by a large lady called 'Henney', where we all used to gather for 'elevenses'. Another flight of stairs led up to the little theatre, which had just been opened with the all-star professional matinée for which Barrie wrote *Shall We Join the Ladies?*

Claude Rains was an enormous favourite with us all—his vitality and enthusiasm made him a delightful teacher, and most of the girls were in love with him.

I worked as hard as I could, and imitated Rains's acting until I became extremely mannered. I felt sure I had some sort of instinct for impersonation, but the imaginative part of my playing came too easily, and the technical side was non-existent. I strained every fibre in my efforts to appear violent or emotional, and only succeeded in forcing my voice and striking strange attitudes with my body. Rehearsing every day in a small room, with rows of girls sitting round on chairs staring at me, made me acutely self-conscious, and it was not until the performances at the end of the term that I was able to let myself go with any degree of confidence. But I was very lucky. At the end of the first term, Nigel Playfair, who knew my mother (more influence, I fear), came to a performance given by my class. The play was *The Admirable Crichton*, and I played the silly ass, Woolley, in the first two acts and Crichton himself in the last two. We gave the performance, not in the theatre, but in the Rehearsal Room, which was a glorified classroom with a small rickety stage at one end of it. After the performance I was sent for, and found Playfair sitting alone among a litter of empty chairs. He offered me the part of Felix, the Poet Butterfly in *The Insect Play* which he was putting on at the Regent Theatre, King's Cross, in a few weeks' time. I was told that after the play was produced, I might continue my classes at the Academy in the daytime except on matinée days.

The rehearsals at the Regent were very exciting. It was thrilling to play a part that had never been played by anyone before, and to see the production taking shape. Claude Rains was in the cast, to my great delight, and also Angela Baddeley, Maire O'Neill, Elsa Lanchester, and Bromley Davenport. Playfair had just discovered at Liverpool Doris Zinkeisen, who was to make her first success in London with her brilliant scenery and dresses for this play. Miss Zinkeisen was very good-looking and wore exotic clothes. She was at that time engaged to James Whale, a tall young man with side-whiskers and suède shoes, who was stage-managing for Playfair at the time. (He was later to direct the first production of *Journey's End* and ended his life and career as a very successful Hollywood director.) These two made a striking pair at the dances to which Playfair, with his charming hospitality, used to invite the company at Thurloe Lodge, a beautiful little house off the Brompton Road which he had just rebuilt, and which Zinkeisen had decorated for him in a very modern style. There was an attractive square hall with a tessellated pavement, a charming staircase, and a white-panelled drawing-room with chandeliers. As a devotee of *The Beggar's Opera* I was of course enraptured to be asked to the Playfairs, to see the Lovat Fraser drawings which decorated the rooms, and to meet, amongst others Violet Marquesita, who had been my special favourite among the Lyric cast.

The Insect Play was a failure, and I created a very bad impression in it. The first act (The Butterflies) was not good, and the weakness of the opening was the more regrettable since the rest of the play was extremely interesting. In the original Czech, I believe, the Butterfly episode had been very improper but very amusing; however, Clifford Bax and Playfair, who translated the play together, removed the indecency but found little material to replace it. The two girls and I, who played the principal parts, were all quite inexperienced, and in spite of our efforts, the act proved ineffective. I wore white flannels, black pumps, a silk shirt, a green laurel-wreath, fair hair, and a golden battledore and shuttlecock—I am surprised that the audience did not throw things at me.

The play ran for six weeks. On the last night, Playfair sat in a box with his back turned to the stage all through the first act. It was a bitter disappointment to him that the play had failed, but my indifferent performance in it did not prevent him from being kind enough to offer me a part in Drinkwater's *Robert E. Lee* which was to follow. In fact, he re-engaged as many of the cast of *The Insect Play* as he possibly could. Zinkeisen was again engaged to design the scenery, but at the dress rehearsal it was found to be far too impressionistic for a straightforward biographical play. Most of it was discarded accordingly, and real trees and bushes planted about the stage. These, placed against a cyclorama, served for the outdoor scenes of the play, most of which took place in woods and on battlefields. Unfortunately, the foliage withered and died after a short space of time, and the stage looked very woebegone as the play dragged on, to increasingly sparse audiences, during the summer months.

The notices were extremely good and the play was full of well-written effective scenes. It was beautifully acted, especially by Claude Rains, but it was never a success and I am sure that Playfair continued to run it chiefly to keep the company in work. He must have lost money every week. One afternoon Claude Rains was taken ill, and I appeared in his place for several performances. As in *The Wheel*, I made a surprising success the first time I played, but lost confidence on subsequent occasions; but I think everybody was agreeably impressed with my ability in the emotional scenes. The 'feeling' of them came to me without much difficulty, and the sincerity of that feeling 'got over' to the audience, despite my lack of technical accomplishment, whereas in the 'walking' part of the orderly, which I usually played, my clumsiness and slovenly movements were conspicuous, and there were no moments of emotion or drama in which I could atone for them.

During the summer my parents went away, and I borrowed a little flat in Mecklenburgh Square, near the Regent Theatre, where I was appearing. I felt very independent with a home of my own, and the flat was charming, with curved corners to the panelled rooms, and a delightful Irish landlady, like Lee White,[1] who wore mob-caps in the morning.

Meanwhile, I was still working at the Academy with Rains. He directed me in Tolstoy's *Reparation*, in which he himself had recently played with Ainley. I had seen it and was wildly excited at the chance of playing the part of Fédya, and we all worked madly at the gypsy scenes, learning songs and collecting 'properties' from home to dress the stage on the day of the performance.

I also played the opening scene of Hotspur, from *Henry IV, Part I*, for a diploma competition, and was complimented by the judges. Next day, one of them sent me a charming letter of congratulation, and summoned me to his office, where he spent half an hour sipping a glass of milk and begging me to change my name for the stage, as no one would ever be able to spell or pronounce it properly. I answered obstinately that if anyone did notice it they would not easily forget it, and so we parted.

I completed my year's tuition at the R.A.D.A. shortly afterwards.

[1] A delightful Australian revue actress, who, with her husband Clay Smith, charmed London audiences during the First World War.

I appeared in *Les Caprices de Marianne*, and in a scene from *L'Aiglon*, endeavouring to act in French. The producer, Mlle Alice Gachet, was one of the most brilliant professors at the Academy. But my French vocabulary is not equal to my accent, and I did her little credit, I'm afraid. It was left to Charles Laughton to become Mlle Gachet's star pupil, and act as brilliantly in French as he did in English. Some years later he was invited to appear, playing in French, at the Comédie Française, and on that memorable occasion Mlle Gachet accompanied him as a guest of honour.

CHAPTER FIVE

1922–23

I remember well the interviews preceding my next two engagements, but I have no idea how my new employers heard of me or why they should have thought me likely to be promising material. My first visit, just before Christmas, after *Robert E. Lee* had come to an end, was to Mrs Brandon-Thomas in Gordon Square; my second, a month or so later, to J. B. Fagan in a charming house in St. John's Wood, just behind Lord's Cricket Ground. Both interviews proved satisfactory, and I went into *Charley's Aunt* for the Christmas season at the Comedy Theatre, and, in the following spring, to Fagan's Repertory Company at the Oxford Playhouse.

Charley's Aunt was rather a disappointment to me. I played Charley, the 'feed' part of the two tiresome undergraduates who provide the juvenile love interest in the play. Finding, when I read the part, that I had few opportunities for distinguishing myself, I arrived at rehearsal fully determined to wear horn-rimmed spectacles and adopt a silly-ass manner, copying as far as I could the methods of an actor whom I had recently admired in a musical comedy called *Battling Butler*. My hopes were rudely shattered by Amy Brandon-Thomas, the producer and daughter of the author, who arrived in a large grey squirrel coat and strode on to the stage bristling with authority. She very soon informed me that the play was a classic—every move, nay, every garment worn by the actors was sacrosanct, and no deviation of any kind was to be tolerated for a moment. It seemed to me a great pity that, in spite of this, the play had been brought up to date. It is full of references to chaperons and carriages (changed in later years rather lamely to 'cars'), and a revival in the original trappings of the nineties would, I am sure, be an enormous success today. The romantic and sentimental scenes alone would be hailed by a modern audience with shouts of joy. Many of the lines have stayed with me ever since; such gems as these:

> 'Oh, to live for ever among these dreaming spires and sculptured nooks—like silent music—a scholar's fairyland!'

and

> 'He never called me "the angel of the watch"; but he did get as far as a stammering compliment and a blush and then——'
> 'And then——?'
> 'Then he was ordered off with his regiment.'
> 'Without ever——?'
> 'Without *ever.*'
> 'Oh! Auntie!'

We played twice daily for six weeks, and I had to dash up and down stairs an innumerable number of times changing my clothes. It was fun at first hearing people laugh so much, but after a few performances it was agony to me to keep a straight face myself, especially as the old actor who had played Mr Spettigue hundreds of times took a particular delight in making us giggle on the stage and then reporting us to the stage management, when Miss Brandon-Thomas would descend upon us again and lecture us severely. Laughing on the stage is a disgraceful habit, and she was perfectly right to make a fuss about it. It is particularly fatal to succumb in farce (the most tempting kind of play to giggle in) for the absolute seriousness of the actors is usually the very thing which makes the situations funny to the audience. My most disgraceful exhibition occurred years afterwards in *The Importance of Being Earnest*, when, at a very hot matinée rather poorly attended, I suddenly noticed four old ladies, in different parts of the stalls, not only fast asleep, but hanging down over the edges of their seats like discarded marionettes in a Punch-and-Judy show. I became so hysterical that the muffins I was eating refused to go down my throat, and by the end of the scene the audience were roaring with laughter, not at the play, but at my hopeless efforts to keep myself under control. I was so ashamed that I hardly knew how to finish the performance.

I had refused the chance of becoming a real undergraduate, and now I had acted one on the stage in *Charley's Aunt*. My engagement with Fagan took me to Oxford after all, with a very nice little salary to live on, and there I stayed for three terms at a time when many of the schoolboys with whom I had been at Westminster were members of the University.

Fagan was an Irishman of great personal charm. Also he was extremely talented as author, producer, and impresario. His death in Hollywood in 1933 was a real loss to the theatre. He and Playfair (whose life also was cut short) were both Oxford men, both Bensonians, and both ardent devotees of Granville-Barker. The productions given by Playfair at the Lyric, Hammersmith and by Fagan at the Court were among the most distinguished and individual of their time, and as a boy I had seen many of them—*The Merchant of Venice* (with Moscovitch as Shylock), *Abraham Lincoln*, *Henry IV*, *Part II* (with Frank Cellier as the King), the Lovat Fraser *As You Like It*, and *Othello* with Godfrey Tearle. I had never read the last play—I only knew that Desdemona was strangled in the last act—and my terror and excitement as the jealousy scenes drew to a climax were almost more than I could bear.

The Playfair-Lovat Fraser *As You Like It* was a commercial failure, but it broke entirely fresh ground in the easy natural way in which the scenes were played, without cuts or traditional business, and in the originality and simplicity of the *décor*. Athene Seyler was a delicious Rosalind, and Herbert Marshall a fine Jacques—his first appearance after the War, in which he had lost a leg. There were unforgettable beauties in the scenery and costumes—a wood scene like a children's fairy tale, with straight white-and-grey silver birch trees and conventionalized curved borders, and a Court Lady in the wrestling scene (which took place in a kind of cloister) with a particoloured black-and-grey fuzzy wig, and a dress belted high up with the skirt billowing out in front in that charming 'pregnant' manner which is typical of the fourteenth-century missals.

The whole production was strikingly simple and bold in its conception, but it was before its time, and at Stratford-on-Avon, where it was tried out, the Press was outraged and the company almost mobbed in the streets. Yet one remembers the success of far more 'advanced' productions by Komisarjevsky in later years at Stratford, and cannot help wishing Playfair had been spared to rival them. Both he and Fagan understood actors very well, and though neither of them seemed to display much authority at rehearsals, their influence on a production was extraordinarily individual and characteristic. Both men really understood Shakespeare and had a wide knowledge of plays of all periods. Besides, they had excellent taste in music and painting, and a flair for discovering unknown talent.

The company at Oxford was a delightful one. Tyrone Guthrie was an actor in those days, and Veronica Turleigh, Flora Robson, James Whale, Richard Goolden, Reginald Denham, Alan Napier, and Glen Byam Shaw were among our number. Mary Grey was the leading lady, and Dorothy Green, Doris Lytton, Minnie Rayner and Raymond Massey were others who joined the company for various productions. We acted on a tiny stage, which Fagan had cleverly built out in an 'apron' several feet in width, with side doors leading on to it. There was no front curtain, except to the inner stage, and any properties needed on the forestage used to be 'set' in view of the audience by a stage hand, dressed in a white coat like a cricket umpire, at the beginning of each scene. In *Monna Vanna*, when the furniture set in this way consisted of a voluptuous-looking couch, with cushions and a leopard-skin, the undergraduate section of the audience could not resist bursting into ironic applause! The prompter was a further difficulty, as there was nowhere in the front part of the stage where he could be effectively concealed. Since we presented a new play every Monday his services were apt to be greatly in demand, particularly at the beginning of the week, and, for fear of not finding him within our reach, we resorted to the old trick of writing out our lines and pinning them about the stage. Disaster came on two occasions—once in *Oedipus*, when a local super stood with both feet and a spear firmly planted on the all-important piece of paper, and Jocasta had to shove him aside with her elbow and then stoop to the ground apparently overcome by a sudden onrush of emotion; and another time, in *Captain Brassbound's Conversion*, when Massey, who played the American Captain, upset an entire bottle of ink over the table on which had been carefully pinned three pages of the dialogue for the final scene between Sir Howard and Lady Cecily.

We had to be very careful in our diction at the Playhouse. The hall, for it was little more, was situated near the junction of the Banbury and Woodstock Roads, and any lorry or bus which passed outside during the play drowned our lines with its vibrations, while inside the cane chairs placed in rows, with slats of wood running underneath them to keep them in position, groaned and squeaked in a running commentary whenever anyone sat down or got up or moved their legs into a more comfortable position. There was no foyer, and smoking was not allowed, so that it is little wonder that our audiences varied in number and that we relied principally on the faithful few who patronized us regularly with season tickets. On the other hand we presented a very interesting programme and the company acted increasingly well together. Reginald Denham and James Whale helped Fagan with the producing, and Fagan and Whale took turns in designing the scenery, which we all used to help paint and construct between Saturday night and Monday afternoon. Some of the effects were quite ambitious. Whale did a wood for *Deirdre of the Sorrows* consisting almost entirely of a few light tree-trunks cut in three-ply, and we had a most regal tent scene in *Monna Vanna*, contrived from the rose-coloured curtains used by Fagan at the Court Theatre for the Moscovitch *Merchant of Venice* Trial Scene.

We acted plays by Congreve, Sheridan, Wilde, Pinero, Milne, Shaw, Ibsen, Chekhov, Pirandello, Synge, Sierra and Benavente during the two eight-week seasons when I was in the company, and the biggest success of the first season was *Love for Love*, which shocked North Oxford and a lot of our regular patrons, but delighted a large section of the University and drew many people to the Playhouse for the first time, chiefly, I am afraid, on account of its scandalous dialogue and improper situations.

It was very pleasant to live in Oxford, to have meals with people in College, and drinks at the O.U.D.S.[1] We actors used to march home together along St. Giles' with linked arms after the play at night, singing army marching songs at the top of our voices, in the hope of being mistaken for undergraduates, pursued by the bull-dogs, and brought before the proctors. 'Your name and college, sir?' 'Not a member of the University!'

Gyles Isham was the 'star' of the O.U.D.S. that year. Fagan produced twice for the Society at this time, first *Henry IV, Part I* in which Gyles played Hotspur, and then Hamlet. Gyles was greatly helped in both performances by 'J. B.', who set the *Hamlet* in Dürer scenery and costumes, and lit his scenes most beautifully. There was a dawn, faintly pink and pearl grey, in the scene of the swearing after the exit of the ghost, that was unforgettably lovely—and the last scene was splendidly arranged and unusually moving and poetic.

[1] Oxford University Dramatic Society.

Gyles had beautiful rooms at Magdalen, once occupied by Oscar Wilde. I lunched with him there one day towards the end of the first season, and he was full of a plan to play Romeo during the vacation for a special performance in London, at the R.A.D.A. theatre in Gower Street. The Juliet was to be a well-to-do young woman, who was in love with Gyles and had theatrical ambitions and a rich mama.

The day after our lunch my face and neck began to swell, and the doctor told me I had mumps. There was nothing to be done but resign myself to going home. Fagan read my part at the Playhouse that night (and developed mumps himself a few days later), and Mother, always prompt in an emergency, arrived at my rooms in St. John's Street and took me home in a hired car, with large pillows on which to rest my face, which looked by this time so like Humpty Dumpty's that I wanted to laugh every time I caught sight of myself in a glass, though it was much too painful to do so.

I recovered in a few weeks, but my luncheon at Magdalen had been a fatal mistake. Gyles went down with mumps just as his *Romeo and Juliet* rehearsals were due to begin. He immediately suggested that I should learn the part and rehearse for him until he was well enough to work himself, and of course I readily consented. The part appealed to me tremendously, and secretly I hoped that he might not recover in time to appear, but a week before the date of production he returned to the cast, and, as I was on good terms with most of the company by this time, I was asked to stay on and appear as Paris at the performance.

I had put down my name at one or two theatrical agents after my *Charley's Aunt* engagement, and all of a sudden one morning I received the following charmingly worded communication from Akerman May:

2nd April 1924

Dear Mr. Gielgud,

If you would like to play the finest lead among the plays by the late William Shakespeare, will you please call upon Mr. Peacock and Mr. Ayliff at the Regent Theatre on Friday at 2.30 p.m. Here is an opportunity to become a London Star in a night.

Please confirm.

Yours very truly,
Akerman May.

I rang up everyone I knew who might give me further information on the subject and discovered at length that Barry Jackson was putting on *Romeo and Juliet* shortly at the Regent Theatre with Gwen Ffrangcon Davies, and was searching for a Romeo to act with her. As I had studied and rehearsed the part so recently and was word-perfect in it, I took my courage in both hands and went to King's Cross to apply for the engagement. Another letter followed a few days later:

April 11, 1924

DEAR MR. GIELGUD,

I am feeling quite excited (as an old Actor) to hear this morning that it is most likely we have fixed you to play in 'Romeo' in London.

Best hopes and congratulations.

AKERMAN MAY.

So it was largely owing to Gyles Isham and the epidemic of mumps at Oxford that I was lucky enough to play my first big Shakespearean part in London at the age of nineteen.

I had to endure the agony of three auditions and a great deal of uncertainty before I was finally engaged. Walter Peacock was advising Jackson at the time and seemed inclined to believe in me from the first, but I was so young and inexperienced that there was every reason to doubt my capacity to sustain such an important part. Jackson was kind and non-committal—his very pale blue eyes twinkled, and he smoked countless cigarettes through white cardboard holders during our interview. H. K. Ayliff, his producer, was rather terrifying, immensely tall and thin like a Franciscan Friar, with brown boots and very long-waisted green tweeds. These three were to decide my fate. Several other young actors besides myself were under consideration, I knew, and I was determined to defeat them all. I gave one audition at the Kingsway and another, more hopefully, at the Regent, where I felt a little more at home as I had acted there so recently. There I stood, with a working-light casting its hard cold beam on to the empty stage, trying to give some sort of reading of the passionate farewell scene with Juliet, whose lines Ayliff read from the wings in hollow tones. In the shrouded stalls Jackson and Peacock were sitting in hats and overcoats. My voice echoed bleakly in the cold theatre, and I felt that in the circumstances I could have done better justice to the sentiments of Juliet in the Potion scene:

'I have a faint cold fear thrills through my veins,
That almost freezes up the heat of life——.'

At last the committee seemed to be satisfied, and I was engaged. I was wildly excited, of course. Rehearsals were not to begin until the following week, and meanwhile I took my father to the Regent, where *The Immortal Hour*[1] was being played at night, to see Gwen as Etain. It was my second visit. Now that I was to work with Gwen I was impatient to see her performance again, and the beauties of her acting and singing enchanted me even more than before —her silver dress, her braided black hair, and those lovely stylized movements of her hands! Her high, clear voice seemed to belong to another world as she glided through the forest in the first act and up the steps in the final scene, hardly seeming to touch the ground. I could not believe that in a few days' time I should be holding her in my arms as Juliet.

The Gwen that appeared at the first rehearsal was a very different person. She wore an old dress and carried a business-like overall on her arm. Her face was no longer pale, and she was brisk and impulsive in her movements. We were introduced. I thought she looked strangely at me for a moment. Then she began rather nervously to talk. After a few minutes she suddenly gasped and said, 'Thank God'. Then she explained that she had seen me in *The Insect Play* as that wretched butterfly-poet. I had made a most unfortunate impression on her, and when she had heard that I was under consideration for Romeo she had been appalled at the idea. She told me all this in the most sincere and charming way, and I was relieved to find that she seemed to like me after all, though at the same time it was a nasty shock to my vanity to find that my performance had affected her so unpleasantly. We started to rehearse. Both of us were word-perfect from the beginning (for Gwen had played Juliet at Birmingham some time before) and we plunged into the work at once. There is usually some excuse for restraint at early rehearsals while one still holds the book in one's hand, but here there was no chance of postponing the moment when I must let myself go. I had to attack my scenes at once with power and confidence, and try and convince everybody that I was worthy of my big chance.

[1] An opera by Rutland Boughton, which had a rather highbrow vogue for a time.

When I had understudied in *The Wheel*, Phyllis had come down once or twice to rehearsals and shown me how to hold her in a love scene. I had been amazed to find how skilled a business it was to handle a woman effectively on the stage, to avoid cramping her movements, disarranging her hair, or turning her awkwardly away from the audience at some important moment of the dialogue. Of course I had played love scenes at Lady Benson's and at the Academy too, and very embarrassing they were. Clinging self-consciously to a girl as shy as oneself in front of a classroom full of sniggering students at half past ten in the morning is a cold-blooded business; but it is probably just as well for the beginner to realize as early as possible how difficult (and how unromantic) the craft of stage love-making can be.

Gwen was wonderfully helpful. She herself was so extraordinarily keen and unselfconscious. From the very first rehearsal she threw herself wholeheartedly into every moment of her part, running the whole gamut of emotions, experimenting, simplifying, but never losing for an instant the style or the pictorial aspect of the character she had so vividly imagined for herself. She told me not to be frightened of our 'clinches', and when the moment came to embrace her passionately, I was amazed to find how naturally she slipped into my arms, sweeping her draperies in the most natural and yet artful way so that they should neither lose their line nor impede her movements, and arranging her head and arms in a position in which we could both speak and breathe in comfort, and extricate ourselves easily when the action demanded.

I know *Romeo and Juliet* by heart, and I have played Romeo three times, yet I cannot say that I ever pleased myself in the part. I always felt I knew exactly how the part should be played, but I had neither the looks, the dash, nor the virility to make a real success of it, however well I spoke the verse and felt the emotion. My Romeo was always 'careful', and I loved the lines and revelled in them too obviously. My big nose and sliding movements were accentuated by the costume and wig, however carefully designed, and in this early Romeo I looked a sight. I was given white tights with soles attached to them underneath and no shoes. My feet looked enormous, and it was most uncomfortable to fight or run about. My wig was coal-black, and parted in the middle. Wearing an orange make-up and a very low-necked doublet, I look, in the photographs, a mixture of Rameses of Egypt and a Victorian matron.

Romeo has only three scenes in the play with Juliet, and I think I was best in those scenes, thanks to the help Gwen had given me at rehearsal and her unfailing co-operation throughout the performance. Most of the others in the cast were not good, and the small parts were really badly played. Paul Shelving's scenery was hard and rather crude, though it solved the problem of speed very satisfactorily, and the production was commendably free from cuts or extraneous business. I lost confidence badly a few days before the first performance. It was a trying time. The clothes, made in the theatre wardrobe, were only half finished. They smelt abominably of the gold paint with which they were lavishly stencilled and fitted very badly. Gwen's dresses alone were most successful. She sat up in the wardrobe and finished sewing them herself in the few hours she could spare, and when the dress-rehearsal came she looked a vision. She wore a red-gold wig with small sausage curls at the neck, a wreath on her head, and high-waisted Botticelli dresses with flowing skirts, each one more becoming than the last. The stage was still in chaos, and the whole production so unfinished that Ayliff cleared the theatre, which was full of invited guests, and conducted the dress-rehearsal with the safety curtain down, a proceeding which did not increase our confidence, especially when I found in the ball scene that Gwen and I could not kiss for the pins which were still holding my costume together and pricking me in various parts of my anatomy.

The notices were very mixed, though Gwen was tremendously and deservingly praised. A. B. Walkley was very encouraging to me in *The Times*, and some of the other critics were amiable about my performance, but on the whole I was not a great success. Ivor Brown said I was 'Niminy-Piminy—Castle Bunthorne'. A weekly paper had a notice which I have always cherished. It said, 'Mr Gielgud from the waist downwards means absolutely nothing. He has the most meaningless legs imaginable. . . . At times he reminded me of that much better actor, Philip Yale Drew [then playing Young Buffalo in a melodrama at the Lyceum]. He has the same sort of hysterical laugh, which is almost a giggle, and quite meaningless!' Some people thought that I was promising, spoke the verse well, and understood the character. Considering my lack of experience, I think it is remarkable that I was let off so lightly. It was too soon for me to dare to play Romeo in London—even at King's Cross.

The people who liked *Romeo and Juliet* liked it very much. Although the theatre was not often full, the production created a good deal of interest. Small bands of faithful admirers came again and again to see it and I met some interesting people.

We were asked out to smart parties once or twice. A rich lady who lived a little way out of London invited us to play the balcony scene on her lawn one Sunday night. We were too shy to ask for a cheque, which no doubt she would have been delighted to give us, but we were pleased to accept her invitation. Mrs Gordon Woodhouse, dressed in purple scarves and a turban, was playing Bach and Mozart on a clavichord when we arrived, and the drawing-room was crammed to suffocation and looked like a scene from one of Aldous Huxley's novels. Ernest Thesiger was sitting about on the lawn, and Lopokova[1] was eating cherries out of a big straw hat. After supper we went up to dress, and then the outdoor performance began. I ran across a flower-bed to my place below the window from which Gwen was leaning (her wig looking strangely orange in the moonlight), and found that I had to risk life and limb on a very rickety espalier before I could touch her hand with mine. I looked round desperately to invoke the moon, but realized at last that it was shining on the wrong side of the house. Our lines were punctuated by our hostess's voice murmuring in a rich Dutch accent, 'Oh! it's so r-r-romantic!' and the wrigglings and slappings of the other guests who were vainly battling with mosquitoes.

One day at the matinée I felt extremely ill. The balcony scene is always a very tiring one to play. It is not easy to produce one's voice correctly while standing and gazing upwards in a strained position. That afternoon I found it particularly exhausting. Suddenly in the middle of it, everything went black. There was a long pause, and the curtain slowly fell. Poor Gwen was left in her balcony with a crumpled Romeo on the floor below. The house applauded, thinking, I suppose, that I had swooned with ecstasy. I came to after a few minutes and finished the two performances somehow. But I had pneumonia, and could not play for a fortnight. I had two understudies, neither of whom was competent to appear (one of them, being sent for to rehearse with Gwen, became stone deaf from sheer terror), and Ion Swinley stepped into the breach

[1] Ballerina in Diaghilev's company. Afterwards married to Maynard Keynes, the great economist.

and played the part with the book in his hand for a few performances. Then Ernest Milton played for a week till I was well enough to act again. A month later the production came to an end after being played for six weeks altogether, but I was away for two of them. My baptism of fire was over.

CHAPTER SIX

1924–25

I went back to the Oxford Playhouse for another season. I was tired of living in 'digs', and I had taken a two-roomed flat on the second floor of a house in the High, opposite the 'Mitre'. It was simply furnished and had sloping wooden floors and a charming view. I was very proud of it as it satisfied all my instincts for tidiness and space. I used to get my own breakfast, boiling an egg and making tea on a gas-ring by my bed, and eat it while I studied my next week's part propped against the looking-glass. While I was putting on my clothes I would wander about between the two rooms reciting my lines, shouting above the noise of the gramophone, which, for some unknown reason, I always played after my bath. Sometimes on Sunday evenings following our dress rehearsals, I gave small parties, and we drank a great deal of beer and shouted out of the windows.

Fagan allowed more rehearsals than usual for *The Cherry Orchard*, which he had determined should be the most interesting production of our new season. He talked to us at some length about the play, but at the first reading it mystified us all considerably. There was little time for discussion, however, and we set to work as best we could. The work was utterly different from anything I had attempted before, but, even though I understood so little the style and construction of the play, I saw at once how effectively my part was placed to make the greatest possible effect in the simplest way—the first entrance of Trofimov, peering in to the nursery through his spectacles, and Madame Ranevsky's emotion at seeing him again, because he was the tutor of her little boy who was drowned—his idealistic scene in the country with Anya—his clumsy efforts to comfort Madame Ranevsky at the party when she hears that the orchard has been sold, and his exit when he rushes from the room in confusion and tumbles downstairs—finally the scene where he burrows among the luggage for his goloshes, and leaves the deserted house with Anya, hallooing through the empty rooms.

Making up for Trofimov, I put on a black wig, very thin on the top and in front, a little beard and steel glasses, and found myself looking like a shabby bleary-eyed caricature of my brother Val. I was very pleased with my make-up. It acted as a kind of protection from my usual self-consciousness and I felt easy and confident when my turn came to make my appearance on the stage. For once I need not worry whether I was moving gracefully or looking handsome; I had not to declaim or die or express violent emotion in fine language. Instead, I must try to create a character utterly different from myself, and behave as I imagined the creature would behave whose odd appearance I saw in my looking-glass.

Of course, all acting should be character-acting, but in those days I did not realize this. When I played a part of my own age I was acutely aware of my own graces and defects. I could not imagine a young man unless he was like myself. My own personality kept interfering, and I began to consider how I was looking, whether my walk was bad, how I was standing; my attention was continually distracted and I could not keep inside the character I was trying to represent. As Trofimov, for the first time I looked in the glass and thought, 'I know how this man would speak and move and behave', and to my great surprise I found I was able to keep that picture in my mind throughout the action without my imagination deserting me for a moment, and to lose myself completely as my appearance and the circumstances of the play seemed to demand. I suppose the truth of the matter was that I was relaxed for the first time. The finest producers I have worked with since have told me that this relaxation is the secret of all good acting but we were never taught it at the dramatic schools. One's instinct in trying to work oneself into an emotional state is to tighten up. When one is young and nervous one tightens the moment one attempts to act at all, and this violent tension, if it is passionately sincere, can sometimes be effective on the stage. But it is utterly exhausting to the actor and only impresses the audience for a very short space of time.

In playing Shakespeare one is bound to be conscious of the

audience. The compromise between a declamatory and a naturalistic style is extremely subtle, and needs tremendous technical skill in its achievement.In Chekhov, provided one can be heard and seen distinctly, it is possible, even advisable, to ignore the audience altogether, and this was another reason why I suddenly felt so much more at ease in playing Trofimov than I had as Romeo.

I have extremely good eyesight and I am very observant. From the stage, if I am not careful, I can recognize people I know eight or ten rows back in the stalls, even on a first night when I am shaking with nervousness: late-comers, people who whisper or rustle chocolates or fall asleep, I have an eye for every one of them, and my performance suffers accordingly. I once asked Marion Terry about this difficulty and she said, 'Hold your eyes level with the front of the dress-circle when you are looking out into the front'. It has taken me years to learn to follow her advice. But in Chekhov, whose plays are written to be acted, as Komisarjevsky used to say, 'with the fourth wall down', I have always been able to shut out the faces in front even when I look in their direction and am conscious of no one but the other characters round me on the stage.

The Cherry Orchard made a stir at Oxford, and Playfair, who came to see it, offered to transfer the whole production to the Lyric, Hammersmith,[1] at the end of the Oxford season. The prospects of success were not very hopeful, however. People remembered how the audience had walked out at the original Stage Society performance some years before, and at the dress-rehearsal at Hammersmith the backers smoked many cigarettes and shook their heads over the booking sheets. But Arnold Bennett[2] and Playfair were still hopeful and enthusiastic, and the play went very well on the first night even though the theatre was not as full as it might have been. There was a mixed press and several very empty houses afterwards, and Playfair hastily arranged for a revival of *The Beggar's Opera* and engaged his cast. All of a sudden the business began to improve. James Agate wrote a most helpful and illuminating notice in the *Sunday Times* and also spoke enthusiastically about the play over the radio. Basil Macdonald Hastings, on the other

[1] The Lyric was managed at this time by Playfair and he produced a number of brilliant successes there until his death. This charming old theatre was pulled down in 1971, and I gave a television interview from the empty stage there just before it was destroyed. It has of course been recently rebuilt and reopened with success.

[2] Bennett and Duff Taylor were partners with Playfair in the management of the theatre.

hand, wrote a violently denunciatory notice, saying *The Cherry Orchard* was the worst play in London. Fagan and Playfair printed Hastings' and Agate's notices together on the same posters and in the advertisements in the newspapers, and the curiosity of the public was aroused. We began to play to really good audiences at last and, though a few people walked out at every performance, the general verdict was enthusiastic. We could not remain at the Lyric, of course, as *The Beggar's Opera* was already in rehearsal, but moved to the Royalty[1] where the play ran through the summer.

The committee of the Phoenix Society had lately been very successful with their Sunday night and Monday afternoon performances of Elizabethan and Restoration plays. Isabel Jeans had made one of her first big successes for the Phoenix in *The Country Wife*. Now Norman Wilkinson[2] asked me to play Castalio in Otway's *The Orphan* for the Society and I jumped at the opportunity. I had a very good declamatory part, and there was a curious plot, in which the heroine, Monimia, came in mad like Ophelia and everybody died in the last act. I remember nothing else about the play, except that Melville Cooper (who afterwards made such a success as Trotter in *Journey's End*) played somebody's old father and had a line beginning very dramatically 'Ruin like a vulture' which he delivered at the dress-rehearsal 'Run like a vulture' and paralysed us all with laughter. At the Monday afternoon performance I saw two figures outlined in the stage-box, and at one moment during the play I distinctly heard a voice which I recognized at once, saying in a loud stage-whisper, 'Now I know how he must have looked as Romeo'. It was Ellen Terry.

I had seen her four or five times on the stage as I was growing up, but one of my most vivid memories is of an evening when I went to hear her read Beatrice in a private house in Grosvenor Square. I had never seen *Much Ado About Nothing* acted on the stage, and here there were only gilt chairs placed in a semicircle, a hushed, respectful audience, and a company of nervous amateurs in evening dress reading their parts from little books. In an armchair in the middle sat Ellen Terry, provided with a large book with very big print. Off she started, spectacles on nose, eyes on the text—no showing off to frighten the others. Just a sweet old lady with a

[1] In Dean Street, Soho. The theatre was bombed in the Second World War.
[2] A brilliant designer for Granville-Barker in his Savoy Shakespeare seasons, 1912–13, was one of the promoters of the Phoenix Society.

lovely voice—but not for long. The words of the play seemed to catch her by the throat, she rose from her chair and she began to act. A few more lines and she had mastered her forgetfulness completely. She was old no longer. She needed no lights or scenery or costume to show us how divinely she could play Beatrice. 'No, sure, my lord, my mother cried; but then there was a star danced, and under that was I born', and then with such a tender change of tone, 'Cousins, God give you joy'. There was nothing frail about her now, no hesitation in her sweeping generous movements and the strong expressive movements of her hands,[1] now at her lips, now darting to her lap to bunch up her skirts as if she were poised for flight:

> 'For look where Beatrice, like a lapwing, runs
> Close by the ground, to hear our conference.'

One could see how she must have glided across the stage. Then, in the Church scene, when Hero swoons, Ellen Terry rushed across the platform, upsetting several of the little gilt chairs on the way, and clasped her 'cousin' in her arms to that young lady's considerable embarrassment.

I saw her act another time in a theatre on one of the piers at Brighton. She gave the Trial Scene from *The Merchant of Venice* and two scenes from *The Merry Wives of Windsor*. The orchestra played a gay little tune and Ellen Terry came dancing on, dressed in the wimple and head-dress and flowing gown of Collier's famous picture.[2] Among the company who appeared with her and had the privilege of learning from her was Edith Evans, who played Nerissa and Mistress Ford on this occasion. 'A girl after my own heart' Ellen wrote once in a book she gave her, and Edith's own lusty performance of Mistress Page a few years afterwards (for Playfair at the Lyric, Hammersmith) showed what an apt pupil she had been.

It was very cold at Brighton when I saw the performance, and I was told that Ellen Terry, well wrapped up against the wind, had been wheeled down the pier in a bath-chair, past the empty benches and penny-in-the-slot machines, to the stage-door. But when she swept in to the court as Portia half an hour later, the

[1] Her hands were not beautiful, but she used them with marvellous fluency.

[2] With Sir Herbert Tree and Dame Madge Kendal in the 1902 Coronation Performance of the *Merry Wives of Windsor* at His Majesty's Theatre. The picture is now in the Garrick Club.

elderly lady of the bath-chair was forgotten, though her hair was unashamedly white under the scarlet lawyer's cap. Like Duse, whom she loved and admired so much, she needed no artificial aids to bring the spirit of youth with her on to the stage. The Trial Scene was her favourite in her last years, and in that one scene her memory seldom seemed to fail her. But I have heard that one night, when she was playing it at the Coliseum during the First World War there was a Zeppelin raid. No one could keep Ellen Terry from seeing everything that was going on, and she insisted on being taken up on to the roof to watch the raid until the time came for her to appear. She made her entrance towards the end of the programme and was received tumultuously by the excited audience, but the bangings and poppings outside the theatre were not helpful to her concentration. When she came to the line, 'This bond doth give thee here no jot of——' she stopped dead. The actor standing nearest to her on the stage, realizing what had happened, was preparing to whisper the missing word into her ear, when the voice of Edith Craig, her daughter, shattered the silence from the prompt corner with the words 'Blood, Mother, blood!'

The newspapers were full of Noël Coward's triumph in *The Vortex* at the Everyman Theatre in Hampstead, and off I went to see it with my parents. In that tiny auditorium the atmosphere was extraordinarily tense, and the curtain of the second act, with Noël sitting in profile to the audience, his white face lifted, chin jutting forward, head thrown back, playing that infuriating little tune over and over, louder and louder, till the curtain fell, was one of the most effective things I ever saw in a theatre. The night we were there Noël was not at the door when the moment came for his entrance in the last act—the call-boy had missed his cue, or perhaps there was no call-boy at the Everyman—and there was an agonizing stage 'wait' while Miss Braithwaite trod the stage like a baulked tigress, holding the excitement as best she could until he arrived some moments later. We in the audience were so engrossed by this time, however, that the unfortunate hitch seemed hardly to affect us, and after the performance, clattering back in the half empty tube on the long journey home to South Kensington, we all sat silent, in that state of flushed exhaustion that only a really exciting evening in the theatre can produce.

When *The Vortex* was transferred to the Royalty (and later to the Comedy and the Little), someone must have suggested that I might be suitable to understudy Coward, as it was essential to have an actor who could play the piano. Fagan released me for the second time. I hope I thanked him properly—looking back on that time I realize what an extraordinarily kind and thoughtful manager he was. I was introduced to Noël one evening as he was making up. In those days I was used to seeing a few sticks of Leichner greasepaint in an old cigarette-box and a shabby tin of talcum powder on actors' dressing-tables, and Noël's room looked very glittering, with large bottles of eau-de-Cologne on the wash-stand and an array of dressing-gowns hanging in the wardrobe. Noël was charming to me. He said it was a great relief to him to have someone reliable in the theatre, and that he would help me in any way he could. I shared a room with three other understudies with whom I played games and did crossword puzzles, and I went into the pit every night to see the last act from the front and watch as carefully as I could the way Noël and Lilian worked up the very long difficult duologue which made the last act so exciting to the audience.

Noël Coward used to arrive late at the theatre for *The Vortex*, as his entrance in the play did not occur until forty minutes after the rise of the curtain. He was rehearsing his revue *On with the Dance* all day long, and enjoyed sitting over his dinner as long as he possibly could. I used to stand at the stage-door looking down the street with a stick of greasepaint in my hand, ready to rush off to his dressing-room and make up if he should fail to appear. At last my patience was rewarded. Noël wanted to go to Manchester to see the opening of his revue, and told me I was to play his part on the night he was away. He gave me two rehearsals beforehand with Lilian Braithwaite and all the principals. I was naturally very nervous. Some of Noël's lines are so extraordinarily characteristic that, when once you have heard him deliver them himself, it is almost impossible to speak them without giving a poor imitation of him. Lines like:

> 'The last time I saw you you were at Sandhurst.'
> 'Such a pretty place.'
> 'You know, the very nicest type of Englishman.'
> 'I hate the very nicest type of Englishman.'

I thought I had studied minutely, during the many performances of the play I had watched, all the gradations of voice and inflection that the actors used in their big scenes, but I found that technically I had a very poor idea of how to reproduce them. The only moment I managed well at the rehearsal was the boy's final outburst against his mother, when he sweeps the glass off her dressing-table and flings himself into her arms. Even then I was so excited that I cut myself with the bottles, but in spite of my clumsiness Noël and Lilian seemed very pleased at my obvious sincerity, and their good opinion encouraged me to play my very best when the important night arrived.

There are few occasions more nerve-racking than playing a leading part in the absence of a principal. Before I went on that evening some kind person knocked at my door to tell me that several people had asked for their money back because they saw the notice posted at the box-office announcing that Noël was not appearing. But audiences are extraordinarily fair and well-disposed towards young understudies, especially if the play is an interesting one. At the end of the evening the applause was just as warm as it had been on other nights, and Lilian Braithwaite, who had helped me so generously all through the performance, sent for me to her room to meet Mr and Mrs George Arliss who had happened to be in the audience. Violet Loraine[1] also wrote to Noël, saying how much she had regretted finding him out of the bill, but how well she thought I had filled the breach. Altogether I felt that I had made a good impression.

The play was moved again, first to the Comedy and then to the Little Theatre.[2] The last weeks were announced, as the production was to be done in New York in the autumn and Noël needed a six weeks' holiday. But the management asked Miss Braithwaite whether she would consent to continue the run for another four weeks after Noël had left the cast, with me replacing him as Nicky. It was characteristic of her to think of my chances and the company's salaries instead of her own much-needed holiday—for, of course, she was to appear in the play in America too.

[1] A great and popular revue artiste, who created with George Robey the immortal popular song of both World Wars, 'If you were the only girl in the world', written by Nat D. Ayer for 'The Bing Boys'.

[2] The Adelphi in John Street, destroyed by bombs in the Second World War.

CHAPTER SEVEN

1925–26

Chekhov's *The Seagull* provided me with my next part. The manager of this venture, Philip Ridgeway, was a curious man. The success of Fagan's production of *The Cherry Orchard* had led him to consider putting on several of Chekhov's plays, and after *The Seagull* he proposed to do productions of *Three Sisters, Ivanov* and *Uncle Vanya.* He had taken a lease of a tiny theatre at Barnes, across the bridge by the gates of Ranelagh Club, and for the first production there he had presented a rather indifferent stage version of *Tess of the D'Urbervilles.* This occasion was the signal for a good deal of publicity. Thomas Hardy was too old to come to London, and Gwen Ffrangcon Davies and Ion Swinley, who were in the play at Barnes, went down to Max Gate one afternoon and acted a scene for the great man on the hearthrug of his drawing-room. Photographs and descriptions followed and the play opened with a good deal of éclat. The acting was good enough to make the version seem a good deal better than it was, and the critics were kind to Ridgeway's enterprising scheme of running a theatre so far from the West End. *Tess* played for many weeks, and *The Seagull*, which had been planned to follow at Barnes, was produced instead at the Little. Then *Tess* moved to the Garrick, and *Three Sisters* followed it at Barnes.

The Seagull seemed to me to be written in a more conventional manner than *The Cherry Orchard.* There are 'big scenes' in every act, and the four principal characters carry the interest in a far simpler method of exposition than in the later Chekhov plays. Konstantin is a very romantic character, a sort of miniature Hamlet, and a very exciting part for an ambitious young actor. I was given very good notices on the whole and thought at first that

I was very well suited to the part. I resented the laughter of the audience when I came on in the second act holding the dead seagull, but on a very small stage it did look rather like a stuffed Christmas goose, however carefully I arranged its wings and legs beforehand. The last act used to go magnificently, thanks to the really beautiful acting of Valerie Taylor, whose performance of Nina made her reputation overnight. It was largely owing to her success that the play was a good deal talked about, and people came to see it for quite an unexpected number of weeks.

In contrast to the praise I received in some quarters for my performances, I received a good deal of personal criticism from a few discriminating friends, who told me that my mannerisms were becoming extremely pronounced, my walk as bad as ever, and my diction slovenly and affected. In one scene I had to quote Hamlet's 'Words, words, words'. My critics were perfectly right when they said I pronounced the line to sound like 'Wirds, wirds, wirds', but I found it surprisingly difficult to rid myself of this habit of closed vowels. I had begun to learn something of pace and the way to build up to a climax, my emotional outbursts were sincere, and I found I could make a great effect at times with pauses carefully timed and spaced, or with a suddenly simple delivery of a line at a pathetic moment. But as soon as I made one of these momentous discoveries I could not resist showing off what a clever technician I had become. The audience was quick to notice my self-satisfaction, and my acting became alternately shamefaced and 'tricky', according to the way I felt I was failing or succeeding in that particular part of the play.

At the end of the run of *The Seagull*, Philip Ridgeway sent for me to meet Theodore Komisarjevsky.

What prompted Ridgeway to engage Komis to produce the other three Chekhov plays for him I cannot imagine, except perhaps the fact that he was, like Chekhov, supposed to be a highbrow with a Russian name. He had, of course, done a number of interesting productions in London before this and he was a friend of the Fagans, for whose productions he had designed costumes. But I doubt if Ridgeway knew much about his work.

Komis was one of the most contradictory and fascinating characters I have ever met in a theatre. He was bitter and cynical about the English stage and the English public, destructive, pessimistic, and at the same time a real artist, a wise and brilliant teacher, and often an inspired director. He had an odd sense of humour quite unlike anyone else's, and would often spend thousands of pounds with less perfect results than he could achieve (as he did at Barnes when I was working under him) with a hundred or two as the outside limit of his expenditure. He loved to work with young people, adored enthusiasm, and inspired the greatest devotion from his actors and staff. His knowledge of painting, music and languages was considerable, and he had produced plays and operas in Berlin, Paris, Rome and Vienna, as well as in London and New York. He nearly always designed his own scenery and dresses, and his lighting was brilliantly clever. He was an architect as well as a painter, and designed all the decorations for the Phoenix Theatre and for a number of big cinemas in the suburbs of London. He was also the author of several fascinating books about the theatre.

Komis's sister, Vera Komisarjevskaia, had been one of the finest actresses of the Moscow Art Theatre, and had created the part of Nina for Stanislavsky. After a brilliant career she died of consumption at an early age. Komis had been to see our *Seagull*, and he had thought the production 'very funny'. But in spite of the fact that he was amazed to find us all playing in such a welter of gloom and Russian blouses and boots (and I dare say we should have been equally astounded at a Russian production of *The Importance of Being Earnest*), he decided that Margaret Swallow, who played Masha, and I were both conceivably promising material, and offered to engage us both for *Three Sisters*, in the parts of Masha and Tusenbach respectively.

Rehearsals started in a flat in Bloomsbury where Komis was living at the time, having rented it from the actor, Franklin Dyall. There we all sat, crowded round a table at first, reading the play for many days on end, then laboriously trying to 'set' our complicated movements by keeping to chalk marks carefully drawn all over the floor to mark the exits, entrances, etc. Some five weeks later, when we reached a more advanced stage of rehearsals and arrived at the Barnes Theatre, we realized why so much care had been taken in dealing with the limited space at our disposal. Komis's ingenuity in making use of a tiny stage on a restricted budget was quite extraordinary. He arranged the first and last acts on a sort of terrace. Through big open windows, stretching right across the stage, one could see the room within—the dining-table (to seat thirteen) angled off-stage into the wings. In front, a clothes-line on one side and the shadow of a tree on the other (a branch tied with a piece of string to the front of a strong lamp in the wings was responsible for this effect) gave the feeling of outdoors. For the two middle acts the windows were removed, and the same back walls suggested the interiors, hung with different lamps and pictures and arranged at a different angle. In the sisters' bedroom the beds were not seen, but a chintz-covered partition some four feet high stretched across the stage, dividing it in two. At the end of the act the girls retired behind this partition with their candles, and one saw, on the wall above, their huge shadows as Irina sat up in bed crying and Olga came across the room and leaned over to comfort her.

Three Sisters can be produced and played with many different interpretations, just as a play of Shakespeare's might be quite differently conceived by, say, William Poel and Granville-Barker, Komis's production certainly emphasized the romantic quality of the play, and he made some curious cuts and alterations in the text. He dressed the play twenty years earlier than the author intended, and the sisters wore the bustles and chignons of the eighties, which looked very attractive and certainly heightened their picturesque appearance. But his principal change affected me particularly, as he cut all references to the Baron being an ugly man—which is Chekhov's reason why Irina cannot love him—and made me play the part in a juvenile make-up, with a smart uniform and side-whiskers, looking as handsome as possible. I have never been able to discover why he did this—but I have a suspicion that he felt that a juvenile love-interest was essential in any play that was to appeal to an English audience. He persisted in casting the part in this way in every subsequent revival of the play, and it was extraordinary to me that not one of the critics, who went into ecstasies over the beauty of the production, noticed this very marked divergence from the express stage-directions and dialogue of the author. Of course I much preferred playing the part as a handsome young Lothario, and it did not then occur to me for a moment to question Komis's validity on any point in such a brilliant ensemble as he had achieved in his beautiful production.

Actors loved working for Komisarjevsky. He let them find their own way, watched, kept silent, then placed the phrasing of a scene in a series of pauses, the timing of which he rehearsed minutely.

Very occasionally he would make some short but intensely illuminating comment, immensely significant and easy to remember. Martita Hunt once rehearsed for him a scene of Charlotta, the German governess in *The Cherry Orchard*. When she had finished Komis patted her on the shoulder and murmured the one word 'Irony'.

There were some wonderfully good performances in the Barnes *Three Sisters*. We played twice daily for eight weeks, and the road from Hammersmith was crowded with cars every night. Chekhov was a hit. Komis was very pleased with the tremendous appreciation both of the press and the public, and I think he was pleased, too, at our delight in working with him. When the scenery and effects were revealed for the first time at the dress rehearsal there was a spontaneous burst of applause from the whole company.

The next production at Barnes was a play called *Katerina* by Andreyev. It was a sensational play, and nearly a very good one. I played Katerina's husband, a sort of Slavonic Othello. At first when Komis showed me the play I was amazed that he should dream of entrusting this strong character-part to me, but, as it turned out, it seemed to be one of the best performances I gave in my early years. There were some magnificent moments of 'theatre' in the play, and Komis arranged them superbly. The curtain rose in the first act upon a darkened stage, faintly lit under the door of a room on the right, where the husband and wife could be heard quarrelling. Their voices, muffled at first, grew louder and louder, till after nearly a minute they reached a climax. Then two shots rang out, and Katerina threw open the door and rushed across the stage. I followed her and fired again, missing her, and from this exciting opening the act proceeded. This first scene was difficult to get right, as the quarrel off-stage was not written in the text, and Frances Carson and I used to make up our lines every night, following the rough outline of a quarrel which we had carefully rehearsed for volume and climax. Punch had a delightful cartoon the following week, representing me with my forehead pressed against the wall, with the smoking revolver in my hand, and the caption 'O, how I miss my wife!'

The theme of the play was interesting. A madly jealous husband suspects his innocent wife of infidelity. She leaves him, and, her mind infected by his suspicions, commits adultery with a very insignificant man, a friend of her husband. The husband comes to beg her to return to him, and she confesses what has happened. In his shame he takes her back, but her mind is completely poisoned, and she begins having affairs with a number of other men, until in the last act, we see her dancing half naked at a studio party, while the husband sits helplessly looking on. At the end of the play she goes out for a drive in the sledge of a drunken artist who makes advances to her, and the husband is left on the stage, amid the débris of the party, mechanically accepting a cigarette from the insignificant little man who was his wife's first lover.

My part began on the very highest note of violent emotion—which then became lower and lower in tone as the play proceeded. There was a beautiful scene of reconciliation in the second act, when Katerina confesses her guilt. Afterwards she goes into the house and plays Debussy on the piano, leaving her husband and her first lover sitting in the garden outside. As the curtain falls the lover offers his cigarette case, but on this first occasion the husband ignores it. There was a fine duologue between the husband and an artist friend (who, later in the play, has also become Katerina's lover) when the husband tries to find courage to kill himself—the whole play was Slav and intense. Ernest Milton played the artist, and we both used to find it hard to keep a straight face in this very dramatic scene if the house was not sympathetic. The dialogue ran:

> 'There's a fine view from that window. Is it high?'
> 'The sixth storey. A precipice.' (*Long pause.*)
> 'Could you kill yourself, Charles? I'm just interested to know.'

Komis cut up the floor of the tiny stage for this production, so that in the garden of the second act people seemed to come up from below on to a terrace, and in the studio scene of the third and fourth acts there were steep stairs ascending to the stage, giving the effect of a very lofty attic. But, as usual, I was rather too conscious of the good effect Komis had created for me, and James Agate remarked: 'Mr Gielgud is becoming one of our most admirable actors; there is mind behind everything he does. Only, he must avoid the snag of portentousness, of being intense about nothing in particular. Twice in this play he has to make an entry upstairs from below stage. The first time is an occasion of great solemnity, but on the second he is merely paying a friendly call, to do which it is unnecessary to put on the manner of one rising from the grave.'

About this time I had the honour of meeting Mrs Patrick Campbell. She had been to see *Katerina*, and when I was introduced to her she was very complimentary and said: 'You acted beautifully. And you should always wear a goatee.' I was introduced to her at the late Lord Lathom's beautiful flat in Mount Street, where I used sometimes to be asked to luncheon parties. Ned Lathom was a tremendous enthusiast about everything to do with the theatre, and he was always putting money into plays as well as writing them himself. If he had not been so rich (and so delicate in health), he might have become a very successful playwright, for he was inventive and had a real flair for good stage-situations and caustic, witty dialogue. I was quite bewildered by the elegance of his flat, with the Romney portraits, the library filled with lovely hand-bound books, the thick carpets, the burning sandalwood which scented the rooms, the exquisite food and fascinating company. Here I met Marie Tempest and Gladys Cooper for the first time, and Ned also introduced me to H. M. Harwood, the playwright, through whose kind offices I acted shortly afterwards, for a special Sunday night performance, in a version he had made of *L'École des Cocottes*, in which I appeared with Gladys Cooper and Leslie Faber.

It was exciting to meet some famous West End stars, and still more exciting to act with them. Ned Lathom used to laugh at my 'highbrow' tendencies, and my enthusiasm for Chekhov and Shakespeare—and indeed my career seemed to have been curiously diverted towards intellectual plays since the days of *Charley's Aunt*. I was longing now to earn a bigger salary and to see my name painted on the boards of a theatre in Shaftesbury Avenue, but at the same time I realized how profitably I had spent my time at Barnes and with the Fagans. Komis's interest and help had encouraged me tremendously, and I began to feel that I could study a part from the inside, as he had taught me, not seizing at once on the obvious showy effects and histrionics, but trying to absorb the atmosphere of the play and the background of the character, and then to build it outwards so that it came to life naturally, developing in proper relationship to the other actors under the control of the director.

The boy in *L'École des Cocottes* was not a big part, but there was a lot of boyish horseplay with the heroine in the first act which embarrassed me acutely (though Miss Cooper did her best to put me at my ease) and two rather charming sentimental scenes towards the end. I was paralysed with nerves at the performance and acted indifferently. The play proved rather disappointing, though Gladys Cooper gave an extraordinary exhibition of virtuosity, and looked absolutely dazzling in a black velvet dress in the third act, and Faber was immense as the Professor of Etiquette, demonstrating to the heroine and her very unsophisticated friend (played inimitably by Dorothy Hamilton) the proper way for ladies to behave on a visit to the Opera. Ned Lathom arranged the scenery for the third act—one of the first 'white' rooms ever done in the theatre. Although the play had been banned at first, it was passed by the Censor after the Sunday performance. When it was done later by Miss Cooper (under the title of *Excelsior*) at the Playhouse, without Faber or Dorothy Hamilton, I thought it not nearly so amusing, though Denys Blakelock was very much better than I had been in the part of the boy.

I appeared for The Three Hundred Club in a play called *Confession* with Cathleen Nesbitt at the Court one Sunday night. After the performance I received a message that Basil Dean was outside waiting to see me. I dressed as quickly as I could and when I came out of the stage-door, there, sure enough, was Dean, standing under a lamp-post by the Sloane Square Underground Station. He murmured something about having liked my performance, thrust a manuscript into my hand, told me to read it and call on him next day, and hurried away into the darkness.

Dean had sent for me once before and asked me to play the effeminate young man in Lonsdale's *Spring Cleaning*. I had always wanted to work at the St. Martin's, which had been the scene of so many of my early thrills as a playgoer—*A Bill of Divorcement*, *The Skin Game*, *Loyalties*—and the prospect of acting with a star cast at that theatre had tempted me greatly. But after reading the part I decided to ask twice the salary I had ever dared to ask before, and was not unduly disappointed when it was refused. I had not forgotten *The Insect Play*, and the bad impression I seemed to have made in it on actors and managers alike, and I was glad that the temptation to play an equally unpleasant character had been summarily removed.

The manuscript which I took home from the Court that night, however, was a very different matter. When I had finished reading

The Constant Nymph, adapted by Margaret Kennedy, with the help of Basil Dean, from her best-selling novel, I could hardly believe it possible that such an opportunity should have fallen to me out of the blue. The part of Lewis Dodd was a tremendously long and difficult one, but it gave wonderful opportunities to the actor; it had comedy, pathos, drama, temperament, scenes at the piano, love scenes. Besides all this, the story was delightful, the atmosphere original and convincing, and the play seemed to demand, and would obviously receive, all the advantages of a first-class West End production.

I arrived next morning at the St. Martin's long before the time for my appointment with Dean, and suffered agonies of apprehension while many other actors and actresses were passed into the inner sanctum ahead of me. The room kept filling up and emptying all the morning, and there were continual comings and goings in the passage through the frosted-glass door. Still my name was not called. I should have been even more dismayed had I known what was going on in Dean's office, for I heard afterwards that Miss Kennedy was violently championing my cause in opposition to that of Ivor Novello, whom Dean had also approached with a view to playing Dodd. At last, when it was nearly lunch-time, I was ushered in, clutching my manuscript to my chest as if I defied the world to take it from me. Dean and Miss Kennedy were very amiable. Dates and salary were mentioned, but somehow I had a feeling that it was all too good to be true. At length I plucked up my courage and said, 'You are quite sure you really want *me* for this part?' Dean was very bland and reassuring. He said I should have a contract as soon as the play was passed by the Censor, and that rehearsals would begin in a few weeks' time. I left the office treading on air, took a fortnight's holiday in the country and, on my return, asked a friend to lunch with me at the Ivy to celebrate my good fortune. Noël Coward was at a table by the door and I nodded to him as I passed. After I had finished my lunch, I noticed that Noël was looking across at me with rather a serious face, and I felt suddenly frightened when he beckoned me to go over to his table. Then he said, very gently and kindly 'I think I ought to tell you before Dean does. I am going to play Lewis Dodd for the first month of the run of *The Constant Nymph*.'

I was bitterly disappointed. I felt Dean had been unfair in not telling me frankly that if he could get a star he would not risk me in the part. Noël had been so kind to me in *The Vortex* that I could not resent his playing Lewis, but I knew how difficult it would be to follow him, and that anyway all the joys of original creation would be snatched from my grasp. I was summoned to Dean's office that afternoon. He offered me half salary to understudy Noël for a month and then the salary he had originally mentioned to play the part afterwards. I swallowed this added insult and then saw that I had been foolish not to have made a bit of a scene, for Dean looked quite relieved and said, 'You are taking this very well'. I smiled sheepishly and retired (wearing a martyr's crown) to seek consolation from my friends.

I sat through all the rehearsals of the play, and very interesting they were, though I was too discontented and depressed to enjoy my first experience of a big new production to the full. There were stormy scenes almost every day. The cast had been brilliantly chosen, but there were complicated ensemble effects, the charades and breakfast scene in the first act, the musical party in the second, and the Queen's Hall scene in the third. In all of these episodes Dean demanded a most complicated perfection of detail to be carried out as if by clockwork. Edna Best had been cast for Tessa (after a great deal of argument during which the part had nearly been given to Tallulah Bankhead) and Cathleen Nesbitt said to me bitterly: 'I am always Basil's last choice. When he can't get any-one else to play a part he sends for me.' Noël disagreed with Dean and Margaret Kennedy on several occasions, and one morning he left the rehearsal at a standstill and retired with them to the bar, whence their voices could be heard in violent argument. Noël came in to the Ivy for lunch with a set face half an hour afterwards telling me he was going to throw up the part, and my heart leapt as I thought my chance was coming after all. Dean asked me that afternoon whether I knew the lines, and I went home and studied them all night—but next morning the row had been patched up, and the rehearsals went on as if nothing at all had happened.

Every day the stage management arrived with piles of 'props'. If the rehearsal was moved to another theatre, everything had to be taken there—siphons, sandwiches, beer-mugs, soup-plates. Over and over again Dean rehearsed the musical party, until the guests went nearly mad, making bright conversation in high-pitched voices, and stopping short with abrupt resignation every few minutes when the same person made the same mistake for the eighth time and the whole scene had to be done all over again.

Dean's efficiency was certainly remarkable and *The Constant Nymph* was one of his most accomplished achievements. He got good results from the actors in the end, but usually after a great deal of heartburning. He would not allow people to think for themselves or develop their characters freely, and his meticulous method of giving them every inflection and tone before they had experimented themselves made them feel helpless and inefficient. As part author of the play as well as director, he was naturally intensely anxious, but his enthusiasm carried the final rehearsals to a remarkable level of perfection.

On the first night I could not bear to watch the play. I slipped off to see Florence Mills in *Blackbirds* at the Pavilion, and only came back between the acts to the stage-door of the New, where they told me that the play was being enormously well received. The Press was unanimous next morning. Edna Best had made the greatest success of her career, Noël had splendid notices, Mary Clare, Keneth Kent, Cathleen Nesbitt, Helen Spencer were all much praised. George Harris's *décor* and Dean's production won superlatives, and the theatre was packed at every performance.

Noël was to have played for a month and I had been promised newspaper announcements and a certain amount of publicity when he left. Ten days before the month was up, however, he sent for me and said he felt terribly ill. He left in the middle of the third week and I opened at a matinée the following day. As I had rehearsed with the understudies, as well as once with Dean and with the principals and once with Noël, I hoped that I should not disgrace myself. At first everything seemed to go well. The houses were still packed in spite of the fact that Coward had left the cast. But I was made to feel rather small. I was billed, after a few days, in the newspapers, but otherwise I was baulked of my hopes for publicity. Noël's photographs remained outside the theatre for the whole year's run which followed, a fact that annoyed me whenever I passed the doors. He had tried to pave my way with the company before he left, but unfortunately I did not seem to be able to live up to the good character he had given me. Dean had gone to America, and there was no one really in control. It was a most unhappy time for me. I acted as well as I could, but at first I was terribly hampered, just as I had been in *The Vortex*, by Noël's reading of the lines, which were so indelibly printed on my mind that I could not easily discover how to play the part in my own way.

It was a very unfortunate thing that, with such a big success and a certainty of a long run, everyone in the company seemed to be at loggerheads with everyone else. At least three of the cast were 'not speaking' to me, and at least three more were 'not speaking' to several others. People accused one another of spoiling their best effects, of cheating on laughs or letting down some important moment. I used to wonder every night how much the general dissatisfaction behind the scenes affected our playing from the point of view of the audience.

My own acting became increasingly self-conscious. Dean returned some twelve weeks after I had opened, saw a performance, and came to my room with 'Very nice for an understudy. You know we want more than that.' The next day he called an intensive rehearsal at which he reduced me to pulp and Edna Best to tears. The rows and complaints continued unceasingly for many months, until at last I got really ill and had to leave the cast for ten days. When I returned, the atmosphere seemed a little more friendly and, to my surprise, several of the company came up to me and asked me why I was not going on tour with the play. I replied rather grandly that nobody had asked me. Next day I was sent for to the office, where I was officially invited to play Lewis in the provinces, upon which I demanded double my salary and star billing. To my amazement, both were conceded without a murmur.

It was extraordinary how often in those early years I seemed to be on the fringe of real achievement. If I had been hailed as a leading juvenile after Romeo in 1922, I might never have played in *The Cherry Orchard* or at Barnes. Again, if I had created the part of Lewis Dodd in 1926 and made a success of it, my subsequent career would probably not have followed the devious route which led me to the Old Vic in 1929. Although my work was extraordinarily varied and I gained a great deal of experience of different kinds, I was always prevented by a series of chances from achieving any spectacular personal success.

CHAPTER EIGHT

1927–28

The Constant Nymph gave me my first experience of a long run. To play the same part eight times a week for more than a year is a severe test for any actor. The routine is nerve-racking, and it is agonizing work trying to keep one's performance fresh without either slackening or over-acting. I am usually guilty of the latter fault, and my tendency to exaggerate every effect becomes more and more marked as the weeks go by. After a long run in London, touring is at first a pleasant change, even in the same play, as one is forced to change the tone and breadth of one's performance to suit the different sizes of the provincial theatres; but by the end of a year's run in London with a six weeks' tour of the provinces to follow, acting becomes a real nightmare, and it seems hard to believe one is ever going to enjoy it again.

Long runs have their advantages, however. To begin with, they are necessary for an actor if he is to attract the notice of a large public. Many people can only afford to go to the theatre two or three times a year, and naturally they are inclined to choose for their visits the plays which are big hits of several months' standing. Young actors can often make personal successes in a series of short runs or even in failures. The critics may indeed notice them with more attention if they distinguish themselves several times running in a series of indifferent plays, as Laurence Olivier did so markedly in the early part of his career. But, though they may be well spoken of in the Press, and 'fancied' in the small world of the theatre, the general public will never have heard of them until their names have once been connected with a big commercial success.

There is also the question of discipline. A long run, with continual good houses, gives the actor confidence and sureness in his technique. He is able to try many different ways of timing, to study the details of tone and inflection, to watch his mannerisms, and to develop his capacity for give-and-take in acting with his partners. He is forced to control his boredom, to discover a means of producing effects of emotion of which the spontaneous feeling has long since deserted him, to resist the temptation to giggle and play the fool, to find a way of rousing a lethargic house, and to remind himself continually that there are many people in every audience who are seeing and judging his acting for the first time.

Long runs are also very useful for making money. As soon as *The Constant Nymph* had settled down to a certain success, I persuaded my parents to let me leave home. Frank Vosper was shortly to move from a little flat in Seven Dials, where he had been living for some time. I greatly admired this flat and arranged to take over from him the rest of his lease.

The flat was full of character and I stayed there for eight years. There was no proper kitchen, and the bathroom, with a rather erratic geyser, was down a very draughty flight of stairs. But otherwise the place was charming. The sitting-room walls had been covered with brown hessian by Vosper, and there was a ceiling in one of the bedrooms painted by an artist friend of his (under the influence, I imagine, of Braque), with large nude figures sprawling about. This I thought very modern and original. Later, when I became a little more affluent, I took over a large attic belonging to the landlord. It had a huge cistern in one corner, windows black with the dust of ages, and an incredible conglomeration of rubbish which had to be taken away by relays of dustmen. When it was cleaned, I painted the floor, silenced the gurglings of the cistern, built in some cupboards, and turned it into a spare room and studio. I acquired a charming Irish cook, and gave small lunch parties at which her Irish stew was the principal attraction.

It was exciting to be in a success in the West End and to be able to afford to take a flat on my own, and I had an exceedingly good time when I was away from the theatre. But I used to get very depressed about my unpopularity at the New, and the strain of the long emotional part of Lewis Dodd was very exhausting. I opened the play, had six changes of clothes, and was hardly ever off the stage except when I was making these changes. Occasionally I saw something of my brother Val. He had been unlucky ever since the

War, and had tried a number of schoolmastering and tutoring jobs without much success. Later, he had taken to the stage, and had even understudied me in *The Cherry Orchard* at the Royalty. Fagan had given him work at the Oxford Playhouse for a time and now he was appearing (as a policeman!) and understudying in *The Ringer*, Edgar Wallace's first big success, which was running at Wyndham's, just across the court from the New where we were playing *The Constant Nymph*.

Naomi Jacob, the authoress, was also acting in *The Ringer*, and very good she was. She left the stage a year or two after this time owing to ill-health which forced her to live abroad. Val and I used sometimes to go to parties at her flat near Baker Street, which were delightful, as she knew a lot of music-hall people as well as 'legitimates'. 'Micky' Jacob was also a great friend of Leslie Faber and his wife.

Faber was playing the Scotch doctor in *The Ringer*, and playing it magnificently. I was already one of his most ardent admirers, having worked with him in *L'École des Cocottes*, in which he was very kind to me. But even before that, I had thought his acting of Henry, the drunken, good-for-nothing husband in St. John Ervine's *Jane Clegg*, which he played with Sybil Thorndike and Clare Greet, one of the finest pieces of character acting I had ever seen. Today I still doubt if I shall ever see a better. So I was in the seventh heaven of delight when, after a gruelling matinée of *The Constant Nymph*, Leslie Faber walked into my dressing-room, said a few immensely gratifying words about my acting, slipped away again, and then wrote me a long letter which he sent across by his dresser during the evening performance.

A week or two after this, Faber took me to supper at the Garrick Club, where I admired the lovely theatrical pictures, the Zoffanys and Hogarths, met Allan Aynesworth, and listened with wonder to some of the older actors reminiscing about Irving. One story, which deeply impressed me but which may be quite apocryphal, described 'the old man' sitting in front of the fire at the Garrick very late one night, crouching apathetically in his armchair with the night's return for *Peter the Great* clutched in his hand, and murmuring bitterly, half-aloud, 'Henry Irving. Ellen Terry. Lyceum Theatre. Twenty-five pounds'.

Leslie Faber's belief in my possibilities carried me through a very difficult time in my career, and I was deeply flattered to have the honour of his friendship. But soon he showed his kindness in a more practical way than by coming to see me act or taking me out to supper. I was summoned to the Gilbert Miller Offices, where 'Tommy' Vaughan, Miller's famous business manager, told me that I was offered the part of the Tsarevitch Alexander in Alfred Neumann's *The Patriot*[1] in America. Leslie Faber, Madge Titheradge and Lyn Harding had already left for New York to rehearse the play. The actor engaged for the young Prince had proved inadequate, and Leslie had put forward my name. If I was to accept the engagement, I must sail in forty-eight hours, learn my short part on the boat, and arrive just in time for the dress-rehearsal. I demanded a good salary and a six weeks' guarantee, packed my trunks, and sailed on a small German boat, the *Berlin*, with only two other English-speaking passengers on board.

I had planned a big New Year party at my flat, but it had to be given without me. The guests sent me a wire to the boat wishing me good luck, and I hoped I should not be very homesick and seasick. I detest uprooting myself and imagine a million disasters and miseries whenever I have to go to a strange place, especially if I am alone. It was just as well, therefore, that on this occasion I had had to make up my mind at once. In New York I was met by a very tall coloured gentleman called John (from the Gilbert Miller offices) and was driven straight to the theatre, where the final dress rehearsal was already in progress.

The very striking scenery and dresses for the play had been designed by Norman Bel-Geddes. The scenes were set on three trucks mounted on castors—one placed at the back of the scene dock and one on each side of the stage. These were 'set' separately, each with a full scene, and then rolled on and off alternately, as they were needed, by stage hands pulling ropes attached to the corners of the trucks. A loud roll of drums in the orchestra covered the noise as they were being moved, and the changes were accomplished in a few seconds. The device is common nowadays in a big production, but in those days it seemed a marvel to me.

When I arrived the theatre was in a state of pandemonium. Miller was rushing about in his shirt-sleeves, with two or three secretaries and stenographers behind him. Bel-Geddes, who looked as if he ought to be playing Lewis Dodd, was gesticulating and

[1] Translated by Ashley Dukes.

shouting through a megaphone, also attended by a retinue of assistants. The stage was covered with scenery and strewn with débris, and Faber was walking up and down, in costume, calling angrily for his dresser.

I did not know how to announce my humble presence and slipped through the pass door to the corridor where the dressing-rooms were, nervously clutching my manuscript in my hand. I knocked at the door marked 'Lyn Harding' and a rich voice bade me enter. Mr Harding, dressed in a very tight but magnificent uniform and made up as the Tsar of All the Russias, was eating a plate of huge oysters from a tray balanced on his knee. I said rather timidly: 'I've come from England to play the Tsarevitch. Shall we go through our lines?' This we proceeded to do.

I had only two or three short scenes in *The Patriot*, but Faber and Lyn Harding gave me every kind of help and generously yielded me the stage in the few effective moments provided for me in the part. It was an alarming prospect to appear after only one rehearsal, but my costume was a great help. My uniform was superb; I wore a beautiful wig, which looked like natural chestnut hair powdered, and a magnificent cloak with an ermine cape, so that one way and another I hoped to cut a dash.

On the first night the play appeared to go very well, though there seemed to be less enthusiasm than at a successful London *première*. I thought this was accounted for by the fact that there was neither pit nor gallery. Miller gave a big party afterwards at his father-in-law's house, and on our way home, in the small hours, Leslie and I sat in Childs' Restaurant drinking coffee and composing hopeful cablegrams to send off to England.

The Press next day was not enthusiastic. The notices ranged from expressions of mild approval to complete boredom. It seemed that a great many people had walked out on the first night—the New Yorkers' polite method of expressing disapproval. Certainly very few walked in to see the eight performances that followed. Then the play was withdrawn. The film rights had been sold beforehand for a large sum, so that the management's losses were covered; all the same, a huge amount of money had been wasted. Some months later the play was done in London under the title of *Such Men are Dangerous*. Matheson Lang appeared in Faber's part, Robert Farquharson in Lyn Harding's, and Isobel Elsom followed Madge Titheradge. Gyles Isham played my part. Aubrey Hammond's *décor* and the production generally were less effective, in my opinion, than ours had been in America. Yet the play was a great success with English audiences and ran for many months.

Faber and I stayed in New York for a day or two in icy weather. The Fagans were playing *And So To Bed* in the theatre next door to the Majestic, where we had been in *The Patriot*. I went with Yvonne Arnaud and young Emlyn Williams to parties, and we had drinks in 'speak-easies', descending steep flights of slippery area steps to little doors, where there would be countersigns and passwords, and faces peering through gratings, before we could be admitted.

I was interviewed during the next few days by one or two managements, the Theatre Guild among others, and promised work later in the season if I would remain in New York. But I could not afford to stay on indefinitely and decided I had better return to try my luck again in London.

Leslie Faber was very much depressed by the failure of the play. The critics had said he looked like George Washington—he did, in fact, resemble him slightly with his powdered hair—and completely failed to appreciate the skill with which he had conceived and executed his performance. I had watched him rehearsing one scene in which he entered a boudoir in his dressing-gown, and forced his mistress to write a letter at his dictation. All the time he was speaking he had to move in and out of the room, tying a complicated neckerchief and completing his toilet in elaborate detail. The scene could have been commonplace enough. As Faber played it, it was a miracle of timing and dexterity.

I saw a great deal of Leslie during the following year in London. He found the play *By Candle Light*, which had been adapted from the German by Harry Graham, produced it brilliantly and played it with Yvonne Arnaud (whom he adored) and Ronald Squire.

While it was running, I acted in a Sunday night performance of *Hunter's Moon*, an adaptation from the Danish. Leslie was very enthusiastic about this play. He directed it superbly, and spent a lot of his own money on accessories, costumes, etc., which otherwise could not have been afforded for one night by the society under whose auspices the play was given. I had a very effective part as a neurotic young coward, and Phyllis Neilson-Terry looked and played radiantly as the heroine. But there was something wrong with the play. I told Leslie I thought he did not take the stage with sufficient *bravura*. He played a kind of Sydney Carton part, all villainy at first with love-scenes and sacrifice to follow, and he was too retiring and generous in the way he acted it. Uncle Fred came to the performance, and I thought how he would have—quite rightly—acted us all off the stage if he had been playing the part instead of Leslie. At the end of the play I was in my dressing-room with a crowd of friends, when there was a knock at the door, and Fred came in. We all stood up, and I said, 'How very kind of you to come round to see me!' I think mine was the best kind of pride when he answered grandly, 'My dear boy, you are one of the Family now'.

I was not long without a regular engagement. Anmer Hall asked me to play two parts in some Spanish plays which he was presenting at the Court Theatre—*Fortunato* and *The Lady from Alfaqueque*, by the brothers Quintero, translated by Helen and Harley Granville-Barker. James Whale was to be the producer. James had had an increasingly interesting career since those first days when I had met him at Oxford. He had worked for Playfair and for Fagan, designed scenery, acted, stage-managed and produced plays; but one could not have foreseen that only a few years later he would go to Hollywood, make the film of *Journey's End*, *Frankenstein*, and then direct *The Invisible Man* and other pictures.

Anmer Hall had cast James Whale for Fortunato, and we were hard at work when we heard one morning that the Granville-Barkers were coming to a rehearsal. When the day arrived and Barker appeared in the stalls, we were all extremely nervous. Everyone whispered, people smoothed their hair and walked about, and Miriam Lewes sat, dressed in her best frock, beating a tattoo with her fingers on the arm of her chair. Barker was certainly a revelation. He rehearsed us for about two hours, changed nearly every move and arrangement of the stage, acted, criticized, advised, in an easy flow of practical efficiency, never stopping for a moment. We all sat spellbound, trying to drink in his words of wisdom and at the same time to remember all the hints he was giving us, none of which we had time to write down or memorize. Everything he said was obviously and irrefutably right. Even when he announced that James could not possibly play Fortunato and that O. B. Clarence must be engaged, everyone gasped but nobody ventured to disagree.[1] Finally we came to my last and best scene in *Alfaqueque.* The young poet who has been found fainting on the door-step has been looked after by the kind lady of the house, and is then discovered by the other characters to be a frightful humbug. But in the last act he brings off another coup and the play ends as he sits in the middle of the stage reading a poem aloud to an admiring circle.

Barker showed me exactly how to play this scene—the business, the timing, everything which would make it effective in performance. I implored him to wait a moment and let me rehearse it two or three times running, but he looked at his watch, signed to Mrs Barker, who was concealed somewhere in the dress-circle, bade us all good-morning, and disappeared through the front of the house never to return.

Shortly after the Court season came to an end, Leon M. Lion decided to contribute to the celebrations that were being arranged for Ibsen's Centenary with some special performances of *Ghosts.* Mrs Patrick Campbell was to appear for the first time in the part of Mrs Alving, and I was asked to play Oswald.

Peter Godfrey, who was running the Gate Theatre at the time, was to be the director, and our first rehearsals took place on the minute stage in Villiers Street.[2] Mrs Campbell arrived and sat in our midst, enthroned in a low wicker armchair which creaked, with her Pekinese on her lap, reading her part from an exercise-book in which some devoted handmaid had copied it out in a large distinct hand. When anybody else was reading she lowered the exercise-book and stared mournfully and intently at the speaker.

We soon found that she knew far more about the play, and every part in it, than any of the rest of us. Mrs Campbell could have been as fine a director as she was an actress. She helped me enormously with the emotional effects of my difficult part, couching her advice in graphic terms. In the scene where Oswald tells his mother of his terrible disease, she said: 'Keep still. Gaze at me. Now, you must speak in a Channel-steamer voice. Empty your voice of meaning

[1] By this I do not mean to disparage the admirable acting of Clarence in the part. But the decision was naturally a sweeping change for us all, and Whale, who had cast and started to direct both plays, as well as designing the scenery, was deeply disappointed of course.

[2] In the arches underneath Charing Cross Station. Now Ridgeways Late Joys.

and speak as if you were going to be sick. Pinero once told me this and I have never forgotten it.'

Mrs Campbell herself gave a very uneven performance as Mrs Alving. For several days she appeared not to know a line of her part, yet at the dress-rehearsal, when we expected her to be temperamental and inaccurate, she astonished us by arriving punctual to the minute, word-perfect, and in full control of her brilliant talents.

We played eight matinées of the play at Wyndham's Theatre following the special Sunday night performance. But the play did not seem to interest the public and the houses were very indifferent. Mrs Campbell used to say to me in her best party voice as she turned away from the audience, 'The Marquis and Marchioness of Empty are in front again'. To add to our difficulties, Charing Cross Road was being repaired with pneumatic drills and the noise in the theatre nearly drove us mad.

I used to take Mrs Campbell to lunch at the Escargot Restaurant in Greek Street, where she taught me to eat snails and discoursed to me on all kinds of topics. I think she was almost the best company in the world, particularly if one was alone with her. The famous stories of her temperament, her 'impossibility' in the theatre, and her brilliant wit, are not at all exaggerated, but, in speaking about these idiosyncrasies to someone who never met her, one is liable to miss giving any impression of her greatness as a woman. It is not often that beauty and success in the world of the theatre are allied to genius. Few people would deny that Mrs Patrick Campbell was one of the really great figures of her theatrical generation. Everything she said or did has been repeated and publicized. She never suffered fools gladly and she was immensely temperamental. But so are all first-class artists. One must remember that Irving and Sarah Bernhardt had their own theatres and could make their own rules of conduct and break them if they felt so inclined. Authors, managers, producers and actors naturally resented being overridden by a personality more powerful than their own, and refused, in her later years, to shoulder the responsibility which the engagement of such an artist as Mrs Campbell involved.

In 1928 Ellen Terry died. St. Paul's Church, Covent Garden, where a service was held in her honour, was a memorable sight. The floor was strewn with sweet-smelling herbs, and in the middle of the aisle was a catafalque covered by a golden pall, with candles burning round it, but there was no coffin and nobody was wearing mourning. At the close of the service the organist played 'The Londonderry Air', and then the huge congregation in its light suits and gay summer dresses streamed out into the sunshine . . .

I thought of the Christmas parties at Gledhow Gardens, and the fairy-Godmother who said 'Read your Shakespeare', and I remembered how once she had read Shakespeare for me herself, not many years before her death. There was a matinée at the Haymarket Theatre and when the curtain rose there were only tall grey curtains and masses of flowers on a table and a lectern with a big book. I still loved scenery and I was rather disappointed. Then Ellen Terry came with her white clubbed hair parted in the middle and her beautifully-lined generous face, bunching up her long white dress with her graceful restless hands. First she talked rather seriously, like a professor, reading out the lecture she had prepared so carefully, but every now and then she slipped her eyes from her book and made some delightfully ordinary comment or improvised some little joke to keep us all happy and amused. Then, cunningly distributed amidst the talk, came the scenes from Shakespeare. There were speeches from many of her great parts, from Juliet, Portia and Beatrice, and there were a few lines from *As You Like It*, in the scene when Rosalind is banished by the Duke. When Ellen Terry came to this, she snatched the big book down from the lectern and walked up and down the stage hugging it in her arms. Of course, she was acting all the parts herself, Frederick and Celia as well as Rosalind.

> 'Mistress, dispatch you with your safest haste, and get you from our court.'
> 'Me, uncle?'
> 'You, cousin.'
> 'Oh, my poor Rosalind, whither wilt thou go? . . .'
> '. . . To seek my father in the forest of Arden'—

—Down she plumped on the table, the book in her arms, swinging her foot in the air. Over went the vases, the tall lilies, the masses of carnations, and the water fell dripping down over the velvet tablecloth, across the stage, down into the footlights, while Ellen Terry sat there, peering over her spectacles and laughing like a schoolgirl.

I saw her appearing once again before the public. She was announced to recite at a charity matinée at the Palladium one afternoon and I went up into the gallery to see the performance. She seemed to be blinded by the lights when she came on, and held her hands behind her, touching the curtains with her fingers to make sure she had not stepped too far forward on the stage. She spoke the title of a poem that every child in the audience knew by heart, 'The Burial of Sir John Moore', but almost as soon as she began the first verse she started to look round wildly for the prompter. She fumbled, muddled two more lines and then stopped dead. It was agonizing to watch her struggling with her memory. One felt sure she did not remember what she was doing or even where she was. Suddenly she lifted her hands towards the audience and smiled. 'Oh, dear,' she said, 'I can't remember it.' Then she threw back her head and began, 'The quality of mercy is not strain'd'— her face lit up, her voice grew strong and beautiful as of old, and on she went triumphantly to the end of the speech.

I have only one more picture of her, and in some ways it is the most vivid of all. I had never in my life been alone with Ellen Terry. Always I had met her at parties, in crowded rooms or theatre boxes or in public. This time, which was the last time that I should ever see her, there was no one by to distract her or to disturb my vision of her.

I was driving one summer day near her lovely Elizabethan cottage at Smallhythe in Kent, where the garden looks across the marsh. It was very hot. I wondered if I dared to call on Ellen Terry all by myself. At last I stopped the car, plucked up my courage and knocked at the door. They told me yes, she was getting up and would be down in a moment.

I went into the farm-kitchen that had been made into a sitting-room. There was a poster of Irving as Becket on the wall. The house was furnished very simply. I like empty, simple rooms myself, but I was rather surprised to find that Ellen Terry did too. Fred and Marion were great hoarders, and towards the end of their lives it was difficult to move in their crowded quarters. Here was a brick floor with rough mats and rugs, a few simple chairs, and a table by the window. Everything was spotlessly clean and airy, and on the table there were big bunches of flowers from the garden, which smelt delicious. There was a steep staircase leading to the rooms above, and I could hear someone moving about, speaking to a servant in a gruff voice, husky but frank and distinct: 'Who is it? Where's my bag?'

Her companion came in and whispered to me quickly: 'Please don't stay for lunch. She is sure to ask you to, but don't, because there's not enough.' Then Ellen Terry came slowly down the staircase. She wore a grey dress like a pilgrim's gown, with long sleeves and something white at her neck. She carried the big worn leather handbag with the padlock that I remembered from my childhood, and there were still red coral combs in her white hair.

She asked me who I was and I told her. She seemed to remember for a while and asked if I was acting now and whether my parents were well. I had on a bright-blue shirt, and she said how gay it was and that bright colours always cheered her up. She asked me to stay to lunch but I pretended I had to go on somewhere else. She seemed suddenly to grow inattentive and I knew I must not tire her any longer. As I turned to go she said: 'Oh, it's so exciting. They have promised to drive me out tomorrow night. I'm going to see the swans at Bodiam Castle. They look so beautiful by moonlight.' I kissed her, and she came with me down the path as far as the gate. As I got into the car she was still standing there, shading her eyes with her hand against the sun. Then she smiled and lifted the other hand to wave goodbye. I looked back from the car for a last sight of her before I turned the corner, but she had disappeared.

CHAPTER NINE

1928–29

I seemed to be getting on well in my profession. I had doubled my salary since the days of *The Constant Nymph* and several managers appeared to know of my existence. I began to be asked to Lady Wyndham's[1] *thés-dansants* in York Terrace on Sunday afternoons, where many well-known stage people were to be seen. I was much flattered by these invitations, for I had never met Lady Wyndham except to say how-do-you-do, and could not imagine that she knew anything about my work, as she very seldom went to the theatre. It was not till after her death, some years later, that I was told that she had 'spotted' me when I was acting in *The Constant Nymph* at the New Theatre, of which she was the owner.

I played in a revival of *The Seagull* for a few performances at the Arts Theatre. The cast and production were almost exactly the same as they had been at the Little in 1925, and Miriam Lewes was very angry with me when I said, over a cup of coffee between the acts at the dress rehearsal: 'It's very boring not to have got any further with this play after all these years. We ought to have found out far more about it this second time.' When I said to the producer: 'I've never played this scene right. Do let me try it some other way', he merely shrugged his shoulders and replied, 'What a pity you always want to gild the lily', which was meant, I believe, as a compliment, but infuriated me none the less.

I acted for several other clubs and private societies which flouri-

[1] Mary Moore, well-known comedienne, wife of James Albery, the playwright, who wrote *Two Roses*. Afterwards she married Sir Charles Wyndham, the actor. She was the mother of Irving Albery, and of Bronson Albery and Howard Wyndham, to whom she bequeathed the three theatres built by Wyndham, The New (now the Albery), The Criterion and Wyndham's.

shed about this time. For the Stage Society I played in O'Neill's *The Great God Brown* with Hugh Williams, Mary Clare and Moyna Macgill.[1] We held masks to cover our faces in certain scenes and speeches which seemed to me rather a pretentious and unsatisfactory convention.

At the Arts Theatre, too, I acted in a play called *Prejudice*, by Mercedes d'Acosta. This was a rather effective melodrama about the persecution of a Polish Jew living in a small town in the Middle West of America. I had a showy and dramatic part, and Gwen Ffrangcon Davies gave a moving performance as the girl, assuming an extremely clever accent for the occasion.

Ralph Richardson played a small part in *Prejudice*, but we did not take much notice of one another. I should have been amazed to be told that we should one day be friends. Leslie Banks directed the play, and I liked working with him enormously. I had great hopes that some enterprising manager might transfer us to another theatre for a regular run, but it was not to be.

Red Sunday, by Hubert Griffith, was another disappointment. The play was much liked by the critics, and several managers made offers for it, but the Censor refused to pass it because the principal characters—the Tsar and Tsarina, Prince Youssoupoff, Rasputin, Lenin and Trotsky—were not then allowed to be shown on the English stage. In this production I again worked with Komis, and admired his methods as much as ever. The scenery was simple to a degree, but brilliantly suggestive and beautifully arranged and lit. There was a most vivid little vignette of the Tsar and Tsarina (Nicholas Hannen and Athene Seyler) in a room in their palace, seen from the audience as if through a balconied window. Komis conveyed exactly the atmosphere of grandeur and ceremony, in contrast to the mean room, lit by an oil-lamp, where I sat as Trotsky, dressed in shabby clothes (and looking even more like Val, in my black wig and spectacles, than I had as Trofimov) at a table littered with books and papers, while Robert Farquharson, amazingly made up as Lenin, leered down at me over the rickety banisters. The scene of Rasputin's murder in the cellar of Youssoupoff's house was macabre and thrilling too, with the big supper-table strewn with dishes where the officers sat, watching with strained panic-stricken faces while Rasputin ate the poisoned cakes. My part went right through the play from youth to middle age,

[1] Mother of Angela Lansbury.

and I enjoyed working out my make-ups, wearing a padded uniform in the later scenes to give the effect of a middle-aged 'spread'.

I hope I have not given the impression that Komis's greatest talent lay in lighting and *décor* and the arrangement of the stage, though he excelled in all these departments. I was more than ever impressed with his handling of the actors, and with his acute musical sensitiveness, which always enabled him to 'orchestrate' a scene to perfection, allowing the actors to feel instinctively that the pauses and business sprang naturally out of the dialogue and process of the action. The result was closely patterned rhythm flowing backwards and forwards between the characters, covering any weakness in individual performance, and shifting the focus of attention continually without breaking the illusion of continuous life and movement on the stage.

These Sunday performances were tremendously interesting but my professional career during the same period was disastrous. I played in three hapless plays in quick succession. First a farce, in which I was 'starred' for the first time in Shaftesbury Avenue, called *Holding out the Apple*, with Hermione Baddeley and Martita Hunt—'You have a way of holding out the apple that positively gives me the pip! !'—Then a thriller at the Shaftesbury called *The Skull*, in which I played an incredible detective who turned out to be the arch-villain. The scene throughout was a deserted church, with an organ played by ghostly hands. There was a comic spinster in difficulties, a somnambulistic *ingénue*, an old professor with a cloak, and a cockney sexton with a club foot. Finally I was in *Out of the Sea* at the Strand, a pretentious poetic melodrama by the American poet, Don Marquis, in which I played the Liebestod from *Tristan* by ear on the grand piano in the first act. In the last, the heroine, who was the reincarnation of Isolde, threw herself off a cliff while I sat glooming in a mackintosh on a neighbouring rock. This last excursion only lasted a week.

Meanwhile *The Lady with a Lamp*, Reginald Berkeley's play about Florence Nightingale, had been produced at the Arts Theatre, and I had attended a few of the rehearsals as I was originally cast for the part of Sydney Herbert. Then something happened to prevent my appearing, and I dropped out. The play was bought and moved to the Garrick, where it achieved a successful run, but Leslie Banks, who played Henry Tremayne (who, in the play, is in love with

Florence Nightingale and is mortally wounded at Scutari), had to leave the cast, and suggested that I should take his place. The part was a short one and I was able to open with only a few rehearsals.

Gwen Ffrangcon Davies gave a most lovely performance in this play as Lady Herbert. It was only a sketch of a part, but she made it such a vivid thing that it seemed to stand out, in every scene in which she appeared, as a perfect foil to Edith Evans's performance as Florence. I had never acted with Edith before, but she and Gwen were old friends. I had seen them playing together brilliantly as Eve and the Serpent in the first part of *Back to Methuselah* at the Court, and had rushed home after the performance and written Gwen a five-page letter of wildly enthusiastic appreciation. Edith Evans fascinated me, but I did not get much opportunity of knowing her at the time of this first meeting. I was chiefly concerned in covering my arms and body with a large quantity of fuller's earth, so that I might appear convincingly filthy when I was borne in dying on my stretcher. Edith had sent strict orders that I must not present a romantically clean appearance, and so shatter the illusion of dramatic fitness which she had conceived in her playing of the scene.

One day, as I was lunching in the restaurant of the Arts Theatre, Harcourt Williams came across the room and asked me if I would consider going to the Vic, where he was about to begin working as director. I suppose I had met him before. Now it hardly seems possible that there was ever a time when I did not know 'Billee' Williams. At any rate I asked him to come and see me at the Garrick Theatre and we would talk the matter over.

In the meantime I asked the advice of most of my friends, as I always do on these occasions (though I can never decide whether I act on the opinions of others or merely use them to strengthen my own). I believe I was really attracted from the first by the idea of going to the Vic. I had had a drifting, unsatisfactory time since *The Constant Nymph*. It was no fun earning a big salary in a bad part, and although I had tried to do character work and act in as many different sorts of plays as possible, I found that managers thought of me chiefly as a 'type' for neurotic, rather hysterical young men. I was not gathering much strength in the West End theatre, and I believe I was secretly determined to reach a position where I might have some say in the handling of a production. I do not think I had ambitions yet to become a director, but I did not want to be nothing but a leading man, and I had begun to feel that acting eight times a week was hardly a full-time job. I was quite prepared to spend all day and all night in a theatre so long as I was making myself really useful and achieving results. Watching Banks and Faber and Komis and Granville-Barker, I realized that, in addition to their individual technical brilliance, a real passion for the theatre was the driving force behind all their work. If I could use my own enthusiasm, or find someone to teach me how to use it constructively, I might perhaps learn in time how to handle plays and actors too, and experiment in putting some of my own ideas to a practical test.

I went down the stairs after the matinée one day and knocked at Edith Evans's door. Edith always slept between the performances, and I am sure she must have been very much annoyed at my intrusion. But she was kind and helpful in discussing my problem, which was similar to the one she had solved so triumphantly for herself, not many years before, in her enormously successful Vic season. She had decided to go there, she told me, because, after playing Helena for Basil Dean in *A Midsummer-Night's Dream* at Drury Lane, she felt that she did not know how to act Shakespeare and wished to gain further experience in his plays. Edith's early career had been an extraordinary one. She was working in a hat shop in London when her acting in an amateur performance brought her to the attention of William Poel, under whose direction she afterwards appeared in some special performances of *Troilus and Cressida*. Then she met George Moore. He also was greatly struck by her talents, and spoke about her everywhere. But even the recommendation of these two brilliant men did not bring her any immediate success. During the First World War she toured in the provinces with Ellen Terry, and afterwards worked in London, playing many kinds of character parts—elderly ladies in *Out to Win* and *Daniel*—and understudying with Dennis Eadie at the Royalty. Here another of Ellen Terry's pupils shared her dressing-room, a young actress named Lynn Fontanne. Edith made further successes as the governess, Charlotta, in *The Cherry Orchard* for the Stage Society, and as the old maid in Brieux's *Three Daughters of M. Dupont*. She played Nerissa at the Court with Moscovitch. Then Fagan and Shaw cast her for Lady Utterword in Shaw's *Heartbreak House*, and she had her first big commercial West End success in Sutro's *The Laughing Lady* at the Globe with Marie Löhr. Refusing to be typed in 'silly society' parts, she boldly refused the offer to play the character of the Duchesse de Surennes in Somerset Maugham's *Our Betters*, in which Constance Collier afterwards made such a great success. At last, at the Lyric, Hammersmith with Playfair, following her success at Birmingham, when she acted the Serpent and the She Ancient in Parts 1 and 5 of Shaw's *Back to Methuselah*, she achieved her greatest triumph as Millamant, and later as Mistress Page. But even at the end of all this varying experience, when her hard struggle had won her recognition and success, she had risked a year out of her West End career and salary to go and play for next to nothing in the Waterloo Road in Shakespeare.

Next day I went to meet Lilian Baylis and discuss my contract. I arrived at the stage door, and was shown into Lilian's office which has so often been described in the stories and descriptions of her. The Vic seemed cleaner than in the old days when I had walked on there, and all the dressing-rooms and most of the offices were new. Morley College was gone, and there was a big airy 'wardrobe' at the top of the new building, replacing the funny old warehouse round the corner, where I remembered rehearsing at nights in murky gloom amidst dusty piles of dress-baskets. Now the corridors behind the stage were painted and swept, and there was a faint smell of size from the painting dock, and of steak and tomatoes from the purlieus of the office, where Lilian's lunch was being cooked.

I was ushered in through the glass door, and found Lilian sitting behind her big roll-topped desk, surrounded by vases of flowers, photographs, two dogs and numerous cups of tea. I had on my best suit, and tried to look rather arrogant, as I always do when money has to be discussed. 'How nice to see you, dear,' said Lilian. 'Of course, we'd love to have you here, your dear aunt, you know—but of course we can't afford stars.' By the end of the interview I was begging her to let me join the company. We both evaded the question of salary as long as possible, and a little matter of fifty shillings, over which we both obstinately failed to agree, was settled by letters some days afterwards.

As soon as matters were arranged, I went to supper with Leslie Faber, whose advice I had asked. He had urged me to accept the engagement, and was delighted to hear that matters were agreed.

I told him that the parts I was to play were not yet settled definitely. I was to open as Romeo, and I was promised Richard the Second, one of Leslie's favourite parts. But I was to play Antonio in *The Merchant of Venice*, which did not appeal to me very much, and the rest of the casting was to be decided later in the season. Lilian was not taking anything on trust. She always wanted to see how the Old Vic audience would respond to the new actors she engaged. 'I expect you'd like to play Hamlet, wouldn't you, dear, but of course Gyles Isham is coming to us too, and we shall have to see.'

Leslie Faber had moved into a new flat in Dorset Street. He had always loved music, and I had sometimes seen him at concerts or at the opera, sitting by himself. He had recently bought a gramophone and we shared our enthusiasms for new records and discussed hotly the respective merits of Bach and Wagner. Leslie gave me records of the enchanting songs from *Mariette* and *Mozart* made by Yvonne Printemps, and also some German recordings of Moissi's speeches, the 'To be or not to be' soliloquy from *Hamlet*, and a scene from Goethe's *Faust* with a background of bells. Even though I do not understand a word of German I realized that the vocal skill and power of these records was remarkably impressive. We would sit up very late at night over a cold supper talking of Gladys Cooper and Yvonne Arnaud, whom Leslie thought the two best actresses he had ever worked with, of the Danish actor Poulsen, of Wyndham and Hawtrey and Du Maurier.

Leslie Faber was making the film of *White Cargo*, playing the part he had also acted in the stage version. He took me to a studio in Wardour Street where we saw the picture in its silent form. It was an excellent film but, as talkies had just come in, it was decided to remake many of the scenes with spoken dialogue. The work was very tiring, and Leslie was still acting in *By Candle Light* eight times a week in addition to his long hours in the studio. He was very much fascinated by film work. He had just made a film for Rex Ingram, *The Three Passions*, in the South of France, and was very good in it. With some of the money he had been earning while doing this work he had bought a boat. He was passionately fond of sailing, and pictures of sailing-boats always hung over his dressing-table in the theatre. After a particularly tiring week's work, he went away for the week-end to enjoy a day's holiday in his new craft, and caught a serious chill.

I had been staying in the country, and read in the newspapers as

I travelled back to town that he was ill and out of the cast at the Criterion. I called at his flat next morning, and inquired if he was better. The man answered, 'Mr Faber died this morning'. I turned mechanically and walked away down the street. It was not till five minutes later that I realized I should never see Leslie again. The doctors had performed the same operation which saved King George the Fifth, but it was too late to save Leslie's life.

I was surprised to read the obituary notices that appeared in the Press after his death. They described him as an actor who had always been eminently successful from his earliest days, and gave an imposing list of plays in which he had appeared as leading man. But I knew that Leslie's career was not in any way equal to his ambitions or his potential talents. He was almost too versatile, and had a curiously ascetic quality which prevented an audience from warming completely to his personality. He excelled as villains and seducers; in plays like *The Letter* and *The Sign on the Door* he was superb. As a character actor, his Dr Lomax in *The Ringer*, his mysterious Count in *In the Night* and his Henry Clegg were all equally different and equally brilliant performances. He failed, however, in heroic tragedy—as Jason, for instance, in *The Medea*—and, to my mind (though he himself thought it his finest performance), as Shakespeare's Richard the Second. On the other hand his Macduff, to James Hackett's Macbeth, was a beautiful piece of work.

He was not a happy man. Difficult, proud and shy, he antagonized many people, and I think he was conscious of this. He was vain, too, and hated the idea of getting old, but perhaps that was why he sought the friendship of younger people like myself, and gave them the privilege of his company so often. He had two unhappy marriages, and he must have been deeply affected by the blindness of his younger daughter, to whom he was devoted. And while he was in the trenches during the War, he received a telegram saying that his son had died suddenly of meningitis at the age of twelve.

By Candle Light had seemed to promise him a new era of success, and, if he had lived, he would, I am sure, have continued in management, surrounded himself with actors whom he admired and trusted, and perhaps he would have achieved at last, both as actor and director, some of the great ambitions he had always cherished.

There is no friend that I have more often missed, no actor whose loss I have more often regretted, than Leslie Faber. His death made me more determined than ever to show at the Vic that I was really worthy of the confidence he had placed in my ability, and to try and emulate his artistic integrity.

CHAPTER TEN

1929–30

I have always been fascinated by theatrical advertisements. When I was a child I used to stand staring in at the window of a ticket agency in the Gloucester Road, learning all the bills by heart. Later, when I went to Westminster School every day by tube, I used to stoop down as the train passed through Sloane Square Station, brushing all the nap off my topper and butting my fellow-passengers in the ribs, while I tried to catch a glimpse of the poster for Fagan's Court Theatre productions, printed in blue, with the picture of Shakespeare—or, was it Malvolio?—drawn in the right-hand corner of it.

When it came to the pleasure of seeing my own name on a theatre bill this obsession became more intense than ever. I was almost run over as I stood, speechless with delight, gazing at my name blazing in lights for the first time.

One evening, some weeks before rehearsals at the Old Vic were due to begin, I decided to walk across the river and look at the outside of the theatre. I pretended that my reason for going was that I had not been there for a long time, but all I really wanted was an excuse to see my name in print.

There are several ways of getting to the Vic. Another of my childish preoccupations, dating back, I fancy, to my dislike of those unswerving walks to kindergarten with Father, is my distaste for following the same route every day in travelling to and from my place of work. Going home from school I used to walk to different stations, Westminster, St. James's Park, or Victoria, on different days, and got out at either South Kensington, Gloucester Road or Earl's Court Station at the other end. Today I still go to the West End from Westminster, where I now live by different sets of streets on succeeding days, avoiding the same route with as much care as I avoid, if possible, wearing the same suit of clothes two days in succession.

From St. Martin's Lane to the Old Vic it is possible to go by several different roads—Northumberland Avenue—Whitehall and Westminster Bridge—the Strand and Waterloo Bridge—Villiers Street and Hungerford Bridge, the last my special favourite. There is something romantic about the steep wooden gangway below Charing Cross Station, leading up through murky Dickensian arches on to the narrow bridge, with its echoing wooden floorboards and iron balustrade. Steps and bridges have always been a passion of mine. I used to think a design of Craig's called *Wapping Old Stairs*—a lovely and characteristic drawing—one of the most perfect ideas for a stage-setting that I had ever seen. Hungerford Bridge somehow reminded me of it. I used to love walking slowly home after rehearsal through the empty slummy streets behind Waterloo Station, climbing the bridge steps until I reached the top where the magnificent stretch of sunset river suddenly burst into view. There were never people about in the late afternoons, and I was able to slouch along mumbling the words of the part I was studying for the next play, without having to drag myself back to earth every few minutes to avoid attracting the attention of astonished passers-by.

It was by Hungerford Bridge that I reached the Waterloo Road that first September evening. I thought the whole place looked tidy and clean in comparison with the rather squalid, naphtha-lit thoroughfare I seemed to remember eight years before. There were still barrows and fish-shops round the corner in the New Cut, but the theatre itself looked bare and almost prim with the front entrance locked and no one going in or out of the stage-door. I scanned the bills on the walls excitedly. They announced a new season with opera in English and Shakespeare, but not a single name.

I walked home (across Waterloo Bridge) in a more mercenary and less romantic frame of mind. Was it for this that I had forsaken a good salary in the West End, a comfortable dressing-room to myself, new suits, late rising, and suppers at the Savoy?

Our first rehearsal took place in a big room at the top of the theatre, next to the wardrobe. It had iron girders in the roof which reminded me of the dormitory at Hillside, and there was a dreadful echo which Harcourt Williams silenced after some weeks by hanging canvas on the walls. A long high shelf ran down one side of the room, and on it perched the 'students', about twenty girls and two or three men. They carried Shakespeares of various shapes and sizes, and stared hungrily at us throughout the early rehearsals of every play. When they began to get bored with the production they all furtively, whispered, or fell asleep. It was rather like the classes at the Academy all over again.

Lilian Baylis arrived that first day and made her usual motherly opening-of-term speech, while we all stood sheepishly round summing each other up—Billee Williams with his eager, harassed face and the tin of Bemax under his arm, Martita Hunt and Adèle Dixon, both very smart and West End, little Brember Wills, Gyles Isham, Donald Wolfit, Leslie French. Billee discussed the opening play with us (*Romeo and Juliet*) and the Granville-Barker preface to it which he told us to read. He himself had just spent a week-end with Barker who had sent us his good wishes, and Gordon Craig had written wishing me luck. 'Stick absolutely loyal to H. W.,' he wrote, 'then great things are possible.'

Martita and I went out in the lunch hour and discussed everything excitedly. As we came back we looked into the auditorium together. The long empty rows of seats lay shrouded in dust-sheets, the boxes stood primly uninviting, with their ugly mouldings and hard gilt chairs, and the horse-shoe circle curved above our heads as we stood by the narrow lincrusta pillars underneath it.

I remembered Russell Thorndike as *Peer Gynt*, straddling like a scarecrow over Ase's deathbed, the painted beehives in Shallow's garden, Andrew Leigh singing his sad little snatches under the table in Goneril's hall, and, above all, Ernest Milton's tragic posturings as Richard the Second. I could see him crouching pitifully on the ground in the scene before Flint Castle, and standing alone, self-pitying but defiant, to give away his kingdom, dressed in a long black velvet robe with great ermine sleeves hanging to the floor.

As we climbed the stairs back to the rehearsal room, we passed the wardrobe door. I left Martita and slipped inside. Behind the nearest counter, like a magnificent grocer, stood Orlando Whitehead the wardrobe master, bald-headed, grinning, with a strong Yorkshire accent, wearing a white apron round his waist. Behind him and all around stretched the shelves and boxes and glass cases with their store of robes and crowns, helmets and swords and armour. Hanging among the other clothes, easily recognizable by its rich simplicity, was that same black velvet robe that had left its impression so vividly on my mind. The sleeves, at close quarters, were only made of rabbit, but their long sweeping folds were still sufficiently imposing and picturesque. In a few weeks, I thought, I shall be wearing that dress myself as Richard. The romantic tradition of stage finery, handed on from one actor to another in classic parts, moved me strangely, and I went back to the rehearsal bursting with a great desire to prove myself worthy of the noble inheritance I had come to the Old Vic to try and claim.

We were very busy. We were often very tired, but we never had time to be bored. We had our failures—in fact the first season opened in an atmosphere of gloom amid the execrations of most of the critics and many of the regular audience. Our great strength and rallying-point was Harcourt Williams. He ruled us by affection and by the trust he had in us, which was almost childlike in its naïvety. Any little instance of selfishness, of disloyalty to the theatre or to the play, would merely throw him into a mood of amazement or disbelief. I am sure we all still remember his little notes of good wishes and thanks to the company and staff on first nights (why were there never notes of abuse and disgust to balance them?), his vegetarian lunches which we could regard with such anxious interest, the occasional cigarette which he would light with an air of recklessness in a moment of extreme crisis, and his frenzied attempts to concentrate on the last rehearsal of a play, when the cast of the next one, to say nothing of the setting for the one after next, must have been causing him sleepless nights.

I know that Ellen Terry thought Harcourt Williams one of the most brilliant young actors of his generation. Her influence over his life showed itself in his straightforward manners, and in the fact that nothing which he accomplished in the theatre was tainted by cheapness or vulgarity. I am sure it must have been her sublime shrewdness and her artist's vision that guided his hand on the occasions during his four strenuous years at the Vic when his acute sensibility was often strained almost to breaking point.

Harcourt Williams quickly won our affection and loyalty, and we were all tremendously keen, for his sake as well as our own, that his plans should succeed. His ideas at that time seemed to be revolutionary,[1] though later it turned out that his Elizabethan productions, which preserved the continuity of the plays by means of natural and speedy delivery of the verse, and light and imaginative settings allowing quick changes of scene, were very suitable for modern needs. His work was to influence my own productions enormously in after years.

I have sometimes called *Romeo and Juliet* my 'milestone'. Four times in my career it has been an important play for me—but never a very satisfactory one from the acting point of view. For Romeo is a difficult, ungrateful part, needing wonderful natural qualities in the actor as well as skilled technique. In spite of the fact that the very name of Romeo would seem to arouse expectations of glamour in the breast of every schoolgirl, the opportunities which the part affords the actor are distinctly limited, and I don't believe anyone has been known to make stage history in it.

The production of the play at the Old Vic was very nearly a disaster. We gabbled in order to try and get pace and we were not yet used to working together—but our unfavourable reception seemed to draw us closer together, and we ranged ourselves behind Harcourt Williams with increasing devotion. Of course he felt that most of the blame fell on him, and he was much disheartened and hurt by the many angry letters he received, and by the rude remarks of a few furious fanatics who used to waylay him by the stage-door. His methods were to be carried to success, and he was to be hailed as an innovator before he left the Vic; in the meantime, we did our best to cheer him up and tried to conceal from him the worst of the notices.

It was in *Richard the Second* that I began to feel at last that I was finding my feet in Shakespeare. I seemed to be immediately in sympathy with that strange mixture of weakness and beauty in the character. I had seen both Faber and Milton play Richard, but, although their pictorial qualities had impressed me greatly in the part of the King, I had taken in nothing of the intellectual or poetic beauties of the play. But as soon as I began to study the part myself, the subtlety of the characterization began to fascinate and excite me.

The audience became a little more friendly towards us in

[1] Though Robert Atkins had already done fine pioneer work of this kind at the Vic in the twenties, producing every single play of Shakespeare, and doing away with cuts and traditional business

Richard the Second. We thought that we had conquered some of their prejudices, and were rather dismayed to find that most of the critics were still in resolute opposition. I was astonished, in reading the notices again the other day, to find how unfavourable they were. Afterwards, when I had played *Richard of Bordeaux*, which was of course so much more popular, this earlier performance of the more difficult Shakespeare part was taken for granted. Actually, at the Vic few people saw me, as I only played Richard about thirty or forty times. In those days we only acted nine times a fortnight—an admirable arrangement for the actors in a repertory company, as we had occasional nights off, more time to study, and never two performances on the same day.

Our first real success came with *A Midsummer Night's Dream*. This time the public and critics alike applauded us enthusiastically. We were delighted for ourselves, for the theatre, but chiefly for Harcourt Williams, who had come through some dark hours before this splendid vindication of his methods. No one was more delighted than Lilian Baylis. She had left us alone and kept her own counsel, but I fancy she must have been slightly perturbed by the mixed reception and poor box-office returns with which our earlier efforts had been rewarded. All the same, she was not altogether in sympathy with farthingales in Athens and folksongs instead of Mendelssohn, though she never actually said so in public. But Billee was a little hurt when he overheard her say in a dressing-room, just before the dress-rehearsal, 'Well, I suppose I'm old-fashioned, but I do like my fairies to be gauzy'.

I was very happy in the part of Oberon. It is one of the few fine parts I have acted in Shakespeare that is not also a great physical strain, and I was learning to speak verse well at last. It gave me a wonderful sense of power to feel that I was beginning to control the lovely language which at rehearsals moved me so much that tears would spring to my eyes. I am always embarrassingly emotional at the early stages of a play, but Sybil Thorndike once told me at the R.A.D.A. that the proper time to give way to emotion is at the early rehearsals. Afterwards one must put it behind one, study it objectively and draw on it with discretion.

The first season came to an end with two very important parts for me, Macbeth and Hamlet. I fancy that few people considered that Macbeth was within my range, and I was rather surprised myself when Billee allowed me to attempt it. But audiences are tolerant and helpful at the Old Vic once they have accepted you and are convinced that you can be trusted to do your best. I think I must have been successful up to a point for I have met several people since who liked me in this play.[1] I remember that it was a very exhausting part, but I don't believe I ever stopped to think how daring I was even to have attempted it at the age of twenty-five.

My physical picture of Macbeth was derived principally from the drawings by Bernard Partridge of Irving which I had seen in a souvenir of the Lyceum production. I made up for the last act with whitened hair and bloodshot eyes, trying to resemble as nearly as I could 'the gaunt famished wolf' of Ellen Terry's description of Irving, and in the opening scene of the play I carried my sheathed sword on one shoulder as Irving carries his in the picture. I knew this would look finely picturesque for my entrance but could not think how to get rid of it afterwards, until it suddenly occurred to me at rehearsal one day to drop it to the ground when Macbeth is hailed as King by the witches. This seemed to give Banquo a good reason for his line:

> Good Sir, why do you start; and seem to fear
> Things that do sound so fair?

It is always important to me, in a character part, to be able to satisfy myself with my visual appearance. I imagine at rehearsals how I hope to look, but if my make-up comes out well when I put it on for the first time, my confidence is increased a hundredfold. In the same way, the right clothes—especially in a part where they must be heavy and dignified—help me at once to find the right movements and gestures for the character. One's expression in a character part develops tremendously quickly after the first few times of making up. Photographs taken at a dress rehearsal only show a kind of mask, a sketch of the actor's intention, just like his performance at an early rehearsal. Photograph him again after he has been acting the part for a fortnight and the whole expression has deepened and developed into something much more complete, revealing the mental conception of the part in the eyes and mouth as well as in the lines and shadows that are painted over them.

[1] Far more, on the whole, than in 1942 when I played the part again, directing the play myself, with Gwen Ffrangcon Davies as Lady Macbeth.

One afternoon, the famous critic, James Agate, bustled into my dressing-room half-way through the matinée performance. Although I knew him very slightly in private life, I was naturally never very much at ease in his august presence.

He began by saying that he had dragged himself to the theatre full of the direst presentiments; that I should fail as Macbeth had seemed a foregone conclusion to him. He then remarked: 'I have never seen the Murder Scene better done, and so I have come to congratulate you now. At the end of the performance I shall probably have changed my mind, for you can't possibly play the rest of it.' I murmured my thanks, and he went back to his seat. All through the second half of the play I was acutely self-conscious. I felt sure that I was over-acting every scene. I was amazed to read a favourable notice in his column the following Sunday.

In spite of the happy outcome of this particular visit, I never feel at ease if a critic comes to my dressing-room. Critics, like clergymen, always seem out of place behind the scenes.

Marion Terry was in a box one afternoon to see *Macbeth*. She had not appeared on the stage since she played the Princess in *Our Betters* in 1923. Six months later, illness had obliged her to leave the cast. Martita had been her understudy and had taken her place when she left. Soon afterwards, calling with flowers to inquire for Marion, Martita was shown into her bedroom. 'I hope, dear, you are playing the part exactly as I did,' said Marion and sank back on the pillows.

Both Marion and Fred suffered a great deal from ill-health during their last years, but they were both firm believers in the recuperative powers of 'Doctor Greasepaint'. Their work helped them to battle against weak hearts and exhausted nervous systems, which would have laid them low many years sooner if they had not both been people of quite extraordinarily determined character, with amazing powers of endurance and will-power. Fred would sometimes carry a stick during the first two acts of *The Scarlet Pimpernel* when his gout was troubling him, but by the middle of the play his indomitable spirit would have asserted itself and he would discard the stick and stride about the stage like a young man.

It was sad to see my wonderful Terry relatives sinking at last under the ravages of time. Marion could not manage the stairs to my dressing-room when she came to see *Macbeth*, and Martita and

I went instead to her box, still in our make-up, at the end of the performance. She still looked immensely distinguished, though it was sad to see her with her back bowed and her hair quite white. It was the last time I ever saw her, and I do not think she was ever again inside a theatre.

The last time I saw Fred was in a theatre too. He came to see *Musical Chairs* two years after this time, in 1931, and sat in a box with his wife Julia. Frank Vosper and I dispatched a dresser to buy a big bouquet of carnations and sent them round with our love, and afterwards Fred and Julia came behind to see us. In the old days I am sure the frankness of Mackenzie's play would have shocked and disgusted Uncle Fred profoundly. I have never forgotten hearing him once hold forth on the vulgarity of the character of Linda, as played so grandly by Mary Clare in *The Constant Nymph*. But he had mellowed and softened in his last years and he was fond of Frank and me. He complimented us warmly and said he had enjoyed the play. I never saw him again, but I always think of him if I go down the long narrow corridor at the back of the Criterion Theatre. There he stood, framed in the iron pass-door leading from the stage, leaning on his stick, looking like a benevolent Henry the Eighth, with Julia by his side, still looking radiantly beautiful, with the flowers we had sent her held loosely in a dark mass against her light dress.

The last production of my first Old Vic season was *Hamlet*. It was exciting to have the chance of playing it after all, but I did not think it likely that I should give an interesting performance. I had no longer much confidence in playing 'romantic juveniles'. I had not made a success of Romeo, though I had played the part before, and I considered Richard and Macbeth, in which I had done better work, were both character parts. From my childhood I had had some sort of picture in my mind of these two personages. I could imagine myself at once dressed in their clothes and tried, in rehearsing and acting them, to forget myself completely, to keep the imagined image fresh and vivid. To some extent I felt I had succeeded. Hamlet was different.

We began to rehearse. Some of the scenes came to me more easily than others; the first appearance of Hamlet particularly—one of my favourite scenes of all the plays I have ever read or acted—sincerity, real emotion, and marvellously simple words to express them in; the second scene, when Hamlet first sees the ghost, violent, sudden, technically hard to speak; the following ghost scene terribly difficult, intensely tiring to act, nothing to say then, after the ghost disappears, too many words. Impossible to convey, even with Shakespeare's help, the horror and madness of the situation, the changing tenderness and weary resignation.

The mad scenes. How mad should Hamlet be? So easy to score off Polonius to get laughs, so important not to clown, to keep the story true—then the intricate scene with Rosencrantz and Guildenstern, and my favourite prose speech in the play, 'What a piece of work is a man! . . .'—The arrival of the players easier again, natural true feelings, but the big soliloquy is coming in a minute, one must concentrate, take care not to anticipate, not begin worrying beforehand how one is going to say it, take time but don't lose time, don't break the verse up, don't succumb to the temptation of a big melodramatic effect for the sake of gaining applause at the curtain —Nunnery scene. Shall it be a love scene? How much emotion? When should Hamlet see the King? I feel so much that I convey nothing. This scene never ceases to baffle me.

Interval—The Advice to the Players. Dreadful little pill to open the second part, all the people coming back into their seats, slamming them down; somehow try to connect the speech with the rest of the play, not just a set piece; tender for the tiny scene with Horatio, a moment's relief—then into the Play scene. Relax if possible, enjoy the scene, watch the Gonzago play, watch the King, forget that this is the most famous of famous scenes, remember that Hamlet is not yet sure of Claudius, delay the climax, then carry it (and it needs all the control and breath in the world to keep the pitch at the right level)—No pause before the Recorders scene begins, and this cannot make the effect it should unless Rosencrantz and Guildenstern pull their weight and share the scene with Hamlet—Half a minute to collect oneself, and on again to the praying King. Such a difficult unsatisfactory scene, and how important to the play—but the closet scene is more grateful, and a woman's voice helps to make a contrast in tone and pitch. The scene starts at terrific emotional tension though, and only slows up for a minute in the middle for the beautiful passage with the ghost. The 'hiding of Polonius's body' scenes (this is The Entirety tonight —called The Eternity by actors)—and then grab a cloak and hat in the wings and rush on to speak the Fortinbras soliloquy as if it wasn't the last hundred yards of a relay race.

Now the one long interval for Hamlet, while Ophelia is doing her mad scene and Claudius and Laertes are laying their plot and the Queen is saying her willow speech. Last lap. Graveyard scene, with the lovely philosophizing and the lines about Yorick, and that hellish shouting fight and the 'Ossa' speech at the end, which takes the last ounce of remaining breath—Now for Osric, and a struggle to hold one's own with the scene-shifters banging about behind the front-cloth, and a careful ear for the first coughs and fidgets in the audience, which *must* somehow be silenced before the 'fall of a sparrow' (I remember one night a gentleman in the front row took out a large watch in this scene, and wound it up resignedly). And so to the apology to Laertes, with half one's mind occupied trying to remember the fight (which has been so carefully rehearsed but always goes wrong at least once a week) and on to the poisoning of the Queen and Claudius's death, and, if all has gone well, a still, attentive audience to the very end.

In rehearsing Hamlet I found it at first impossible to characterize. I could not 'imagine' the part and live in it, forgetting myself in the words and adventures of the character, as I had tried to do in my best work in other plays. This difficulty surprised and alarmed me. Although I knew the theatrical effect that should be produced by each scene, I could only act the part if I felt that I really experienced every word of it as I spoke. The need to 'make an effect' or 'force a climax' paralysed my imagination and destroyed any reality which I had begun to feel. I knew that I must act in a broad style, that I must be grander, more dignified and noble, more tender and gracious, more bitter and scathing, than was absolutely natural—that I must not be as slow as I should be if I were really thinking aloud, that I must drive the dialogue along at a regular moving pace, and, above all, that every shade of thought must be arranged behind the lines, so that nothing should be left to chance in presenting them to the audience correctly and clearly in the pattern which I had conceived. All through rehearsals I was dismayed by my utter inability to forget myself while I was acting. It was not until I stood before an audience that I seemed to find the breadth and voice which enabled me suddenly to shake off my self-consciousness and live the part in my imagination, while I executed the technical difficulties with another part of my consciousness at the same time.

Maurice Browne came to the Old Vic. He was an American

actor and director who had made money from the phenomenal success of *Journey's End*, and had taken over two theatres, the Globe and the Queen's, in Shaftesbury Avenue. He thought that the West End ought to see our *Hamlet* and arranged to transfer the production to the Queen's Theatre as soon as the Vic season came to an end.

The first night in the West End gave the stage management some alarming moments. The scene in the churchyard was played on a platform. Below this was the real stage, which served for the bottom of the grave. Here the skulls were carefully placed. It seemed to me, when I walked on with Horatio, that an air of thoughtfulness, one might have said of strain, hung over the First Grave-Digger. I suddenly saw what had happened a few lines before we came to the best part of the scene. The skull was missing. And soon I must begin the 'Alas, poor Yorick' speech, holding it in my hands. Should I orate over an imaginary skull? I dared not hope that the audience's imagination would follow me so far. I suddenly decided to cut out thirty lines. I jumped to 'But soft, but soft awhile—here comes the King', the words which introduce Ophelia's funeral procession which was fortunately forming in the wings at that very moment. There was a short pause while the surprised mourners hurried to their places, then the procession entered. I learned afterwards that owing to the rake of the stage the skulls had rolled out of the grave-digger's reach. There was nothing to be done, though the distracted stage manager had tried, without avail, to borrow another skull from the Globe Theatre next door, where Alexander Moissi was playing *Hamlet* in a German version.

Unfortunately, it turned out that Maurice Browne's faith in the drawing power of *Hamlet* in the West End was misplaced. Besides Moissi, Henry Ainley was also playing *Hamlet* at the Haymarket at the same time, so I had two rivals on this occasion. (Later, when I played Hamlet in New York in 1936, I was to have another rival in Leslie Howard.) It was only slightly gratifying to hear that the business at the other two theatres was no better than at ours. Our cheaper seats were always full, but the stalls and dress-circle public obstinately kept away. I was very much disappointed. What was the use of being praised, extravagantly perhaps, by the critics if one was to fail with the public? The cheers at the Old Vic had been so hopeful and encouraging that the atmosphere of failure at the Queen's Theatre seemed the more depressing by comparison.

I was somewhat comforted by an elderly friend of mine, who said she had been too much impressed to move during my death scene, although a pipe had burst during the performance and water was creeping along the floor from one side of her stall and a mouse from the other!

The public was to flock to see me four years later as Hamlet at the New Theatre. But many people told me then, of course, that I had been much better in the earlier production which so few came to see. We tried to put the blame on the rival companies and on the heat-wave which added to our troubles but it was no use. I accepted another engagement, upon which the management immediately said (more in sorrow than in anger) that if I had not been so hasty they would have kept *Hamlet* on after all.

I was very sorry when the Old Vic company disbanded for the summer, but I was glad to know that I should be returning in the autumn. I had asked for a rise in salary as a condition of a second season, and when it was given me without a murmur—at the Vic, where money really was a most earnest consideration—I felt I must surely be something of a 'draw' at last. I had enjoyed our rehearsals, a new play every three weeks, the quick lunches at the Wellington Bar or the station buffet at Waterloo, during which we stopped arguing only when our mouths were too full of sandwiches and sausage-rolls to speak, and the rush back to the theatre to work until four o'clock. Afterwards I would go back to my flat and rest until the evening performance, play my gramophone, and perhaps have a drink with a few friends. On the evening when the Opera Company held the stage at the Old Vic we were free, and I was able to learn my lines or go to other theatres.

At our week-end dress-rehearsals at the Old Vic the company were permitted to invite friends and relations. My mother, I am sure, did not miss one of these functions. Besides friendly criticism she brought large supplies of food which she pressed on all the actors, and especially on Harcourt Williams, who used to say that her provisions saved his reason several times on these trying occasions.

Before our first nights it was a sort of ritual with some of us to have dinner at Gow's, a chop house in the Strand, but we were usually too nervous to eat very much. Old Vic first nights, although they occurred with such frequent regularity, never seemed to lose their novelty and excitement. There was a feeling of anticipation at the Vic which I have never encountered anywhere else, for the spirit of the place seemed so much stronger than any of the separate personalities who served it.

Before I went home after a first night I sometimes showed myself at the Savoy Grill for supper. This was pure snobbishness on my part, but I felt that it preserved my status as a West End actor, giving me the right to return one day to the bright lights of Shaftesbury Avenue, and I liked to be seen there with Martita Hunt. She and I were inseparable during this first Vic season, and besides her own brilliant performances in a variety of parts—especially as Helena in *A Midsummer Night's Dream*, Gertrude in *Hamlet* and as a vivid Lady Macbeth—she was unfailingly kind and wise in helping me in all my work.

I was not idle during the summer. Nigel Playfair proposed to revive Oscar Wilde's *The Importance of Being Earnest* in a stylized black-and-white production, and offered me the part of John Worthing. I accepted eagerly. Here was the sort of comedy-character I longed to play. I had once attempted the part when I was still an amateur, and it was amusing to change the black weeds of Hamlet for the top-hat and crepe band of Worthing's mourning for his brother. My recent association with the tragedy gave further point to Wilde's joke. I was very proud to have the opportunity of appearing for the first time in this production with my mother's sister, Mabel Terry-Lewis, who made a notable success as Lady Bracknell. Mabel was an instinctive actress, with a grace and skill which she inherited from her family. Her dignity and her beautiful voice reminded one of Marion, and she shared with Marie Tempest and Irene Vanbrugh that rare distinction of style, deportment and carriage which is so seldom seen on the stage today. Like Kate, her mother (and Ellen Terry too), a long retirement from the theatre after her own marriage did not seem to have impaired in the slightest the freshness and skill of her stage technique, and she took up her career at a higher point than she had left it. Her reappearance in H. M. Harwood's *The Grain of Mustard Seed* at the Ambassador's Theatre in 1920 after her husband's death was an immediate and distinguished personal success.

When I had worked with Playfair before, I had been very small fry indeed. I had been grateful for a smile or a nod from the other actors, and when Playfair had once asked my opinion on some detail or other at a rehearsal, I had been too shy to speak. Now it was gratifying to play a leading part opposite such fine actresses as Mabel and Jean Cadell and to appear at the Lyric, where I had so often sat enraptured among the audience. Nigel Playfair was the first manager who ever made me feel that I was a star in his theatre. Of course, the Lyric, Hammersmith was too far west to be considered real West End, but this made the success of the revival all the more flattering.

The parts I played during the first Vic season were as follows: Romeo, Antonio, Cléante (in *The Imaginary Invalid* of Molière), Oberon, Richard the Second, Orlando, the Emperor in *Androcles and the Lion*, Macbeth and Hamlet.

It was a changed company that assembled at the Old Vic for the first rehearsal in the autumn. Martita Hunt had left. Her place as leading lady was taken by Dorothy Green. I had seen her play all the big parts in Shakespeare at Stratford-on-Avon in 1925, and had always hoped to act with her one day. Ralph Richardson now joined the company and I am delighted that I went back for another year if only for the reason that I was able to meet Ralph and win his friendship. He has told me since that my acting before this time used to keep him out of a theatre, and the knowledge that he would have to act with me almost prevented him from accepting the engagement. So are many good friendships brought about! Ralph and I formed ourselves into a kind of subordinate committee, and discussed and hinted and interfered generally over the productions. During the first season, Leslie French, Martita and I had always lunched with Billee and pestered him with our suggestions and advice, but he seemed to like talking over his plans beforehand, and we tried to make ourselves useful and not to let our enthusiasm run away with us too far. These 'conferences' about the Vic productions eventually gave birth to an intense longing in me to produce plays myself.

Ralph is a stimulating person in the theatre, and although we have not many tastes in common, with the exception of our love of Shakespeare—and of music, which he says he never cared for till I played my gramophone to him—we soon became fast friends. I found him in many ways curiously similar in temperament to Leslie Faber (who also shared my fondness for music). Ralph Richardson has great integrity both as an artist and as a man. He is, I think, one of our very best actors. He is inclined to despise the petty accessories of theatrical life which appeal so strongly to me—the gossip, the theatrical columns in the newspapers, the billing and the photographs in the front of the house—and it is probably only by chance that he has found a creative outlet on the stage. He might have succeeded equally well as a mechanic, a doctor, or an airman. Unlike me he is intensely interested in machinery and in all the intricate details of science and engineering. Once, when I was motoring in Cornwall, I met him unexpectedly. I had been enjoying myself quietly in my own way, admiring the scenery without inspecting any of it too closely, enjoying the air without wondering from which direction the wind was blowing, puzzling over various signs of industrial activity, such as slag-heaps, which I thought added to the picturesque effect though I had no idea what use they were.

Ralph soon transferred me from my own comfortable car to his long, low, wicked-looking racer, and proceeded to rush me through the air at ninety miles an hour. He could never pass a hill without insisting that we should get out and scale it on foot. Once, on the top of a cliff, he immediately decided that we should both struggle down it to the beach. We visited tin mines, salt mines, pottery works, and listened attentively for several minutes (at one of the slag-heaps I had noticed) while a workman explained the technical details of his occupation to us. Ralph never seemed to tire of long mechanical discussions, though I found these matters entirely beyond my grasp and felt painfully conscious of my one-track mind. Though I missed him as soon as he had left, I was secretly relieved when, later in the day, Ralph climbed back into his car alone, and almost immediately disappeared from view like a shell shot from a cannon.

Harcourt Williams introduced some plays of Bernard Shaw to Old Vic audiences for the first time while I was there. We had already given *Androcles and the Lion* and *The Dark Lady of the Sonnets* the season before. I had enjoyed myself immensely in the former playing the Emperor, with a red wig, a lecherous red mouth, and a large emerald through which I peered lasciviously. Now I was cast as Sergius, the mustachioed conceited major to whom Raina is engaged, in *Arms and the Man.* We were all very much flattered, and considerably awed, when we learned that Mr Shaw had consented to come and read his play to us. We waited for him in the theatre one winter morning. It was bitterly cold, and we sat muffled up in heavy overcoats and scarves. Punctually at 10.30

the great author arrived, wearing the lightest of mackintoshes. His reading of the play was far more amusing and complete than ours could possibly hope to be. He seemed to enjoy himself thoroughly as he illustrated bits of business and emphasized the correct inflexions for his lines. We were so amused that we forgot to be alarmed.

Later Mr Shaw came to a dress rehearsal. We could not distinguish him in the darkness of the stalls, but we saw the light of his pocket-lamp bobbing up and down as he made his notes. He assembled the company in the first interval, produced his written comments, and reduced everybody to a state of disquiet. Then he departed. Unfortunately I was not able to gather from him any hints about my own performance, as Sergius does not appear until the second act.

During my second and last season at the Old Vic, Lilian Baylis made the ambitious decision to re-open Sadler's Wells Theatre which had been restored after many years of disuse. The play chosen was *Twelfth Night*, in which I played Malvolio. There was a grand inauguration at our first performance. Sir Johnston Forbes-Robertson declared the theatre open and spoke of his master, Phelps, and Dame Madge Kendal was in the stalls. It was one of the last times either of them was to appear in public. The stalls bulged with celebrities, and the four front rows were like all the gossip columns come to life. The play was wedged between two grand celebrations, the first of which was almost an hour of speeches before the curtain went up, with rows of aldermen, mayors, and other officials sitting upon the stage, shirt-fronts and chains of office glistening above the footlights. But I was feeling that the play was the thing, and itched to speak my line, 'Have you no wit, manners, nor honesty, but to gabble like tinkers at this time of night?'

At the close of the performance the audience remained seated, and, after the curtain had been lowered for a few minutes, it went up again revealing the line of celebrities once more. Miss Baylis, imposing and academic in her robes of Master of Arts, with the Cross of a Companion of Honour on her breast, marched to the middle of the stage to make her speech.

The audience waited politely, and the line of celebrities sat, stiff and white-faced, rather like a cricket team about to be photographed. Lilian carried a huge basket of fruit in her right hand, and when she began her oration her gestures were somewhat hampered by her burden. However, she ploughed bravely on until, enthralled by the force of her own argument, she swept her right arm out impulsively. An enormous apple fell from the basket with a thud. There was a slight titter from the audience. Lilian looked at the basket, and then, edging towards the truant apple, tried to hide it with her robes. She went on with her speech, but soon sincerity overcame technique, and the basket shot out to the right to accentuate another point. This time a pear fell on to the stage. I gave one look at it and burst out laughing. The audience followed suit, and the solemnity of the occasion was irrevocably shattered.

How we all detested Sadler's Wells when it was opened first! The auditorium looked like a denuded wedding cake and the acoustics were dreadful. The only obvious advantages lay in the cleanness and comfort of the dressing-rooms. But we were never able to remember at which of the two theatres we were supposed to be acting or rehearsing, and no sooner did we begin to play to good business in one than we were transferred to the other, where the audiences promptly dwindled away. Patrons of the two theatres got muddled, and the famous green slips with details of the programmes which Lilian always insisted on enclosing in every letter that was sent from either theatre, became more complicated than Old Moore's Almanack. There were all sorts of debts incurred, and all sorts of economies invented to pay them off, but it always seemed that if Shakespeare was making money Opera was losing it, or vice versa. In later years the founding of the Ballet and a great deal of ambitious innovation on the Opera side made it possible for the Wells to be devoted entirely to the musical side of the enterprise.

It was a great triumph for Lilian to have carried through her cherished scheme of rebuilding and reopening Sadler's Wells, but it made my second season less successful and more exhausting than it might otherwise have been. We played eight times a week, instead of nine times a fortnight, and the weeks at the Wells were particularly strenuous, what with scanty houses and the strain of accustoming our voices to the pitch of the new theatre.

Still, *Henry IV, Part I, Antony and Cleopatra, The Tempest* and *King Lear* were all particularly successful, and Billee did some of his very best work in these productions.

CHAPTER ELEVEN

1930–31

The second season was drawing to a close. There had been a revival of *Richard II.* I had acted Hotspur, Benedick, Malvolio, Sergius, Lord Trinket in *The Jealous Wife* (great fun—I had almost forgotten him) and Antony in *Antony and Cleopatra.* This was one of Billee William's very best productions, founded on Granville-Barker's preface, and staged with Renaissance-Classical scenery and dresses in the style of Veronese. Needless to say, all this grandeur was achieved for a very few pounds by the ingenuity of Billee and Paul Smyth, the resident designer. Ralph was superb as Enobarbus. I wore a Drake beard and padded doublet and shouted myself hoarse but was very miscast all the same. I loved playing Prospero in *The Tempest* and thought I was good in that, helped by Billee, by Leslie French (who played Ariel beautifully), and indirectly by Komisarjevsky, who had suggested to me that I ought to look like Dante and not wear a beard. Ralph hated himself as Caliban but he was excellent in the part, with a wonderful Mongolian make-up that took him hours to put on every night.

My last part at the Old Vic was King Lear. It was distinctly ambitious of me to dare, at the age of twenty-six to try and assume 'the large effects that troop with majesty' as eighty-year-old King Lear. But I felt it would be a more exciting close to my two seasons than a revival of *Hamlet*, which was the alternative proposed. I was wholly inadequate in the storm scenes, having neither the voice nor the physique for them. Lear has to *be* the storm, but I could do no more than shout against the thundersheet. The only scene I thought I did at all well was the one with the Fool when Lear leaves Goneril to go to Regan: 'O, let me not be mad, not mad, sweet heaven——'. Ralph was fine as Kent and Leslie French moving and effective as the Fool.

It was not considered in keeping with the austere traditions of the Old Vic for audiences to applaud an actor's first entrance. But as Lear I came on in such splendour that, from the moment when Gloster announced 'The King is coming', the stage was mine. Trumpets blared in the orchestra and my way was cleared by spearmen; lords and attendants kept their distance behind my magnificent white robe. Sometimes the audience could not resist such majesty, especially in a farewell production, and at least three nights a week I came on to applause. This uncertainty started a little joke between Ralph Richardson and myself. He was on the stage before me, and as I prepared to enter, encumbered by my own magnificence, he would look slyly in my direction as I stood in the wings, hiding his smile behind his thick, mask-like make-up. (Ralph always designed elaborate make-ups, made careful drawings for them beforehand, and carried them out in great detail with shadows and highlights, scoffing at our comparatively slapdash efforts at disguise. He achieved striking results, but his method stylized his appearance, and made him apt to look different from anyone else on the stage). In the meantime I was trying to amass my eighty years and my large effects of majesty in the wings. If I failed to get the round of applause as I mounted my throne the expression of amused triumph on Ralph's face would be almost too much for me. It was fortunate that I had to turn away from the audience for a moment before I faced them and began 'Attend the lords of France and Burgundy . . .'.

When *Lear* was over and my white robes were packed away, I crossed the river and came back to the West End once more. I had been asked to play in Edward Knoblock's stage version of J. B. Priestley's *The Good Companions*. How lucky I have been in the opportunity of doing so many different kinds of work! At that moment, I believe, I was almost the only man in England who had not read the book. I spent half the night skimming it through as quickly as I could, and next morning I called on Julian Wylie for the first time. His offices were in the Charing Cross Road. As I climbed the stairs, up which a hundred principal boys had borne their portly hips, I heard the sound of many pianos all being played at the same time. The sheet music of pantomime songs was ranged on racks on every landing, and I caught a glimpse of a boudoir as I

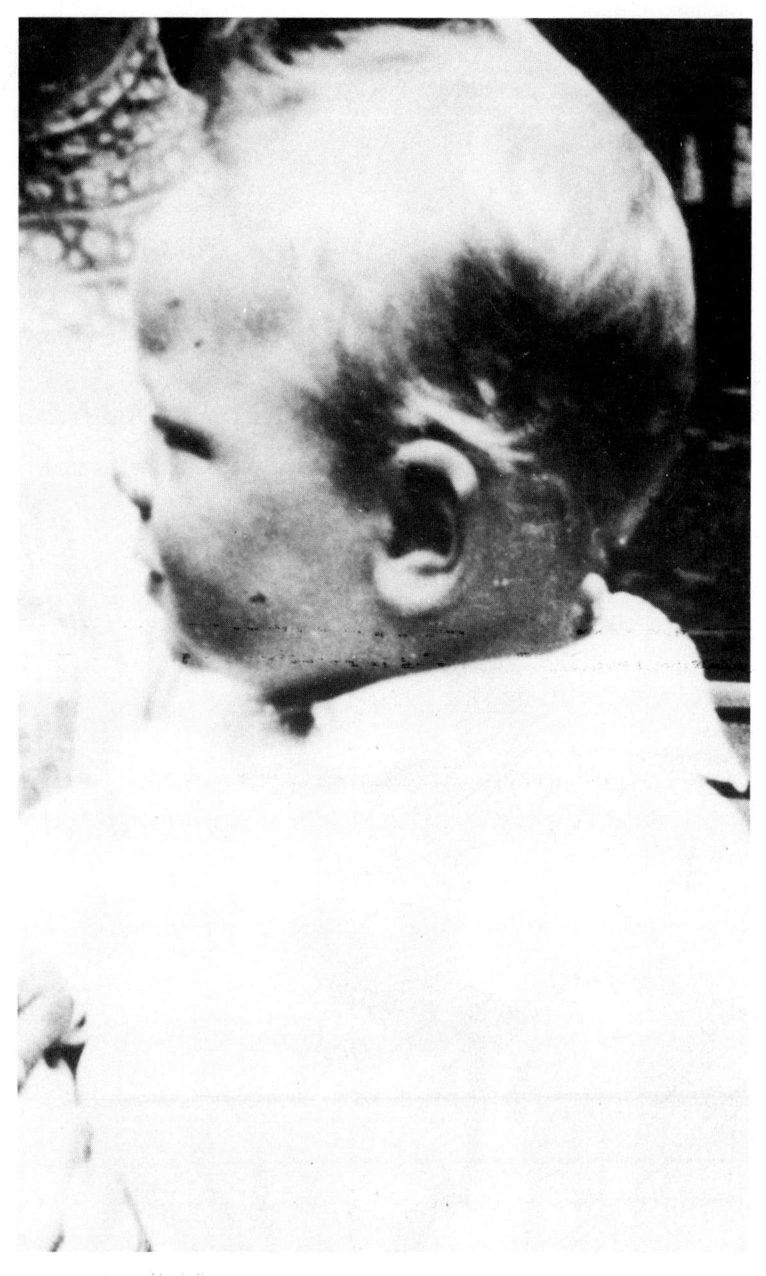

Arthur John Gielgud: one of the earliest photographs

Above: The White Butterfly in *The Insect Play*, 1923. Below: Trofimov in *The Cherry Orchard*, 1925

The abdication scene, Richard II, 1929. Costume design by Elizabeth Montgomery (Motley)

Richard of Bordeaux, 1933–34

Hamlet, 1934

Romeo, with Peggy Ashcroft as Juliet

First major film role in *The Secret Agent*, with Peter Lorre, Madeleine Carroll and Robert Young, 1935

Noah in the play of the same name by André Obey, 1935

passed, with Louis Seize decorations and a ceiling profusely painted with clouds and cherubs, the private sanctum of some lordly music-publisher who reigned in the offices below.

I was ushered in, ahead of the score of people waiting in the outer office. Julian Wylie sat behind a massive table smoking a big cigar, and the walls round him were covered with photographs of pantomime and music-hall favourites. Julian looked the typical impresario, but he was more than that. I liked him immensely—a sympathetic, cultivated man, who made the business of pantomime into a romance. He would digress upon its origins with an exact regard for tradition, pointing out that the Fairy Queen must always enter from the right, and the Demon King from the left—Why? Because it had always been so. But Wylie was not a reactionary, and, since pantomime had fallen upon less successful days, he skilfully led it towards revue and saved it. He was very broad-minded in his enthusiasms. I could not help smiling when I heard that he had been to the Wells to look at me with a view to my playing Jollifant, and had sat through my Lear with apparent enjoyment.

Wylie was very thorough in his methods. For two long weeks we read the play in the boardroom of the Dominion Theatre, after which we rehearsed for four weeks. The company then 'tried out' for three weeks in the Provinces with an understudy in my part but I played once at Birmingham and once at Leeds for single performances on the nights when we did not act at the Vic. Thus I appeared as Inigo Jollifant, King Lear, and Benedick (*Much Ado* was still in the bill for occasional matinées at this time) all in the same week—a record almost worthy of the old stock companies. But it was a mad rush, and I have no doubt that all three performances left a great deal to be desired.

The crowd scenes in *The Good Companions*, which were hailed as marvels of stage-craft, were rehearsed in exactly half an hour by Wylie and Knoblock, who divided the supers into groups and labelled them with numbers. Wylie was thus able to control them like a sergeant-major from his place in the stalls. There he sat, like some passionless Buddha, brushing the cigar-ash from his lapel with two fingers, a favourite and characteristic gesture of his.

I saw no signs of the temperamental storms and rages for which he was said to be famous among pantomime artists. Leslie Henson the great comedian, once told me of a rehearsal of *Dick Whittington*, in which he had appeared under Julian's direction. There was an unusually complicated change of set to be negotiated, from a 'Desert' scene to 'A Staircase in the Palace'. In the first there was a trap-door which had to be closed before the curtain went up on the second, in which a lady was discovered singing on the stairs. After a verse or two she was supposed to descend in stately fashion. But this she dared not do, fearing that the trap might still be open.

'For heaven's sake, come *forward,*' Wylie yelled each time.

But the lady demurred, and the change had to be rehearsed all over again. At last Wylie could bear it no longer. He bounded on to the stage with a roar, and immediately vanished into the still-open trap. There was a murmur of consternation. Then Julian's head suddenly popped up through the hole in the stage. 'I heard you laughing,' he announced, though actually everyone had been too much alarmed to see the joke.

I had to play the piano in *The Good Companions*. The music was by Richard Addinsell, whom I had known when he was an undergraduate at Oxford and used to play at parties. He kindly offered to teach me how to play his tunes, imagining, I suppose, that as I play tolerably by ear his task would be an easy one. Alas, my natural facility is a positive curse when it comes to learning correctly! I slaved away for days, just as I had done in *The Constant Nymph*, when Elsie April had patiently guided my inexpert fingers. I cannot read a note of music from sight, and I can only play in certain keys—but the fact that I can easily transpose a melody and render it inaccurately with my own harmonies seems to make things all the more difficult for me when I have to learn correctly.

The scenes were very short and sketchy, and demanded a considerable readjustment of my style of acting. There was hardly any development of character. Jollifant in the play was a 'type'—a very ordinary juvenile who had to carry off a few slight love scenes and a couple of effective comedy situations with the aid of a pipe, undergraduate clothes, and the catchword 'absolutely'. Here there were no white robes and spearmen and lordly followers to bolster up my first appearance. The sets were enormous, the orchestra vast, and the stage as wide as a desert. I had learned from playing Shakespeare not to be afraid of acting broadly, and the size of the theatre did not dismay me as much as I had feared at first, but the manner and pace had to be very different from anything I had ever done before. I had to try and catch the audience's interest with the first word, and sweep my little scenes along to a climax in a few short minutes. However, though the robes and the large effects that troop with majesty had not come with me from the Old Vic, my followers had. On that exciting first night at His Majesty's, when my performance of Inigo might have been smothered under the reputation of Priestley's book, Knoblock's adaptation, and the immediate success of Edward Chapman and Frank Pettingell, at least a hundred of my staunch friends had crossed the river to greet me. My reception when I first appeared was out of all proportion, and I have no doubt that I deserved Mr Agate's flight of fancy in the *Sunday Times* the following week. He wrote:

> The young man rattling away at the piano was Mr John Gielgud, and perhaps this time some of the applause might be taken as a tribute to all those kings over the water whose sceptres our young tragedian had just laid down.

I learnt some useful lessons during the long run of *The Good Companions*, for I was playing with actors of several different schools. Chapman and I had acted together years before, when we were both amateurs, in a performance of Noël Coward's *I'll Leave it to You*. Adèle Dixon had been my Juliet at the Vic, and some of the others I already knew. But there were one or two members of the company recruited from revue and pantomime.

In one scene a veteran actor ruined my lines by walking up-stage of me and standing against the backcloth. This is a well-known trick, even in straight plays, but not considered good art or good manners in any type of entertainment. I remonstrated politely, but without avail. One day I lunched with Fred Terry and told him of my nightly struggle in this particular scene. Uncle Fred pronounced his verdict grandly, as if it were the correct reading of some obscure phrase in the classics: 'Walk in front of him while he's speaking, my boy. He'll have to come down level with you then so that the audience can see him.' Next night I did as I was told, with immediate and gratifying results.

The Good Companions brought me my first real taste of commercial success. I was being well paid, and the play had a long run. Suppers at the Savoy were no longer a luxury, and sometimes I enjoyed hearing people say 'That's John Gielgud' as I passed. While I was basking in the comparative idleness of my leisure hours another piece of luck came my way. I was beginning to attract the attention of playwrights, and manuscripts arrived in increasing numbers. I was flattered to receive a few from established authors, bearing the exclusive stamps of the more expensive typewriting firms. Their pages were tidy and perhaps a trifle too self-assured. Others, from writers whose names were unknown to me, seemed more impressive because they were already printed, but I soon learned to become wary of these neat volumes. There was something cold and stillborn in their completeness. Most of the plays, however, came from beginners, some carefully typewritten, others tattered and covered with illegible handwriting. I perused them with an increasing sense of despondency as time went on. All actors must have shared my feelings. One can never dismiss a new play-script for fear that it may contain the seed of something good. Within a few weeks two packages arrived in my dressing-room at His Majesty's. One contained *Musical Chairs* and the other *Richard of Bordeaux.*

A letter arrived with the manuscript of *Musical Chairs*. The writer reminded me that he had been at 'prep' school with me at Hillside. At the end was the signature, R. A. Mackenzie. I remembered the initials at once, but at first I could not clearly envisage their owner. I picked up the play, however, and was intrigued to find that the action took place in Poland, the country of my father's family. I began to read. The first scene, with its masterly introduction of the characters and explanation of their relationships, interested me at once. When I reached the end of the first act I was enthusiastic, and I finished the play in a mood of great excitement. I wrote to the author immediately, inviting him to lunch.

I am afraid that our reunion was not a great success. I found Mackenzie waiting for me in a quiet room upstairs at the Gourmets restaurant in Lisle Street and at once recognized his blunt Scottish features and dark curly hair. He looked very much the same as the little boy who had been in my dormitory at Hillside. But he had had a hard time since our last meeting and he was bitter and cynical in his attitude towards the world. Also he was as shy as I was. I attempted to meet the somewhat aggressive air which he affected with a little charm. This he probably found thoroughly patronizing and obnoxious. I hoped the atmosphere might improve when we had ordered our lunch. Unfortunately, it turned out that

Mackenzie was an uncompromising vegetarian. I felt greedy and superior as I tackled my steak. He glowered darkly at me over his carrots.

Towards the end of the meal he told me that he had been wandering all over the world, trying various professions with little or no success. He had never been able to make any money. He had worked on farms and in the logging camps of Canada. Then, on his return to England, chance had brought him in touch with the stage. He had been engaged as tutor to Owen Nares's two sons. He spoke to Mr Nares one day of his interest in the theatre, and obtained from him an introduction to Edgar Wallace, who gave him a job as assistant stage manager to a company playing *The Case of the Frightened Lady.* Later he occupied the same post at Wyndham's Theatre in another Wallace play called *Smoky Cell.* But he was very contemptuous of the commercial theatre and would sit in the prompt corner scribbling at his playwriting and reading Chekhov and Tolstoy. His own plays were written with tremendous care and the strictest economy. He rewrote every act two or three times and constructed every scene with the most expert skill.

I never got to know Mackenzie at all well. He was a difficult person, but he had tremendous talent and a fine instinct for the theatre. After some time, we discovered that we had musical tastes in common, and we used sometimes to meet in the same gramophone shop and discuss the records we were thinking of buying. The first thing Mackenzie did when his play was a success was to buy a large and beautiful new gramophone, which was still standing undelivered in the basement of the shop a few days after he was killed.

Although I was enthusiastic about *Musical Chairs*, I feared that it was not a commercial proposition. Actors need managers and backers as well as plays so I sent the manuscript off to Bronson Albery. I was very much surprised when he rang me up early next morning to say that he had read the play overnight and was anxious to put it on at the Arts Theatre, of which he was one of the directors, for a trial run of two special performances.

The moment I become excited over the manuscript of a new play I begin casting it furiously. This interfering side of my nature encouraged me later on, as soon as occasion offered, to try my hand as a director. As I had brought *Musical Chairs* to Mr Albery he allowed me to take part in the discussions of the way in which it should be cast and produced. Many actors take little interest in a play apart from their own individual share in it, but I enjoy every minute of the rehearsal period, whether I am directing the play or not, and my passionate interest in every detail compels me to watch and criticize and interfere in all directions. I am frequently a great nuisance, and entirely selfish in my desire to be consulted about everything that is going on.

I thought at once of Frank Vosper for the important part of old Schindler, my father in the play. Frank and I had been friends for four or five years. I had first met him at Lord Lathom's, and later, when I knew him quite well, I had taken over his flat, but we had never worked together before. He had made great successes with Barry Jackson, first as the sailor in *Yellow Sands* (in which he dressed with Ralph Richardson) and then as Claudius in the modern-dress *Hamlet.* He acted with Edith Evans, too, at the Old Vic during her season there—playing Romeo, Mark Antony and Orlando. (Of this last performance he said to me: 'I wore a red wig and looked like Fay Compton with goitre!')

Frank was always wonderfully good company. He loved ragging me about my highbrow activities, and pretended that, even in Shakespeare, he never knew which play he was in, or what the lines were all about. He used his shortsightedness to assist this impression of vagueness, peering at people through his glasses to avoid having to greet anyone he disliked. I was very fond of him. Some people thought him affected and rude, but I loved his sublime disregard for other people's disapproval and his really generous warm heart and sense of humour. When he first read *Musical Chairs* he said he thought it very depressing and difficult to understand, but gradually I discovered that he was quite intrigued with the play and anxious to create the part of Schindler. He behaved absurdly at rehearsals, singing snatches of grand opera to try out his voice, and imitating Fred Terry, for whom he had unbounded admiration. Mackenzie took a great fancy to Frank, and afterwards when he began to write his second play, *The Maitlands,* he built the part of the actor, Jack, round Frank's off-stage personality, with all the tricks and mannerisms he had used at the *Musical Chairs* rehearsals. I was very sorry, when the time came for the play to be done, that Frank was not available to play this part, in which he should have been inimitable.

I suggested that Komisarjevsky should direct *Musical Chairs,* and this turned out to be a most happy choice for everyone concerned.

Although he could sometimes be capricious and difficult when he was dealing with the managerial side of the West End theatre, Komis had real sympathy with artists, and knew exactly the way to deal with awkward but talented young people in order to bring out the very best in them. He found himself in immediate sympathy with Ronald Mackenzie and his work, and at once agreed to direct the play.

There was originally an outdoor scene in the second act when the oil-well catches fire. This would have been difficult to stage in a small theatre. Besides, Komis thought that the change to an exterior setting would destroy the feeling of claustrophobia suggested by the small room in which the rest of the play took place, with the glimpse of mountains and flooded river outside the windows. An attempt to show all this more elaborately would have been most dangerous. So in the end the whole play was acted in the one interior scene. Komis devised this himself,[1] and added a little staircase which led to the door of the girl's room on one side of the stage. He used this with brilliant effect. Mackenzie had written a very conventional curtain to the second act which Komis developed into something subtle and original without adding a word, merely by the atmosphere which he created with pauses and effective lighting and grouping.

He was brilliantly clever in the way he helped me too. The plot of the play concerns a consumptive young pianist, whose fiancée (a German) has been killed in an air raid in which he was one of the bombers on the English side. At the first rehearsal Komis led me to the middle of the stage to explain the arrangement of the furniture. 'There is your piano, and there on it is the photograph of that girl who was killed. Build your performance round those two things,' he said.

He managed Mackenzie with consummate tact. The final curtain of the play was tried in several different ways, none of them entirely satisfactory. Komis had conceived a fine pictorial climax as the characters passed the windows dressed in black, and I begged him to bring the curtain down on this effective general exit. Mackenzie wanted an anticlimax, and had written a short scene to follow, between Anna, the maid, and the American commercial traveller. Frank, Komis, Mackenzie, Albery and I argued about this ending for half an hour after the dress-rehearsal, and

[1] At a cost, I believe, of only £12!

finally two different versions were played at the Arts Theatre performances. I do not remember who thought of the father shutting the piano, which was the final 'curtain' as the play was eventually arranged. I should like to take the credit for it, but I think it is just as likely that it was suggested by Komis or by Frank. The title of the play was certainly mine. It was originally called *The Discontents*, a name which we all felt would not be thought attractive by the public. No one except me seemed to know what *Musical Chairs* meant, but it was an effective title and easy to remember. We always said at the Criterion that people booked for the play thinking it was a farce or a musical comedy. If so, they must have had a nasty shock when they arrived.

Mackenzie was at first inclined to be rebellious and obstinate about the alterations in his script. Then Komisarjevsky would say gently, 'But Mr Mackenzie, I assure you that we are doing this for the good of your play,' and then the young author's troubled frown would disappear, and his obstinate mouth would relax into a smile.

I was very pleased when, shortly after the successful Arts performances of *Musical Chairs*, Bronson Albery offered me a contract to appear in three plays, under the joint management of himself and Howard Wyndham. I knew very little about 'Bronnie's' activities (for he worked in an atmosphere of self-effacing anonymity) and I had hardly ever met him. Albery was the son of Lady Wyndham. She had spoken to him about me, it appears, after *The Constant Nymph*, and he had followed my career since that time at the Old Vic and elsewhere. I owe an enormous debt of gratitude to Mr Albery and his brothers, and I was very happy under their management. They allowed me a large share in the shaping of their policy while I was working at their theatres, and I learnt a great deal about the dangers and risks of management without having to contribute in any way myself towards the financial responsibilities of the productions with which I was so happily associated.

Musical Chairs had been a great success at the Arts Theatre, but we could not ignore the fact that it had attracted a specialized audience. By the time the dress-rehearsal before the regular run at the Criterion Theatre was upon us we were all plunged in gloom. The play was bitter and tragic, and the cast did not contain any dazzling and well-known names to attract people to the box office.

We say in the theatre that it is a good sign if dress-rehearsals do not proceed smoothly. The Criterion dress-rehearsal was chaotic. Throughout the early part of the play the audience had to be aware of thunder booming away in the distance. These noises had been timed most carefully during the previous rehearsals, but on this occasion they persisted in coming in at wrong moments, interrupting our best lines, and failing to materialize at all if we paused to allow them their full effect. The lighting went wrong. During one of my tensest love scenes with Carol Goodner I heard insistent hammering behind the scenes, and I lost my temper and shouted at the stage hands.

Only Komisarjevsky seemed to be satisfied and unperturbed. I watched him walk across the stage, just before the curtain went up on the first night and pin a fly-paper in a prominent position. He seemed delighted with this last-minute touch of realistic detail, quite absorbed and apparently oblivious of the feeling of tension all round him.

True to the traditions of the theatre the opening performance went like clockwork. The audience was delighted; Mackenzie was called for, and made an excellent and modest speech. His pleasure and gratitude were very touching.

One of the luckiest things that ever happened for me, and for the play and its author too, as it turned out, was the engagement of Carol Goodner for *Musical Chairs*. She played the American fiancée of the hero's brother, a distinctly unsympathetic character, who must, however, seem seductive and interesting to the audience.

I knew Carol Goodner by name, but I had never seen her act. Before she joined the cast, the part was offered to an English actress who thought it much too unpleasant. We had no other actress in mind, and we offered the part to Miss Goodner without any real knowledge of her capabilities, chiefly because we knew she was an American.

I had never before tackled such violent love scenes in a modern play, and the smallness of the Criterion Theatre, as well as one or two dangerous lines, had made me nervous at rehearsals. But when these moments held the house successfully on the first night I knew that all was well.

During the long run of *Musical Chairs* I became worried, as I have always done under similar circumstances, lest my performance should deteriorate more and more as time went on. I became very nervy, and looked so emaciated that people used to wonder if I was as consumptive as I appeared to be in the play. A charming lady said to Ralph Richardson: 'I went to see your friend Mr Gielgud act the other night. Tell me, is he really as thin as that?'

The Criterion is a small theatre, and my fatal habit of being too much aware of the audience became increasingly destructive to my concentration. *Musical Chairs* attracted the smart stall-public which likes to arrive late, and people would come pushing into the front rows, peering at us across the footlights. They were so near that we could have shaken hands with them, and we could hear their remarks as they rustled their programmes and asked each other stupid questions about the play.

My impromptu piano-playing in the part served well enough, but I became self-conscious about that too after a while, especially one night when I saw Artur Rubinstein sitting in the second row of the stalls.

Another evening I noticed Noël Coward in front. I recognized him immediately, became very nervous, and played the first act with one eye on him all the time. The curtain rose after the first interval, and I looked again in Noël's direction. He had not returned, and his seat was empty for the rest of the performance. For the next few weeks I was very hurt and complained to all my friends how rude he had been in walking out. At last I ran across him, and he said frankly, 'You were overacting so terribly that I couldn't have borne it another minute, and Frank Vosper's wig was so badly joined that it looked like a yachting-cap!' He also said (though not to me), that he would never have dreamed of leaving the theatre had he known that his exit would be noticed. 'This incident,' he remarked, 'has finally convinced me that I am really famous.' The same incident really broke me for good of my dreadful habit of looking at people in the audience.

I took a short holiday in the summer. While I was away, my part was played by another young man, John Cheatle, who had been at my preparatory school before the War, when he had played Portia to my Shylock. I went off to the South of France for a fortnight, but I did not get much rest. I stopped at hotels in noisy streets and stayed up all night gambling. On my way home I spent a night at Chartres, and happened to pick up an English paper in the lounge of the hotel just before I went to bed. There I read of Ronald Mackenzie's death in a motor accident. He also had gone on holiday (for the first time in eight years), and was motoring in France not a hundred miles from where I was. A tyre burst, the car overturned, and he was killed immediately.

CHAPTER TWELVE

1931–32

During the run of *The Good Companions*, I had been given my first chance as a director. I was asked to go to Oxford and do *Romeo and Juliet* for the O.U.D.S. This production was a first sketch for the one which was to be such a success in London in 1935. 'The Motleys', who designed the dresses, Peggy Ashcroft, who played Juliet, and Edith Evans, who was the Nurse, were all to be associated with me at the New Theatre four years later. Christopher Hassall, the son of the poster artist, was a splendid Romeo at Oxford. It is, in many ways, an ideal part for an undergraduate, whose natural attributes of youth amply compensate for his lack of professional experience as an actor. George Devine, who was president of the O.U.D.S. at this time, was a fine Mercutio, and William Devlin and Hugh Hunt played Tybalt and the Friar respectively, so I had a company bursting with potential talent.

'The Motleys', as we always call them in the theatre, have been associated with me in nearly all my productions, and any success I have had as a director I gladly share with them, for they are at all times the ideal collaborators. Their real names are Elizabeth Montgomery, Audrey and Peggy Harris. During my seasons at the Old Vic they had made some drawings of me as Richard, Macbeth and Lear, which they shyly brought to my notice. They were three silent and retiring young women in those days, and it was some time before I could get them to speak about themselves in their gentle, hesitating voices. I began to visit them in their tiny doll's house of a home near Church Street, Kensington, and, although they were perfect hostesses I thought them strangely silent. They have since told me that my sudden and unexpected arrivals used to throw them all into paroxysms of shyness, as I hurled remarks at them over my shoulder and spoke so fast that they barely understood a word I uttered. At Oxford, when I produced *Romeo*, they did their first work for me in designing the costumes (but not the scenery). They were enormously helpful to me in the production, and tremendously popular with the company. The O.U.D.S. was split that term into rival factions by an intense political partisanship on the occasion of the election of a new president at the end of Devine's term of office. The visiting ladies of the company were taken out by the undergraduates between rehearsals. They listened sympathetically while the rival candidates were praised or abused. Edith would go marching along the Oxford Canal or drive out to Godstow for dinner with two or three members of the cast, while Peggy was soothing another party over an omelette at The George. I was only at rehearsal in the daytime, as I was acting all the week in London, and so missed most of this excitement. George Devine found the Motleys especially sympathetic, and when he went 'down' a few months later and decided to take up acting as a profession he also became business manager to the Motleys, who were then launching out as stage-designers on quite an ambitious scale. Later he married Sophie (Audrey), Harris, the eldest of the three.

Julian Wylie gave me the night off for the opening of *Romeo* at Oxford, and I sat in the pit and nearly died with anxiety and mortification when the curtain fouled, causing a two-minutes' wait towards the end of what should otherwise have been a non-stop production.

I was in an unusual state of nerves when I went on to the stage at the end of the performance. The graceful compliments I intended to distribute circled madly in my head, and I referred to Miss Evans and Miss Ashcroft as 'two leading ladies, the like of whom I hope I shall never meet again!'

In spite of this *gaffe*, my desire to continue as a director was unshaken. Working with amateurs had given me confidence, and *Romeo* was a play which I knew really well. Edith Evans had of course played the Nurse before at the Old Vic, and her superb performance freed me from the least anxiety in any scene in which she appeared. Not only was she friendly and encouraging to everyone, but she rightly insisted on a certain admirable discipline during rehearsals, which was exactly what the O.U.D.S. needed to ensure the best possible results. I knew Peggy's Juliet would be enchanting. I had first seen her as Desdemona, at the Savoy, in what I thought a very disappointing production of *Othello*, with Paul Robeson, Maurice Browne, Ralph Richardson and Sybil Thorndike. When Peggy came on in the Senate scene it was as if all the lights in the theatre had suddenly gone up. Later, in the handkerchief scene, I shall never forget her touching gaiety as she darted about the stage, utterly innocent and lighthearted, trying to coax and charm Othello from his angry questioning. Her Juliet, especially in the early scenes, had this same quality of enchantment, and she made an enormous success at Oxford.

I was happy to find that I got on well with the whole cast, and it was exciting to see some of my long-cherished ideas of production actually being carried out upon the stage. In private life I am never very good at giving orders and getting my own way. As a director I seemed for the first time to gain real authority. One of the most exciting moments came just before the first dress-rehearsal. The lights, the scenery, and the orchestra were all to be used together for the first time. I sat alone in the dress-circle with my note-book and torch. The house lights went down, the music began to play, there was a faint glow from the footlights. A wonderful play was about to be performed, and it was for me alone. I felt like Ludwig of Bavaria. On the other hand, my feeling of utter helplessness on the first night made me far more nervous than if I had been appearing in the play myself.

I began my career as a director of Shakespeare in the professional theatre with *The Merchant of Venice* at the Old Vic. As usual I was doing two things at once, acting in *Musical Chairs* this time, and finishing a film of *The Good Companions*, which overran its schedule, so that instead of having three weeks for my production, I was only able to attend five rehearsals altogether. Once again I found myself indebted to Harcourt Williams, who took the rehearsals when I was kept away[1]. Many people told me that they enjoyed this production of mine, but I was accused of fantasticating the story too much, and of overloading it with dancing, music and elaborate decorations. I was impressed but not wholly convinced by my critics. What was wrong with the production was lack of rehearsal, and it was a marvel to me that the company were able in so short a time to give even a hint of the elaborate ideas which I had conceived.

[1] Again I dropped one of my celebrated bricks in a first-night speech when I referred to 'Harcourt Williams, who has done all the donkey-work in this production!'

In one respect at least we were most restrained. The Motleys' colourful décor, which some people thought affected and extravagant, cost only £90. These practical young artists were more than usually resourceful in discovering cheap and effective materials. Shylock's dress, for instance, was made of dish rags. I used a great deal of music in the play, chiefly from Peter Warlock's *Capriol Suite,* which fitted perfectly with the contrasting moods of the different scenes, bound the action together, and covered many of the deficiencies in my production.

Soon afterwards I directed my first modern play, *Strange Orchestra.* Rodney Ackland's plays have a distinctive rhythm. The moods and subtleties of his characters are delicately woven together. His vision is apt to be limited to his own particular type of atmosphere, but at least he deals with real people, struggling with the circumstances under which they live, unlike the creatures of so many playwrights' imaginations, who wander about the stage, well clothed and fed, with no visible means of practical support.

When I read *Strange Orchestra,* I thought I saw an opportunity of trying to put into practice for myself some of the methods which I had learnt from watching Komisarjevsky. My production was a direct imitation of his style as I remembered it.

I discovered in Rodney Ackland another vegetarian playwright. There, however, his likeness to Ronald Mackenzie ended. Ackland has a restless, excitable mind, and a lack of reserve which is sometimes frank and endearing, although it can be a little embarrassing on occasion. He too has led a struggling, difficult life, but the fact that he has spent many years in that most uncomfortable and nerve-racking region, the fringe of success, has not made him bitter. He tells stories against himself, and makes fun of his misfortunes, but I know that he is sensitive and feels very acutely in the production of his plays. *Strange Orchestra* takes place in a Bloomsbury flat, where the paying guests are young and poor. They are uncertain of their jobs, they quarrel, make love, indulge in scenes of hysteria, behave abominably to one another, perform deeds of unselfish heroism, and dance to the gramophone.

The principal character in the play was the owner of the flat, Mrs Vera Lyndon, a Bohemian, slatternly woman with a heart of gold. This was a gorgeous character, and I saw at once that much of the success of the play would depend on the actress who created it. I was very anxious for Mrs Patrick Campbell to play the part, and finally suggested it to her with some trepidation. She could be very stubborn, and her reasons for rejecting or accepting a part were peculiar to herself. She once came to me in a state of great excitement over a quite unsuitable play to which she had taken a fancy, and when I asked her why she was so anxious to do it, she replied: 'Because I should speak French and German, play the César Franck sonata in the second act, and Vosper could be my father.'

When to my delighted surprise, Mrs Campbell accepted the Ackland part provisionally, new doubts began to trouble me. I knew that she was liable to treat a producer as dust beneath her chariot wheels, and I had heard strange stories of her behaviour at rehearsals. Marion Terry had told me once that, in *Pygmalion*, when Mrs Campbell discovered that Mr Shaw intended coming to a rehearsal, she refused to act while he remained in the theatre. Mr Shaw sat still. Mrs Campbell strode to her dressing-room, locked herself in, and played the piano for hours, while the cast, who could not proceed with their work listened entranced.

When the first rehearsal of *Strange Orchestra* began, 'Mrs Pat' pretended that she did not understand the play. 'Who are all these extraordinary characters?' she demanded. 'Where do they live? Does Gladys Cooper know them?' She invariably arrived late every morning and we would hear her talking loudly all the way from the stage-door to the stage. She said to David Hutcheson, whom we got for a certain part after tremendous trouble: 'Oh, how-do-you-do. I hope you'll stay. We have had four already!' She kept on reminding us, 'I am leaving in a fortnight; you must get someone else to play this part.' Every afternoon she went off to sit with her beloved Pekinese, which had been locked up in quarantine on her return with it from America. Her distress about her pet was quite genuine, and a real obsession with her.[1] In the end she left us, as she had threatened to do, and I was in despair. She had rehearsed the part magnificently and I felt sure that if she would only open in it the play's success was certain. And how wise she was about all the other parts! Here, just as in *Ghosts*, she was extremely well-informed about every detail of the play though she pretended to be quite indifferent to everything that was going on. One day she was sitting at the side of the stage. I thought she was

[1] She said 'I smuggled it once as a false bust, and once as hip-disease'. The third time she put it in her hat-box, and it barked and was discovered!

asleep. I was rehearsing another scene, and asked one of the actors concerned to cut a certain line. Suddenly the famous voice boomed out. 'You know his whole character is in that line; I shouldn't cut it if I were you.' Of course she was perfectly right.

After Mrs Campbell's departure, gloom reigned for several days. Our spirits revived somewhat when we succeeded in persuading Laura Cowie to take her place. I did not like asking another actress to take over a part which Mrs Campbell had given up, but she gave a fine performance, exchanging her own vivid beauty and distinguished manners for the slatternly blowziness of Mrs Lyndon. When the curtain went up on the first night she was spreading jam on a piece of toast. Her hand shook with nervousness and some of the jam fell on to her stocking. Laura stooped down, lazily scraped it off, and put it back on the toast. This unrehearsed piece of business, so perfectly 'in character', opened the play with a roar of laughter.

I was proud to be associated with *Strange Orchestra*. The play was only a moderate commercial success, but it had great quality—'as much superior to the ordinary stuff of the theatre as tattered silk is to unbleached calico'—as James Agate so aptly put it.

Sheppey was the last play of a famous and experienced author, Somerset Maugham. We had some difficulty in casting many of the parts. We finally selected Ralph Richardson for the title part, Angela Baddeley for Sheppey's pretentious, vulgar-minded daughter, Eric Portman for her caddish lover, and Laura Cowie for the street-walker who, in the last scene, appears as Death. Two very successful pieces of casting were Victor Stanley, as a sort of modern Artful Dodger, and Cicely Oates, who gave a lovely performance as Mrs Sheppey.

I have always been struck, in my career as a director, by the all-round excellence of English character-actors. Their discipline is beyond reproach, and their knowledge of their work is an enormous help to a director. Cast them right and they will always be perfect; you need never worry about them. Cicely Oates had played Lady Montague (a part of two lines and a little wailing) at the Regent, the first time I acted Romeo. Though she was a fine actress, it was a very long time before managers seemed to be aware of her remarkable talents. She died not long after the run of *Sheppey*, just at the moment when success seemed to be coming at last to reward her for her many years of unrecognized hard work.

Maugham's play was difficult to direct, though. It was so well written and carefully constructed that any radical changes, except a few cuts, were out of the question. Sir Gerald du Maurier once said of another Maugham play, *The Letter*, which he was directing: 'I don't like this sort of play. There's nothing for me to do.' But *Sheppey* seemed to be conceived in an extraordinary mixture of styles, with a first act of Pineroesque comedy, a second of almost Shavian cynicism and drama, and a third of tragic fantasy. I had neither the courage nor the experience to make any drastic changes in the script, and Mr Maugham did not arrive till the rehearsals had been in progress for a fortnight. I was very nervous when I approached him first. He was charming, but seemed oddly devoid of enthusiasm. He made some practical and useful suggestions but did not comment at all on the work that I had done. He seemed quite untouched by the expectant atmosphere in the theatre.

I discussed deferentially with him the scene where Sheppey's daughter, furious because her father proposes to give away the fortune which he has won in a sweepstake, yet hopeful that, if the family can have him certified as insane, the money may still be theirs, wanders round the stage with her eyes closed repeating a prayer: 'O God, make them say he's potty'. I was doubtful of the effect of some comic lines at this painful moment in the play and said to Maugham: 'Do you want this scene played for comedy or pathos? As it stands, the audience will laugh in the wrong places, and make it very difficult for the actress.' Mr Maugham looked genuinely surprised as he answered, 'But I think the whole scene is very funny don't you?' The scene was played in the end with much power by Angela Baddeley, who gave a brilliant performance of a difficult part, but, though Maugham congratulated her, I never knew if he thought we had harmed the effect of the scene as he conceived it by the way we had handled it in production.

I have nearly always been acting in another theatre on the first night of other plays I have directed, and it is a trying business on these occasions to concentrate on the old work while the new is in progress at a theatre near by. On the first night of *Sheppey* someone rushed across the court separating the stage-door of Wyndham's from that of the New Theatre, where I was appearing in *Richard of Bordeaux*, to tell me that the lights had gone wrong in the last scene when Death appears to the sleeping Sheppey. This mistake must have damaged the play considerably at this first performance.

Later, I asked Mr Maugham to come to a matinée of *Sheppey* with me, as I wanted his approval of a few slight cuts. We sat in a box together and he began to take notes. In the interval I thought, 'Now perhaps he will talk about his play to me'. But Maugham had an odd knack of drawing one out, while he remained practically silent himself. I found that, as usual, I was doing all the talking, and I had a sneaking suspicion that although his manner was studiously correct, my companion was extracting a certain amount of demure amusement from my eloquence.

When Maugham rang me up a few days later and asked me to lunch with him at Claridge's, adding 'I have a little book that I want to give you', I went to keep the engagement with the liveliest expectations. But instead of the quiet *tête-à-tête* meal I had hoped for, I found that a large luncheon party had been assembled. Beverley Nichols and John Van Druten were present, as well as several other brilliant people, and I had to be satisfied with crumbs of polite conversation from my host, who sat right away from me on the other side of a large table. When the meal was over, Mr Maugham drew me into the men's room, where he murmured a few polite words as he pressed the promised gift into my hands. When I looked up to thank him, he was gone. The book was a first copy of *Sheppey*, and I found when I opened it that the author had dedicated the play to me. It was a charming gesture, but I should have been very grateful for an hour's talk with Maugham about the theatre. It is always difficult I find, to get on intimate terms with dramatic authors. I suppose my actor's egotism is to blame. I am not clever at drawing people out, and my friends tell me that I have no real interest in anyone but myself. I hope this is not the exact truth.

CHAPTER THIRTEEN

1932–33

The manuscript of Gordon Daviot's *Richard of Bordeaux*, with its neat pages typed in blue, had lain in my dressing-room for several days before I found time to look at it. I picked it up in one of my waits during a matinée of *The Good Companions* and began to read it through. There was a long cast and a great number of scenes and I knew little of the history of Richard's time except what I had learned from Shakespeare. The opening scene of the new play was light and charming, and the description of Richard's appearance attracted me at once—I thought that perhaps the author had seen me in the part at the Vic[1]—but the council scene which followed seemed rather wordy and I could not at first distinguish the characters of the different councillors and uncles. It was not till I began reading the third scene, in Richard's palace after dinner, with Derby telling boring stories about the tournament on one side and Anne discussing fashions and religion with Lady Derby on the other, that my interest and enthusiasm were thoroughly aroused. I took the play home with me that night, and read it several times during the weeks that followed.

I realized at once that Richard was a gift from heaven, and I felt sure that Gwen Ffrangcon Davies would be exquisite as Anne, if she could be persuaded to play it. Originally the part was even smaller than in the final version, and it was essential that the actress who created it should completely fill the picture in every scene in which she appeared as there was little other female interest in the play. I did not mean to direct it myself as I thought it would be too difficult a task for me in addition to playing such a long, exacting part. I hoped to get Komisarjevsky to undertake

[1] It turned out later that she had!

it, but he was abroad at the time. Bronson Albery liked the manuscript and offered to give performances at the Arts Theatre on two consecutive Sunday nights. I eagerly agreed, and asked Harcourt Williams to help me to direct the play.

These performances took place in the spring of 1932, when *Musical Chairs* was still running successfully at the Criterion. Joseph Schindler was a pretty exhausting part emotionally, but I was grateful for the chance of studying something new. I had shown the script of *Richard of Bordeaux* to the Motleys who were enthusiastic and full of ingenious schemes for saving time and money over the *décor*. Albery allowed us to spend £300 and lent us the New Theatre for the trial performances in order to give us more space to manœuvre the quick changes of scenery. However, what with casting, directing, and acting in two places at once, I was completely exhausted after the performances were over, and, although we had played to enthusiastic audiences, I felt that the middle part of the play was weak, and could not believe it had really much chance of commercial success. Mackenzie, I remember, disliked it intensely, and as I am always inclined to be more impressed by adverse criticism than by enthusiastic comments from my friends after an exhausting first night, I resumed the unbroken run of *Musical Chairs* without much regret and thought no more about the other play.

Soon after Mackenzie died, however, and when the nine months' run of *Musical Chairs* was coming to an end, Albery began pressing me to do *Richard of Bordeaux* again for a regular run at the New Theatre. For some weeks I was not at all enthusiastic about the idea as I still thought that certain parts of the play were weak, and I did not feel I had the energy to tackle it again so soon.

When we had started rehearsing the Arts Theatre production I had not met Gordon Daviot[1] at all. All the business negotiations were carried out by her agent, Curtis Brown, and it was only at the dress-rehearsal that a figure was pointed out to me sitting in the stalls, and I went down to meet my authoress for the first time.

We had already altered her play a good deal when she saw it first, yet she had nothing but praise for everything that we had done,

[1] Gordon Daviot was the pseudonym of Elizabeth Mackintosh whose home was in Inverness. She wrote her plays under this name and, at the same time, wrote many successful thrillers under the pseudonym of Josephine Tey, including *The Daughter of Time*, a book about Richard III.

and seemed ready to fall in with any suggestions for further alteration that might be thought necessary.

Gwen's share in the preparation and ultimate success of *Richard of Bordeaux* was incalculable. With her comedy, her pathos and her appearance in the rich simple dresses which the Motley's had designed for her, she might have stepped out of the pages of a missal. She was responsive to every mood and tone of mine as we rehearsed our scenes together. Every sweep of her dress and turn of her body was contrived with skill and grace. She helped me continually with my difficult part, just as she had done in *Romeo and Juliet* ten years before. In her own performance nothing was left to chance—she always wore a train for rehearsals, studied her costumes with extreme care so as to know beforehand exactly where they would help or hinder her while she was acting, and selected and economized her emotional effects from day to day, working with the other actors to share her scenes with them in the most helpful way possible.

After the two special performances were over, Gordon and I had talked together at some length about the play, discussing certain suggestions for improvements. There was a bad gap in the story at the end of the long first act, there was also a council scene later, after the Queen's death, which I did not think very effective. The last act needed strengthening, and two small intermediate scenes, we decided, ought to be cut altogether. One, describing John of Gaunt's death, seemed too close to Shakespeare, and the other was not very successful in performance. I thought Derby himself should be given another scene instead. There was not enough of him in the play to give the audience a real interest in his final victory over Richard. Richard himself had so much to do that I felt certain it would help him if the characters of Anne, Robert, Mowbray, the uncles, and Derby could be more fully developed in contrast.

Gordon Daviot went back to Scotland after our conversation and I thought no more about it. Some weeks afterwards I said to Albery: 'I am not very keen to do *Richard* again. It will need a great deal of work and alteration, and then perhaps it will not come out right.' A day or two later I received a letter from Gordon enclosing a dozen pages of rewritten manuscript. Every single point we had discussed had been considered and remedied in the simplest and most effective way. There was a new opening to the second act.

The council scene was gone. In its place was a scene at Sheen Palace in the winter, when Richard returns, for the first and last time, to the room where Anne had died a year before. Mowbray's character was elaborated in a few lines. There was a new scene in the last act for Derby and the Archbishop. I was delighted with the changes, and started to discuss the play again.

In the end I directed *Richard of Bordeaux* myself—a big responsibility, but by this time I felt I knew more about this particular play than anyone else except the author.

The cost of the whole production was extraordinarily little, though the scenery and dresses were of course elaborated from the 'one set with a few additions' which had served for the original performances. The final result was beautiful, even spectacular, and the Motleys established themselves, by their exquisitely graded colour scheme, and simple but brilliantly suggestive scenery, as designers of the very first rank.

In the manuscript, the scenes were labelled by the author, 'Conway Castle', 'The Palace at Eltham', 'The Palace of Sheen' and so on. We were therefore able to develop all the details for ourselves. Working with the Motleys, I planned out rough ideas for every scene—the council-chamber with a horse-shoe table, and banners hanging from the roof (I cribbed this effect of grouping, with the King on his throne seen through the backs of the councillors, from a photograph of a Reinhardt production of *Henry IV, Part I*, that had been done in Germany); the Eltham scene in a striped garden pavilion; the Palace of Sheen with white cloisters and a little tree. Then I was obsessed by the idea that I must walk down stairs at the end of the scene when Richard banishes Mowbray:

> 'So you never really trusted me, Richard?'
>
> 'My dear Thomas, the only persons I trust are two thousand archers, paid regularly every Friday,'

—the line seemed to demand a slow descending exit, and so the scene was placed in a gallery overlooking a great hall. We suggested the festivities going on below by music under the stage, and by two or three richly dressed supers walking with us in procession across the front of the stage before the opening of the scene. The scenery throughout the play gave an admirable suggestion of the size and bareness of the mediaeval palaces of those days, with their high roofs and narrow corridors, steep steps, and embrasured windows. There was just the right amount of detail—a few simple pieces of furniture, rich hangings and table appointments, luxurious materials used for the lovely clothes, but nothing distracting or overdone.

There were some moments in the play which obstinately refused to come out right. During rehearsal one afternoon we were struggling with the Queen's death scene in a dark, depressing room in the back-streets of Soho. The stage direction suggested that Anne should be carried from the stage leaving Richard alone in despair as the curtain fell. Though this had seemed, in reading, one of those 'star curtains' which actors dream of, I began to be more and more certain that the audience could not be moved by the spectacle of my grief if the object of it was no longer there. With the centre of interest gone, I could not make anything of the 'curtain' by myself. At last someone suggested that the doctor should arrive and discover that Anne was dying of the plague. We improvised the scene in dumb show to get the right feeling and grouping for the situation, the authoress wrote two or three short lines of dialogue, and the trick was done.

Some of my other ideas were not so successful. I introduced two tableaux which were a complete failure, but had the sense to remove them (rather reluctantly and under pressure) at the dress-rehearsal. Gordon suddenly found her voice and called, 'Oh, don't cut them out, John has taken so much trouble with them'. I had thought it would be effective to show Richard setting fire to the faggots which were to burn down Sheen Palace, and had planned with the stage carpenter a magnificent stage effect, which he had invented some years before to burn Matheson Lang at the stake in *The Wandering Jew!* But this was not quite the same kind of play, and I realized, just in time, that tableaux were a little out of date, and quite inappropriate to this particular production.

The dress-rehearsal was a series of mishaps. I had spent the whole day in the theatre arranging the lighting. The dress-circle, where I sat, was in the process of being reseated by a battalion of workmen hammering and raising dust. I had to shout my directions to the stage-hands at the top of my voice and kept begging the workmen to extinguish their working lights every few minutes, in order to judge the effect I was trying to create on the stage below. By the evening I was too tired even to lose my temper. Instead I wore an expression of royal composure, suitable as I thought to the character I was trying to play. 'Surely there should be a blue spot there?' I said, pointing gently to a corner, as I lay on the floor at Gwen's feet attempting to act and watch together. 'It is lucky someone has a memory in this theatre.' Then came the incident of the tableaux, which I bore with comparative resignation, but in the final scene, as I opened my mouth to speak the last line of the play, the curtain suddenly descended. I was only able to murmur, 'If that happens tomorrow night we are all sunk!' and sweep, sad but forgiving, to my dressing-room. There is a superstition in the theatre that it is unlucky to speak the 'tag' line of a new play at the dress-rehearsal, and afterwards I wondered if there wasn't something in it after all.

The first night was not sensational, though the audience was attentive and enthusiastic. The strain of acting and producing the play had been very great, and I had practically lost my voice. To add to my troubles, I had quarrelled with one of the leading actors, who refused to see eye to eye with me in the way he should play his part. Fortunately, he was very well cast, and the faults in his performance, though irritating to me, were not detrimental to the general effect, as it turned out, or noticeable to the audience.

The notices were enthusiastic the following morning, and I spent the day thanking people who telephoned me their congratulations. However, when I opened the return for the second performance I found that there had been only £77 in the house. Such modest takings did not indicate the great success which some people had so confidently predicted. The tide turned at the first matinée. Business had been quiet all the morning, but at ten minutes past one the telephone bell in the box office began to ring. Queues formed outside the theatre, and so great and unexpected was the rush that it was a quarter-past three before all the members of the afternoon's audience were in their seats.

From that moment *Richard of Bordeaux* became what the Americans call a 'smash hit'. I travelled down to Brighton for the day on the following Sunday, and although I was physically dog-tired I felt so happy and exhilarated that I went for a long walk on the Downs in a heavy snowstorm.

I determined to make a gesture in honour of the play's success by giving a party. I borrowed the Motleys' studio, which had once been a night club, and sent out invitations to everybody I knew.

The party was a great success both in numbers and distinction. 'Heavens, what a salary list!' somebody was heard to murmur. The Motleys' model theatre was on view. A card had been placed in front of it with the words 'Do not touch' attached to the switchboard, but this awakened Leslie Henson's curiosity, with the result that the crowded room was plunged in darkness, and many of the best-known voices in London were raised in protest.

Richard of Bordeaux was the success of the season. From the window of my flat, I could look down St. Martin's Lane and see the queues coiled like serpents round the theatre. I was photographed, painted, caricatured, interviewed. I signed my autograph a dozen times a day, and received letters and presents by every post. White harts rained upon me in every shape and form, designed in flowers, embroidered on handkerchiefs, stamped on cigarette-boxes. When I left after the matinée the court outside the stage-door would be packed with people. It was rather embarrassing to find that some of my admirers had discovered that I lived near by, and I would often stagger up the street to my front door, with my hat over my eyes and my overcoat collar turned up, followed by a crowd of fifteen or twenty members of my enthusiastic audience. Of course I enjoyed it all at first. But after a time it became rather irksome when I could not go out of my flat without finding two or three 'fans' lurking across the street to intercept me, and several times a day I would open the front door to a complete stranger, or answer the telephone only to find that some importunate or impertinent schoolgirl was giggling at the other end, having 'had a bet with a friend that she would manage to speak to me'.

People came thirty and forty times to see the play. There were several changes in the cast during the run and the rehearsals kept us fairly fresh. In addition to this I was always watching the performance and making little additions and improvements which the 'regulars' were quick to appreciate. I was not so pleased when some of them wrote to me that I was becoming mannered and seemed emotionally exhausted. I fought hard against the boredom and fatigue of so many consecutive performances, and was dismayed to find that, in spite of all my efforts, I was becoming exaggerated and insincere. By the end of the run I had become acutely selfconscious in all the moments that people had originally liked best. But I nearly always enjoyed acting the last two scenes of the play, finding a way of playing these scenes in complete control of my own emotions although the audience became more and more affected to the point of tears. At last I felt I was learning to relax, which Komisarjevsky had told me was the secret of all good emotional acting, and to manage my audience instead of allowing the audience to manage me.

Just before Christmas of the *Richard of Bordeaux* year my voice began to give me a lot of trouble. I was given a fortnight's holiday, and went off on a motor tour through the West of England.

I stayed at a remote inn on Dartmoor, went for long walks, and ate enormous teas with jam and cream. I went to Plymouth and strode along the wind-swept Hoe. Next morning I crossed by the ferry and found myself in the strange foreign land of Cornwall. It was here that I met Ralph Richardson unexpectedly. We had dinner together, and drank champagne, and went cliff-climbing in the dark.

I was thoroughly enjoying myself, but I was conscious of a slight feeling of restlessness. Some time before it was really necessary I started back towards London again. At Bath the car broke down, and it was with a sensation which I recognized as relief that I proceeded to Brighton, where I decided to spend the last days of my holiday. But I found it impossible to keep away from the theatre, and rushed off in the evening to see a Charlot Revue which was being played at the Hippodrome. I must have been away from *Richard* for at least ten days, but although there were still several more left before I must return to the cast, I travelled back to London the next morning. Sneaking into the New Theatre in the evening, I sat behind a curtain in one of the boxes watching a performance of *Richard of Bordeaux* with Glen Byam Shaw, who understudied me, playing the King.

Richard was a wonderful part. It was perfectly suited to my personality and even my tricks and mannerisms did not seem to matter as much as usual. I was helped enormously by my costumes, which expressed exactly the development and gradual ageing of the character. Also the work I had been doing during the three previous years had been of great value to my acting taste.

Playing Shakespeare at the Vic had enriched my sensibility and developed my technique. Afterwards I had jumped into a completely different atmosphere and found a way of making the most of my shadowy part in *The Good Companions.* Finally, Komis's subtle production of *Musical Chairs* had demanded yet another method of approach, an inner understanding of character which I was able to carry a stage further than I had ever done before. I no longer fought shy of using my own personality, as I had at the time of the Vic *Hamlet*. On the contrary, I made full use of it for the first time as Joseph Schindler and gained confidence by doing so. Now, in *Richard*, I was able to gather the fruits of all this experience to give light and shade to a long and elaborate character study.

I have often wondered how *Richard of Bordeaux* stands in relation to the notable successes of the past, and what are its chances of survival. The majority of the plays in which Irving, Tree, Alexander and Wyndham appeared could now only be revived as curiosities.[1] I fancy we are unable to accept them today because their period is too close to ours, and also because they are associated in our minds with the great actors who created them. The theatrical successes of the Victorian age were essentially the products of single personalities. *The Bells* was Irving, and the public today would never accept another actor in the play. On the other hand, Gladys Cooper's revival of *The Second Mrs Tanqueray* in the twenties caused enormous interest, and though the play seemed rather old-fashioned it remained a finely constructed vehicle for acting.

In the future new players may interpret afresh some of the more recent works which now lie neglected on the shelf. Will those plays then become what we call 'classics'? I should not care to guess the names of the plays of my generation for which this honour waits—*The Circle*[2] perhaps, *The Vortex* possibly. Will *Musical Chairs* or *Richard of Bordeaux* be among their number? And shall I feel very jealous or only faintly patronizing if those plays are revived during my lifetime with new players in the parts which I created?

Richard came to an end at last. The final performances in London were terribly tiring and emotional. The tour which followed was a triumphant success, and at Golder's Green, where we played the very last performance, the police had to be called to keep back the crowd which surged round the stage-door when Gwen and I tried to leave the theatre.

In the copy of the play that Gordon sent to me she wrote: 'I like

[1] Since writing this we have had a notable spate of successful revivals. *Lady Windermere's Fan*, *Dear Brutus* and *Caste* among them.

[2] I revived this myself in 1944 with some success.

to think that, in time to come, whenever *Richard of Bordeaux* is mentioned, it is your name that will spring to people's lips'. How pleasant it was to be told that! But it was to the brilliant inspiration and sympathy of Gordon Daviot that I owed the biggest personal success of my career.

CHAPTER FOURTEEN

1934

During the run of *Richard* I had made my first venture into management, greatly attracted by the charming atmosphere of a new play, *Spring 1600*, written by Emlyn Williams, who was at that time acting in Edgar Wallace's *The Case of the Frightened Lady* in New York. Emlyn had been an undergraduate at Oxford in the days when I was playing there with the Fagans, and I had sometimes seen him curled up in an armchair in a corner of the Clubroom at the O.U.D.S. But I did not know him at all, though I had greatly admired his performance as Angelo, the Italian secretary to Tony Perelli, the gangster, in Wallace's *On the Spot*. I was aware that Fagan had given him his first chances, both as author and actor, by producing his first play *Full Moon* at the Oxford Playhouse. Since that time he had been acting and writing with equal success.

I was not able to interest Bronson Albery in *Spring 1600*, and after some thought I decided to present it myself, with Richard Clowes, a great friend of mine, as partner. I was also to direct the play. At first we found it extremely difficult to cast. Elisabeth Bergner had just arrived in England and had announced her intention of appearing on the London stage. I found out where she was living, and asked her to come and lunch with me. The childish figure who arrived, wearing a blue beret and a loose woolly coat, did not at all resemble the glamorous star of popular imagination, but she did look exactly like the young girl in Emlyn's play who runs away from the country and joins Richard Burbage's company disguised as a boy. She sat with me at Boulestin's restaurant, with her red hair falling over one eye, talking eagerly in her precise attractive English and looking wisely at me as she picked at her very frugal meal. I was fascinated by Elisabeth Bergner, as I have been ever since.

She told me she had read three hundred plays since her arrival in London and had liked *Spring 1600* best, but she was greatly in the debt of Mr Cochran and could not dream of making her début under any management but his. Why I did not immediately offer the manuscript to Cochran I cannot for the life of me imagine.

Spring 1600 was shelved for several months. I talked it over with Emlyn, and persuaded him to re-shape the last act completely and make other fairly drastic alterations. This method had been very successful in *Richard of Bordeaux*, but in this case my suggested additions overweighted the spectacular side of the play. The slender plot sank gradually deeper and deeper into a morass of atmosphere and detail. The Motleys designed elaborate sets, I engaged madrigal singers, a large orchestra, and a crowd of supers, Isabel Jeans, as Lady Coperario, had a magnificent-looking real negro attendant to usher her on to the stage, and a real black monkey (which promptly bit her) to carry on her shoulder. By the time the curtain rose on the first night we had spent £4000.

The most successful performance was given by Frank Pettingell, who was irresistibly funny as Ned Pope, a middle-aged actor in Burbage's company who had played Juliet's Nurse, and was delighted at the prospect of being offered the part of Gertrude, the Queen, in Shakespeare's new play. He was immensely sedate as he sat quarrelling with the young boys who played the heroines' parts or sewing in a corner of Burbage's bedroom while a rehearsal was going on.

In spite of many hectic days in the theatre Emlyn Williams remained calm. He accepted most of my alterations and cuttings without demur, wrote in the extra scenes which I suggested and kept us all continually amused. One morning I approached him a little nervously and said that I thought the opening scene of the play was unduly encumbered with the names of flowers. Would he agree to my making a few cuts, as these repeated floral allusions rather held up the action? 'By all means', said Emlyn. 'We don't want James Agate to head his Sunday article, "Herrick, or Little by Little".'

We were only once in serious danger of quarrelling. 'The last act is thin. We must try to make the best of it,' I announced through my megaphone from the dress-circle, thinking that our author was miles away.

'I think we all know the act is thin, John,' said a voice at my elbow, 'but you need not announce the fact to the whole cast. You might wait for the critics to do that.' I felt very much ashamed of myself. But when I turned round to apologize I caught Emlyn's eye and we both burst out laughing.

The dress-rehearsal arrived. I was still playing in *Richard of Bordeaux* at night and was terribly tired with the double work. A few professionals came to the rehearsal, Frank Vosper among them. At the end he came to me and said, 'It's a lovely production, but you ought to cut twenty minutes out of the first act.' By some very careless oversight the play had never been timed, but I had chopped the text about so much that I did not dare to impose new cuts and alterations at the last minute, as there was no time left to rehearse them. I rushed off to the New for my own performance, leaving everything as it was and hoping for the best. Alas, I should at all costs have listened to Frank's admirable advice! On the first night, despite a most friendly and enthusiastic house, the first act hung fire badly, and the final curtain did not descend until 11.30.

I heard afterwards that the audience behaved with exemplary patience. They seemed to wish the play to succeed, and seized on the good things in it with pleasure and relief. When I read the notices the following morning, however, I knew the worst at once. The critics praised where they could, but it was obvious that most of them knew that something was amiss. Emlyn spoke to me on the telephone, asking my permission to make some cuts. I heard that afterwards he went straight to the theatre, borrowed the prompt copy of his play, and sat on a chair at the stage-door making the alterations he thought necessary. He had watched the first performance from the top of a ladder in the wings, from which point of vantage he was able to judge the audience's reaction to every single situation.

I had a matinée of *Richard of Bordeaux* that afternoon, and Emlyn came to see me after it was over. We found a subdued company waiting for us at the Shaftesbury Theatre. I think we all realized that our labours of the last four weeks had been for nothing, but the prospect of failure was never even hinted at as we gave out the cuts. How well actors behave on these occasions!

The very definite failures, which are taken off after a couple of nights, are easier to endure than plays which die a lingering death. A fortnight passed while *Spring 1600* perished slowly and miserably. The houses were poor, but not unenthusiastic, and several days of fog enabled us to blame the weather and continue to live in hope. But it was no use. Once or twice I looked in during a matinée, but the sight of so many empty seats drove me out into the murky streets again. But at least I had my own work to keep me occupied in the evenings, whilst poor Emlyn haunted the Shaftesbury Theatre every night. At last he could bear it no longer, packed his bags, and fled to Spain. A few days later the play came to an end.

I knew that Ronald Mackenzie had finished another play just before his death, though he had never shown it to me, and I had heard that he hoped to interest Leslie Banks in playing the leading part. But one matinée day, just before Ronald went on his fatal holiday, I had lunched at Rules with him and Komis. I was slightly disgruntled because I had not been asked to read the new manuscript, and as the conversation was chiefly centred on this topic I was not able to take much part in it. I left for my performance half-way through lunch, leaving Komis and Ronald glowering at each other across the table in a curiously glum but understanding manner.

A few months after Mackenzie died Komis sent me *The Maitlands* to read, and I thought it wonderfully good, though I understood immediately why the author had not thought me ideal for either of the two men's parts. I knew that Albery had bought an option on the play and proposed to present it at some future time. Now, more than a year later, it was decided to produce *The Maitlands* at Wyndham's as soon as I returned from my holiday.

Mackenzie had insisted that only Komis should handle the play, and I was not sure how much they had discussed together the details of the casting and production. I did not like to ask Komis too many questions on the subject, as he might have supposed me interfering. I knew he had been very fond of Mackenzie, and that he believed sincerely in the play.

The rehearsals began without me. I returned from my short rest, ten days later, to find the actors in position and all the preliminary work in hand, never a very satisfactory way to begin studying a new part. Komis orchestrated the action with his usual skill, but I did not think his cuts and rearrangements as successful as they had been in *Musical Chairs*. Again he ignored a change of scene demanded by the stage directions, and designed a composite set of great ingenuity, consisting of a sitting-room in the front of the stage with a dining-room in the background, and a hall, staircase and front door (all visible to the audience) on the right-hand side. There was a strange little door under the stairs, leading to the basement, round which a comic maid popped her head at various moments. The whole pictorial treatment conveyed a rather crazy, unreal atmosphere which I do not think the author intended, as the play was strictly realistic.

We opened on a terribly hot night. All day long the queues had waited patiently for the pit and gallery to open. My name was in large letters outside the theatre. After *Bordeaux*, everyone supposed that I must have chosen another big showy part for my next appearance.

When the curtain went up, I was discovered wearing rather shabby modern clothes, and a moustache (which I had specially grown for the occasion), with a trident in my hand and a paper crown on my head, being fitted for a Neptune carnival costume. There was tremendous applause at first. Then, either because my appearance disappointed those who thought I ought to look romantic, or because the regular first-nighters had been irritated and crowded out by a mass of *Bordeaux* enthusiasts, an uproar broke out in the gallery which lasted for several moments. Meanwhile I stood on the stage, paralysed with nervousness, waiting to speak the opening lines of the play. Calm was restored as soon as the dialogue began, and the performance continued without any other untimely interruptions. But at the end of the play, after many curtains, I stepped forward to speak about Mackenzie, when someone in the gallery shouted 'Rubbish!'

When I came out of the stage-door, half an hour later, the court was full of people looking curiously glum and disagreeable, though there was no demonstration of any kind. Next morning, however, the newspapers had headlines 'Dead author's play booed on first night', 'Wild scenes at Wyndham's' and so on. In spite of this unfavourable beginning, *The Maitlands* ran for ten weeks to average business, but it was never really a success. I hope it may be done again one day under happier auspices. It is a brilliant piece of work, full of observation and bitter wit, with an unerring quality of theatrical effectiveness, which was not, in my opinion, exploited to the full in the performance we gave.

I had an amusing encounter with Lilian Baylis about this time. The Vic was about to open again for a new season, and Lilian sent me one of her characteristic letters (neatly typed, with most of the typing crossed out and her own writing crowded in on top of it) asking me to come down to see her and discuss some of her plans. Delighted and flattered at being considered so important, I stepped into my car and drove to the Vic. I marched in to Lilian's office in my best West End style, with a new hat and yellow gloves held negligently in my hand. Lilian greeted me warmly and we talked enthusiastically together for half an hour. As I got up to go I said grandly, 'I should simply love to come down some time and act and direct again at the Vic for you if you'd let me, but of course I'm awfully busy for the next month or two'. Lilian, looking steadily at my rapidly receding hair, said briskly, 'Oh no, dear, you play all the young parts you can while you're still able to!' I left the Vic in a distinctly chastened frame of mind, determined that I would never again attempt to impress so shrewd a judge of character as Lilian Baylis.

Ever since *Richard of Bordeaux* I had talked about *Hamlet* with the Motleys. We had sat in their studio over endless cups of tea, arguing about the ideal setting for the play, how it should be cast, what period of costume would suit it best, and so on. After the comparatively short runs of *The Maitlands* and *Queen of Scots*,[1] Albery suddenly decided to do *Hamlet* for me at the New. It was lucky that I knew the part and had been making plans on and off for nearly a year for this very play—otherwise I could never have hoped to tackle the tremendous job of acting in it and directing it as well with only four weeks' rehearsals.

Of course I was encouraged by the prospect of choosing a fine cast for myself, and I longed to see if my ideas for the production could be carried out as I had conceived them.

I have a particular aversion to the hackneyed Gothic style of decoration for *Hamlet*, in which the King and Queen look like playing-cards, and Hamlet like an overgrown Peter Pan. I described my ideas on the subject to the Motleys, and shortly afterwards they showed me some of the work of Lucas Cranach, a contemporary of Dürer. These drawings finally inspired the costumes which they designed for our production.

[1] Written for Gwen Ffrangcon Davies by Gordon Daviot. I directed it with a fine cast, including Laurence Olivier, but it only achieved a moderate success.

For the scenery a large rostrum was constructed, revolving on its own axis and moved by hand. It was quite easily pushed round by four or five stage hands. This rostrum (which looked by daylight rather like the body of a denuded battleship) provided slopes and levels, seen at different angles when the position of the rostrum changed, on which I could vary the groupings at different moments in the play. A cyclorama was used at the back for the exteriors—the platform, the graveyard, and the final scene, and painted canvas curtains, covered with a rich florid design in blue and silver, enclosed the stage or draped the rostrum for the other parts of the play. It was easy to raise or drop these curtains with only a few moments' pause between the scenes.

All the dresses were made of canvas, but trimmed with silk and velvet, and with rich autumnal colours patterned on to them with a paint spray. The cost of these clothes was amazingly little, and the result looked magnificent, thanks to the Motleys' labour and ingenuity. The finished costumes had the rich, worn look so difficult to obtain on the stage, where period dresses always appear to be either brand-new from the costumier or else shabby and second-hand. We wore great chains round our necks, which appeared imposing and massive from the front. Actually they were made of rubber, painted with silver and gold, and were as light as a feather.

The success of *Hamlet* at the New was a great pleasure and surprise to me. I have written at some length in Rosamond Gilder's book,[1] about my performance in this part, and discussed there most of my difficulties and conclusions in dealing with the inexhaustible problems of the play. I do not wish to enlarge on them again. As always happens when a production is hailed as a success, there was a good deal of conflicting opinion about the merits of the performance. Many people told me that they had preferred my own acting at the Vic when I had played the part for the first time. In the same way, Frank Vosper's Claudius was not so highly praised as it had been when he played it in modern dress at the Kingsway some years before. Jessica Tandy's Ophelia was dismissed as a complete failure by certain critics and highly praised by others. I liked it enormously myself. Almost everyone was agreed as to the excellence of George Howe's Polonius, Jack Hawkins was an admirable and sympathetic Horatio, and Laura Cowie magnificently sensuous in the

[1] *John Gielgud's Hamlet*, by Rosamond Gilder. Methuen 1938.

part of Gertrude, playing with especially fine effect in her scenes with Vosper. They looked like a pair of cruel, monstrous cats, and their first appearance, seated on dull gold thrones above the bowing ranks of russet-tinted courtiers, with tall Landsknecht soldiers lining the steps behind them, was immensely fine and impressive.

One night, during one of the intervals in *Hamlet*, Frank was visited by an Army major who told him how much he was enjoying the performance. He was not the type of playgoer one would have expected to relish Shakespearean tragedy and we were all delighted to hear that he was enjoying himself. Then came the moment in the final scene when Claudius says, 'Cousin Hamlet, you know the wager'. None of us knew where to look when Frank, still thinking of his visitor and quite unaware of his mistake, demanded sonorously, 'Cousin Hamlet, you know the major!'

Hamlet was the last production in which I was associated with Frank Vosper. His tragic death in 1937 was a great shock to all his friends. He had inimitable gaiety and charm, was generous to a degree, a delightfully Bohemian and charming host and, as an artist, completely free from jealousy of any kind. Often he gave the impression that he behaved selfishly in doing exactly as he liked, but in reality he enjoyed nothing so much as giving pleasure to other people. As an actor he was often unequal, and sometimes his performances became exaggerated in the course of a long run, but his original creation of old Schindler in *Musical Chairs*, his Dulcimer in *The Green Bay Tree*, and his Henry VIII in *The Rose Without a Thorn*, could hardly have been bettered.

It is difficult to write in detail of these last four years of my career, for I was really too busy to observe their passing with much accuracy of detail. My time was taken up with casting, directing, acting. At the end of an exhausting run I was always in the throes of making plans for something fresh. My short holidays barely gave me time to recover from the hectic life I led in the theatre. I spent most of my spare time in sleeping a great deal, in taking care not to eat unwisely or too well (arranging one's menu is a great problem when one is playing exhausting classical parts eight times a week), husbanding my voice, and living in the country whenever I could.

CHAPTER FIFTEEN

1935

While I was playing *Hamlet*, Rodney Ackland brought me a new play, an adaptation of Hugh Walpole's novel *The Old Ladies*. The book had always been a favourite of mine, and I had even been bold enough to call on Walpole himself a year or so before, and suggest with some temerity that I should collaborate with him on a stage version. We had a delightful talk but nothing came of the idea, as Walpole was busy with his Herries saga and I was full of other plans in the theatre at the time.

Again I found it impossible to discover a manager to share my enthusiasm. Albery and Horace Watson (of the Haymarket) both turned down the play, and I could not find anyone else willing to present it, so, for the second time, Richard Clowes and I decided to go into partnership. After a good deal of discussion, we managed to find a really perfect cast. There are only four characters in the whole play—one of them a charwoman who does not speak. We engaged Edith Evans for Mrs Payne, the old gipsy woman who covets the piece of amber owned by the poor faded gentlewoman Miss Beringer (Jean Cadell). The third old lady—Mrs Amorest, a motherly little widow whose hopes are centred in her adored son who is abroad and a tiny legacy which she is likely to receive from a dying cousin—was beautifully played by Mary Jerrold.

We started rehearsals without having been able to lease a theatre, and the cast worked away valiantly while we made every effort to obtain one. I felt sure that the play should be given in a small theatre, preferably the Criterion as, with only four characters, a small stage seemed essential. The faded gentility of the atmosphere, and the macabre scene of Miss Beringer's death in the last act, were considered to be dangerous ingredients for the box-office, and every day our search for a theatre became more and more despairing. We were terrified that our three fine actresses might be tempted by a more concrete offer to leave us in the midst of our rehearsals. The delay over the theatre finally resulted in our rehearsing the play for six weeks instead of the usual three and a half, and I believe this was one of the reasons why the production was such a complete piece of work when it was finished.

The Old Ladies was the first production in which I was able to carry out most fully my original intentions. Usually one begins with a number of exciting ideas which gradually get lost in the stress of 'putting on the play somehow' in a limited time.

The action took place in three rooms of an old house in a cathedral town. The script demanded that both the staircase and hall should be visible to the audience, and at first I pictured the stage with the rooms arranged symmetrically one above the other. One day we were rehearsing doggedly at the New, with our properties for *The Old Ladies* set up on the big uneven rostrum which was used for *Hamlet* in the evenings. Edith was sitting in a low rocking-chair on the highest part of the rostrum. A few feet below her, and a little forward on the stage, Mary Jerrold moved about, making cups of tea among her pathetic little sticks of furniture. The few feet of rostrum which divided them suggested immediately that they were in different rooms, though in reality a twelve-foot wall and a ceiling would have separated them from one another. I suddenly saw an extraordinary effect in this arrangement and rushed to the Motleys' studio, where I sketched them my idea on a half-sheet of paper. By next morning a new set had been designed showing the lower half of the house at the beginning of the play, Mrs Amorest's sitting-room, the hall, the foot of the stairs and the front door. After the first scene there was a short wait. While the curtain was down the top half of the back wall of the sitting-room was taken away to allow the floor of Mrs Payne's room to appear, on a slightly higher level, above and behind it, but several feet lower than it would have been if it had been built on top of the lower room. Miss Beringer's narrow attic was on the right of the stage on another level, sandwiched in between a little landing at the top of the stairs and the room next door where Agatha sat in her rocking-chair.

It would have been impossible for the actress playing Agatha to dominate the play, as Edith Evans did so successfully, if she had been 'skied' at the realistic level of the upper room for most of her important scenes. With the new arrangement of the stage the audience imagined the missing ceilings and found nothing strange, if indeed they noticed it at all, in the fact that the two principal rooms were built in an impossible architectural arrangement, one behind the other. When the curtain went up on the second scene of the play, showing the three old ladies dressing for Mrs Amorest's Christmas party in their three contrasting rooms, the effect was fascinating, like a Sickert picture, full of life and character and quite unlike anything I have ever seen in any other play.

The dresses were equally effective. Edith, on her first appearance, wore a sort of maroon-coloured dressing-gown, and in the last act she shuffled down the stairs wrapped in a dirty yellow velvet robe with a transparent shawl thrown over it on which sequins glittered menacingly. I was pleased with the moment when Agatha sat with her back to the audience, a huddled mass of shadow, waiting patiently outside Mrs Amorest's door till her victim should be alone. There was also a good effect when the two women's silent struggle for the piece of amber was disturbed by a sudden loud knocking at the front door which used to make the whole audience jump.

In the end, we were unable to obtain a small theatre for the play and, rather apprehensively, we opened at the New, which was far too big, though the setting looked very well on the wide stage. But, in spite of some fine reviews and encouragement from a few enthusiasts, the public did not care for the production and it only ran for a few weeks.

André Obey's *Noah* had been a great artistic success when it was played here at the Ambassadors Theatre, in French, by the Compagnie des Quinze, under the direction of Michel St. Denis. I went one afternoon to see it, and was deeply impressed by the dignity and naïveté of the play and by the superb teamwork of the actors. Some time after this I read in an American paper that Pierre Fresnay, a young actor of about the same age as myself, who had originally created the part of Noah in Paris (in London it was played first by Auguste Bovério, then by Michel St. Denis himself), had gone to New York in Noël Coward's *Conversation Piece*, and had afterwards played Noah in an English version there with great success. The account which I read of his performance roused my curiosity, and encouraged me to suggest to Mr Albery that we should try and get hold of the version that had been used in New

York, and that he should present it at the New Theatre with me in the part of Noah. Albery, who had previously presented the Quinze in London, was enthusiastic about the idea, and so was St. Denis, who had lately arrived in England, with the intention of forming a school and a theatrical company here on the lines of the Quinze, which had been recently disbanded. This was a very daring scheme, particularly as at that time he knew very little English, though he immediately agreed to direct the London production.

The version of *Noah* arrived from New York, but it was far from satisfactory; strange Americanisms (among them the expression, 'Hey, you floozies!') had been used to translate the slang French phrases in the text, which, as St. Denis pointed out, was originally written in an alternately poetic and colloquial style. The charming speeches in which Noah talks to the Almighty were especially hard to express in simple English, and these passages were particularly important as they set the whole keynote of the play. We could not decide at first whether to get a completely new version done and to do the play quite differently as an English parallel to the Bible story, or to keep to the spirit and style of the French performance as nearly as possible. Not having very much time, we decided on the latter course, and I fear we were unwise in doing so. Noah, in the French version, was dressed in velveteen trousers, sabots and a fur cap; in fact he suggested in appearance a larger-than-life version of a French peasant. But when I appeared in these clothes people failed to see why the Patriarch, in the intense heat of the jungle, was apparently dressed as if he were ready for a trip to the North Pole! Fresnay, being a Frenchman, as well as a magnificent actor, probably wore this costume with more conviction in the New York performance. I believe now that the only chance for the play in London would have been to engage Charles Laughton or Cedric Hardwicke to play the part, with a costume, make-up, and speech suggesting the typical English country farmer, but this would have necessitated re-writing a great deal of the play.

We tinkered with the dialogue all through rehearsals, but the final English text had neither the charm and simplicity of the French nor yet the slangy vigour of the American. On the first night the play went marvellously, and it seemed that our fears had been groundless: from the moment that I appeared in my terrific whiskers, hammering at the ark and humming 'The Sailor's Hornpipe' (my sole personal contribution to the production), the house seemed to be entirely with us. But the audiences who came later never appeared to understand the swift transitions from comedy to pathos which were so attractive, and which had made their effect so easily at the first performance. The critics complained, with some justification, that the play had been elaborated scenically at the New, whereas at the Ambassadors it had been done in the simplest and most economical way. But at the same time they ignored a great many good points in our production. Though they had raved over the play itself when it was done in French, they never observed that, in our production, a large section had been revised and strengthened by Obey, notably the fourth act, which contained a completely new scene as well as some splendid new comedy at the opening of the second act, which increased the effect of the delightful episode later when the children play games and march round the deck to greet the sun after the forty days of rain.

I never satisfied myself as Noah, though I had many happy moments working at it. Physically, however, it was a perfect misery. The play was produced during a heat-wave in July, and I was covered with thick padding and enormously heavy garments which were completely soaked through at the end of each performance. Vocally and physically the part was a great strain, and in every scene I had to act with my body as well as my voice, swaying to and fro in the gale, balancing my unwieldy form precariously on a ladder, and in the last scene crouching doubled up on the ground.

Every detail of my performance was taught me by St. Denis, and it was several weeks before I found myself sufficiently at home in the part to add anything in the least creative of my own. Some of the critics who had seen the French performance saw at once how greatly I was indebted to my director, and I could not help feeling at times like a young painter trying to copy an Old Master. But it was a fine exercise in technique, and at least I succeeded in concealing my own personality completely, and creating an illusion of age and weight in a part for which I did not really carry sufficient guns.

How hard it is to know when to take notice of criticism, whether it comes from actors, laymen, or professional critics! It is nonsense to say that one is always the best judge of one's own acting. How many actors imagine they were giving their best performance on a night when they were afterwards told by the producer that they were playing particularly badly![1] When I worked at Noah I realized that mere histrionics would be of little use to me in the part, although a breadth and authority were needed which would be difficult for me to achieve without them. The opening speech of the play demanded a great comedian with a very simple, natural method—a man like George Robey, who would have held the audience in the hollow of his hand, and forced them by sheer charm and good-humour to accept the very simple, almost childlike convention of the play. The other parts were not very happily cast in some instances, and St. Denis was hampered by the translation and by the fact that he had great difficulty in expressing himself in English at rehearsals. He was accustomed, with his own company, to a much longer period of preparation than he was allowed with us, and now, in so short a time, he had to try to teach us the special stylized technique, so perfected by the Quinze, which combined miming and rhythmic movements with natural comedy and dramatic emotion.

The performance that we gave on the first night was in some way inspired—largely, of course, by the sympathetic quality of the reception. St. Denis had warned us beforehand that *Noah* was a play of atmosphere, depending for its effect partly on the responsiveness of the audience. He said we could not possibly hope to act it really well eight times a week, and that the ideal way was to play it in a repertoire. We thought this rather a highbrow idea at the time, but when we had been playing for a few nights we realized that it was perfectly true. English people are easily embarrassed and put off by any humorous or fantastic approach to religion, though they will gladly swallow sensational plays on the subject (*Romance*, *The Passing of the Third Floor Back*, *The Sign of the Cross*, *The Wandering Jew*). They will also patronize plays of a more serious kind touching on religion (*St. Joan*, *Robert's Wife*, *Murder in the Cathedral*), but *Noah* did not fall into the same category as any of these plays, and only a superb company could have acted it, with the fullest effect, to the rather scanty and often suspicious audiences that came to see it at the New after the first night.

Stupid people thought it extraordinary that I should wish to disguise myself by such an unrecognizable make-up, and either

[1] Ellen Terry says, speaking of this: '"We all know when we do our best," said Henry once. "We are the only people who know." Yet he thought he did better in *Macbeth* than in *Hamlet*. Was he right after all?'

stayed away or took a dislike to the play in consequence. Others were shocked by the comic scenes and failed to understand the miming.

At the final performance, Michel said to me, 'At last you are beginning to find the way to play the first act'. By that time I had such a respect for his idealistic attitude towards his work that I was encouraged rather than depressed by his remark.

Michel St. Denis was never entirely satisfied with his productions. In *Noah* he made me feel intensely lazy, ignorant, and self-satisfied, but I was terrified at first that he would also kill my self-confidence, and convince me that my talents were completely negligible. On the contrary, these doubts and fears made me work all the harder in my desire to overcome the technical obstacles which stood in my way. I never studied with Michel a part for which I was really well cast. In the two plays (*Noah* and *Three Sisters*) in which he directed me, my own physical and mental attributes were so much at variance with the characters I was trying to represent that I did not really succeed in giving anything but workmanlike character performances in either of them. On the other hand, I know that I learnt more from acting in these two plays than from others in which I have made a greater personal success.

During the rest of the summer following *Noah*, I worked on a version of Dickens's *Tale of Two Cities*, which I had long had in mind. Terence Rattigan, the young author of *French Without Tears*, wrote the dialogue, and I planned most of the scenario. We had various actors in mind for the principal parts, and tried to provide for them accordingly. The first two acts came out quite well, and I showed them to Bronson Albery, who was sufficiently enthusiastic to promise to put on the play for me in the autumn, provided that the last act came up to expectation. Rattigan and I rushed back to the country and completed the script in a little over a week. A number of actors were approached, and the Motleys completed several charming designs for scenery and costumes.

Suddenly I received a letter from Sir John Martin-Harvey asking me not to go on with the play. He said that he intended to revive *The Only Way* again shortly, and that another version of the story would ruin its chances of success. Rather reluctantly we abandoned our project, and our play was shelved.

At the board meeting at which this was decided I suddenly proposed an alternative idea. *Romeo and Juliet* had always brought me luck. Edith Evans and Peggy Ashcroft, whose lovely performances in the production at Oxford I longed to see again, were both disengaged, and I thought it would be interesting for me to alternate the parts of Romeo and Mercutio with another star. Robert Donat's name immediately occurred to me, but I found to my dismay that he was planning to present *Romeo and Juliet* himself. When we approached him he kindly agreed to abandon his own production but could not see his way to appearing in mine. My next suggestion was Laurence Olivier. I could hardly believe my ears when he told me that he too was planning to do the play. His scenery was designed, and he had worked out every detail for an elaborate scheme of production, but I refused to allow my plans to be altered a second time, and at last Olivier very generously agreed to give up his *Romeo* production and appear in mine, playing the two parts alternately with me, as I had hoped. We had only three weeks to prepare and rehearse the play, and I was due to begin filming with Hitchcock in *Secret Agent* directly *Romeo* was produced.

Romeo and Juliet is very difficult to stage from a scenic point of view. I was not altogether satisfied with the triple-arched set we had used at Oxford, yet it had obvious advantages in simplicity and speed. The Motleys worked furiously hard, and at the end of three days they had produced three different projects for a permanent setting. None of them, we all agreed, seemed exactly right. Sadly, we were looking over the neglected designs for the Dickens play lying in a corner of the studio when suddenly it occurred to us to make use of them in another way.

The scenery for the *Tale of Two Cities* was to be arranged on two sides of the stage, the action moving alternately from one to the other, with a few scenes played on an upper stage approached by a staircase in the middle. We adapted this upper stage for Juliet's balcony, always a terrible difficulty both for the producer and scene-designer. If the window is at the side of the stage the lovers can only be seen in profile throughout the scene. If the balcony is too low, it seems as if Romeo could easily climb up, and if it is too high people in the circles cannot see Juliet properly. The ball scene which comes just before requires a clear space for the dancers, and the noise of a heavy piece of built scenery being moved into position is a fatal interruption to the short 'front' scene in which Mercutio and Benvolio shout their bawdy jokes in the silence of the night. We decided to build our balcony in the middle and leave it there, concealing the upper part with shutters or curtains during the ball and street scenes, and adding to it for the second part of the play, when the whole of Juliet's bedroom was to be shown, as well as the balcony outside.

I was determined that the lovers should part, as I am sure Shakespeare intended them to do, on the balcony where they plight their troth in the earlier part of the play. With this arrangement Romeo is able to speak his final lines in view of the audience, whereas with an interior setting he disappears from view and the lines have to be spoken very tamely from behind and below the stage. In Shakespeare's day, of course, the lovers played the farewell scene on the upper stage and Romeo, presumably, climbed down, spoke his lines, and made his exit from the lower stage. Then, at the entrance of Lady Capulet and the Nurse, Juliet herself came down on to the lower stage, disappearing, one supposes, from above, and descending by a staircase behind the scenes. This convention would hardly be accepted by a modern audience, so I took a tip from the *Old Ladies'* set which, after all, had not been seen by many people, and devised that the whole of the interior of the bedroom should be seen above, on a platform, as well as the balcony outside the windows. Belowstairs there was a door leading to the street, and the acting thus moved effectively, helped by various changes of lighting, now from the bedroom to the balcony, now belowstairs where the preparations for Juliet's marriage were going on, and now to the Friar's Cell, which remained in place throughout on the other side of the stage, concealed by a curtain when it was not needed for the action.

Romeo and Juliet opened with great success, and I started on my film, playing Mercutio at night. I hoped, of course, that the filming would be over by the time I began playing Romeo, six weeks later but to my dismay I found the work stretching out day after day, and in the end it was thirteen weeks before *Secret Agent* was completely finished.

Altogether I made five films during the period this book covers. The first, *Who is the Man?* was a very imposing affair, adapted from *Daniel*, in which Sarah Bernhardt made her last appearance in London at the Prince's Theatre in 1921. The play (written by Sarah's godson, Louis Verneuil) centred round the character of Daniel, a morphinomaniac, who did not appear until the third and fourth acts, when he sat in a chair as the central figure in an emotional climax culminating in a dramatic death scene. This was the part offered to me in the picture, but of course I did not sit in a chair. Nothing of the kind. I was a sculptor in a beautiful smock, flinging clay at a half-finished nude lady. I had not sat to Epstein in those days and I had no idea of the way sculptors really work, but I made great play with a sweeping thumb and a wire-headed tool and hoped for the best. I had a wonderful stagey studio with a skylight and a sofa draped with shawls on which I flung myself at intervals and smoked a pipe of opium (in a close-up). It was very hot weather, and I exhausted myself acting in a highly melodramatic manner, inspired in my efforts by a piano and violin which played tear-compelling excerpts from popular melodies.[1] The director acted harder than I did, and exhorted me frenziedly through every 'take', waving his arms and shouting directions above the music. Some scenes at Le Touquet were needed to complete the film, and off we went one week-end to take the necessary 'shots' in the correct backgrounds. I acted in two short scenes, surrounded by gaping and delighted crowds, and suffered acute embarrassment marching about in a yellow make-up and attempting to drive a car (which is not one of my accomplishments) out of the gateway of the Hermitage Hotel. In the finished film, this 'shot' lasted about five seconds (perhaps because of the obviously agonized expression on my face), and the background was indistinguishable, while the second 'shot' taken at Le Touquet showed a strip of sand and a bathing-tent and might have been photographed equally well at Margate. However, I had a very jolly week-end.

My second film was an Edgar Wallace thriller, *The Clue of the New Pin*. In this I played the villain, fantastically disguised in a long black cloak, black wig, spectacles and false teeth, and always photographed from the back, so that I could by no possible chance be recognized, even by the most adept villain-spotter in the audience, as the bright young juvenile whom I impersonated during the rest of the film. There was an endless 'sequence' in a vault in which I had to go mad and reveal myself as the maniac I really was. These were still the 'silent' days, and I thought I should really be sick by the time I had repeated a dozen times the peals of hysterical laughter, the moppings and mowings and extraordinary impromptu dialogue which the director, an actor (who had once appeared in Irving's company), demanded from me at this crucial moment.

[1] This, of course, was a silent film.

My next film effort, *Insult*, was an adaptation of a play by Jan Fabricius that ran quite successfully for a time at the Apollo. This was my first 'talkie'. The director, an American named Harry Lachman, was also a painter. He had a great feeling for photography, and his arrangements of light and scenic composition were admirable—but as a director of acting he was rather eccentric. He had a wonderfully beautiful Chinese wife—who appeared occasionally in the studio—and a violent temper which he displayed four or five times every day. He used to go red in the face and scream at everybody, not so much from real anger, I think, as from a natural desire to ginger things up every now and again. The film was set in the East and Lachman suddenly had the idea of showing all the scenes in a certain 'sequence' through a veil of mist. Ten men would rush on to the set when all was ready for a 'take', brandishing foul-smelling torches filled with some nauseous substance which emitted clouds of smoke. We would all begin to cough and rub our eyes, and then, just as the fog was beginning to clear, there would be shouts of delight from Lachman, and the cameras would begin to turn.

Animals and a native crowd enhanced the charms of my long hours in *Insult*. There was a donkey, a monkey, and several horses, one of which I rode gingerly (in close-up) down a narrow studio village street, while a double stood close at hand to mount and dismount my fiery steed (in longshot).

I was fascinated and horrified by my acting in these three pictures—fascinated, because seeing one's own back and profile is an interesting experience usually limited to one's visits to the tailor, horrified at the vulturine grimaces on my face, and the violent and affected mannerisms of my walk and gestures. In the film of *The Good Companions* I had rather a better idea of what I was about, having played the part of Inigo for several months upon the stage. Also I liked working with Victor Saville, Jessie Matthews and Edmund Gwenn, and such scenes as I had were simple, light, charming and well-rehearsed. It was in this film that I played a short scene with the great music-hall comedian Max Miller. It was one of his first appearances in pictures, but he was quite undismayed by the new technique, rattling off impromptu gags each time the scene was rehearsed or photographed, while I tried to keep pace with rather lame replies whenever he paused for breath or seemed to need a 'feed' line.

There are many things about filming that I detest. The early rising, to begin with. Then the agonies of film make-up, by which a pleasant twenty-minute affair of conscience and vanity in the theatre every night is transformed into a surgical operation in the studio lasting forty minutes every morning. I loathe to be patted and slapped and curled and painted, while I lie supine and helpless in an equivalent of the dentist's chair. I hate the long endless days of spasmodic work—a week or more in the same set, littered with cables and lights and half-dismantled at every point except the small section on which the camera is directed. I detest the lack of continuity, which demands that I should idiotically walk twenty times down a corridor with a suitcase in my hand to enter the door of a room in which I played some important scene three weeks ago. 'Let me see, that was the suit you were wearing. Now do you remember your tie was hanging out, and your handkerchief was tucked into your pocket? Right. Shoot.' How I hate the meals in films, and the heat of the lights which makes them more disgusting! For a week, in *The Good Companions*, we sat round a huge table, with twenty or thirty arcs focused over our heads—two to each of twelve persons—while the food on our plates congealed every half-hour and was replaced by a fresh supply. In one scene I had to eat a piece of chocolate, and the moment I began to unwrap it it melted under the lights. A property man stood by with twenty spare bars and I chewed a bit off a different one in every separate 'take'. Then there is the discomfort of the 'dolly' shots—when a camera pursues you on a track while you are walking or dancing, or swoops down on you from a crane—and the close-ups, when the heroine is not called, and you play the big moment of your emotional scene with her in her absence, with the camera a yard away. 'Now please look just two inches to the right of this piece of paper. That represents Miss ——'s face. Just *think right*, and let the expression come into your eyes.'

Railway-train scenes are misery, because the actors are crowded together in a tiny space, carriages and corridors are just as cramped and uncomfortable as they are in real life, and the heat of the lights is worse than ever. There is also vapour to be blown across the window by a machine at the last moment, just before every 'take'. If I decide to have a cigarette in some scene (in order to make an excuse for smoking on the set, which is forbidden except 'when necessitated by the action') I regret it immediately, for, after several minutes' delay, the cigarette is burnt too far down to 'match' with the previous 'shot', and someone must stand by with relays of cigarettes cut to the right length which I must continue to smoke until my throat is sore. I decide to play a scene in an overcoat, and stifle, not for a few minutes, but for a week, while the 'sequence' drags to its interminable conclusion. If I think of a nice little bit of business to do in the close-up I must remember always to do it again in every 'take' and every 'long-shot' for fear it will not match.

In *Secret Agent* I lay for several days under iron girders and rubbish in a scene of a train wreck. Another day I sat for hours before a blank screen, while a short length of Lake Como was unrolled behind me in 'back-projection', a device which enables studio scenes to be played before backgrounds of places hundreds of miles away.

Victor Saville and Alfred Hitchcock were very good company, and, apart from the work, I enjoyed making films with them.

Hitchcock is famous for his practical jokes, and keeps everyone amused, but I find it quite impossible to rouse myself from the lethargy induced by hours of waiting, hammering and delays of every kind, and to work myself into a state of high tension and sincere emotion for about three minutes, only to follow it with another despairing wait of half an hour or more. The strain under which the director must labour, and the nervous power required by him to sustain the direction of such an enterprise over twelve or fifteen weeks, is more than I can understand. One must remember, too, that he has already worked on every detail of the picture for weeks before anything is photographed or a single actor is engaged.

Film people always think legitimate actors very odd in their enthusiasm for the theatre, much more so, I believe, than we theatre actors do observing their passion for the films. I was interviewed during the shooting of *Secret Agent* by Caroline Lejeune, a well-known film critic, for whose writing in a leading paper I had always had considerable admiration and respect. The Sunday before I met her she had made a thinly-veiled reference to my production of *Romeo* which she had been to see. I asked her immediately why she had not liked the performance. She seemed very embarrassed at my having found out which play she was referring to, and then said: 'Oh, but I always find it difficult to know what I am supposed to notice when the curtain goes up in a theatre.

One is muddled by all the details. In films, anything important is shown in a close-up.' This point of view had never occurred to me before, but I suppose it must be shared by a great many people who go continually to the films, and seldom to the theatre.

Romeo and Juliet was an exciting play, with its street fights (resulting in casualties several times a week) and its murders and poisonings and lamentations, but it was extraordinary restful after the chaos of the studio at Hammersmith where we were making *Secret Agent*. I used to rush away at 5.30, eat a hurried meal, sleep deeply for half an hour, and arrive at the theatre looking forward eagerly to playing before a real audience and to the pleasure of acting in an ordered play performed to schedule. Seldom have I more sincerely enjoyed speaking the words of Shakespeare, and I appreciated, more than ever before, the neatness and punctuality of the routine of a stage performance. I think it is the sprawling, untidy, wasteful atmosphere which gets on my nerves to such an extent in making films, and the mixture of extreme reality and outrageous fake which is combined in their paraphernalia.

CHAPTER SIXTEEN

1936

Romeo and Juliet ran well into the spring. It was a happy time for me, only slightly marred by fatigue from overwork. *Secret Agent*, which had seemed to be finished just before the New Year, went wrong in the cutting-room, and eight weeks later I had to work for two more weeks filming a different sequence to replace one that had turned out unsatisfactorily.

My scheme of alternating the parts of Romeo and Mercutio with Olivier had proved very attractive to the public and showed that it was possible to play two great parts in completely different ways without upsetting the swing and rhythm of the whole production. The only trouble came in our scenes together, when we kept on trying to speak on each other's cues. Larry had the advantage over me in his vitality, looks, humour and directness. In addition, he was a fine fencer, and his breath-taking fight with Tybalt was a superb prelude to his death-scene as Mercutio. As Romeo, his love scenes were intensely real and tender, and his tragic grief profoundly touching.

I had an advantage over him in my familiarity with the verse, and in the fact that the production was of my own devising, so that all the scenes were arranged just as I had imagined I could play them best. I built my Mercutio round the Queen Mab speech, and enjoyed the lightness and gaiety of the part—surely one of the shortest and 'plummiest' in Shakespeare. But I was again disappointed with my performance as Romeo, and resolved after this to be done with it for ever, though I loved acting with Peggy. Her lightness and spontaneity were a continual joy and inspiration, and she won all hearts with her flower-like, passionate Juliet. She had already developed considerably in power and endurance since her first performance at Oxford. To me, acting with her, she seemed utterly natural and sincere.

But, after Hamlet, Romeo was not such a good part as it had seemed when I was young. It is badly placed in the play. The 'Banishment' scene, which would in any case be a difficult one for the actor, becomes doubly difficult following, as it does, right on the heels of Juliet's great lamentation scene with the Nurse, and the Apothecary scene (in which Irving is said to have acted so wonderfully) follows immediately on the long scene of wailing and grief over the supposed dead body of Juliet, which is apt to rob it of much of its effect.

The uncut versions of Shakespeare which we give nowadays show the plays to full advantage, but I suspect that the cuts and transpositions so much favoured by the Victorians were cunningly devised to allow the 'show' scenes of the stars their utmost value. I wonder how audiences today would enjoy a production of *Romeo and Juliet* in which only the principal and well-known *bravura* scenes were acted, tricked out with lavish scenery. In Irving's *Romeo* the 'cords' scene of Juliet and the Nurse was enormously cut, also the scenes with Capulet and the servants, while the final scene in the tomb after the death of the lovers disappeared altogether. Here a tableau was substituted, with the Prince speaking the four 'tag' lines of the play.

My second three-play contract with Howard Wyndham and Bronson Albery came to an end. Guthrie McClintic, the husband of the fine American actress, Katharine Cornell, and one of New York's best directors and impresarios, had spoken to me several times on his visits to London, of my playing Hamlet in America. Now he approached me again with a definite offer to do the play in the autumn, and with some hesitation I accepted. Guthrie was anxious to direct the play himself, and told me flatteringly that he could 'present' my performance to greater advantage than I had done in my own production. Lillian Gish was proposed for Ophelia, and Guthrie brought her to see me in my dressing-room. She was enchantingly dressed in a summer frock with short sleeves, her fair hair crowned with a big white straw hat with black velvet ribbons. I remembered the advertisement that I used to scan so eagerly on the Piccadilly Tube in the old days of the silent films—the backs of two little girls, both wearing straw hats with velvet ribbons, and a big question-mark, with an intriguing caption underneath,

'Two little strangers about whom all the world will soon be talking'.[1] When I spoke of this, Lilian said she had been afraid I should think her too old to play Ophelia, and had 'dressed the part' to make a good impression on me. I also met Judith Anderson, who had come over with Guthrie and was to play the Queen; and Jo Mielziner, who was to design the scenery and costumes, came to supper at my flat with his wife to discuss the *décor*, which was to be inspired by Van Dyck.

Meanwhile we planned to revive Chekhov's *The Seagull* at the New for a limited season. I arranged to leave the cast after eight weeks in order to have a good holiday before sailing to America. I had longed to see *The Seagull* done in the West End again with a fine company, and I had always wanted Komisarjevsky to direct it, as it was one of the few Chekhov plays he had never done in London. Edith Evans agreed to play Arcádina, and Peggy Ashcroft would obviously be well cast as Nina. I had always fancied the part of Trigórin for myself. After Romeo I was anxious not to play another heroic or romantic part before tackling Hamlet for the third time, and anyway I was really too old to act Konstantin again. Stephen Haggard was engaged to play this important part, and the rest of the cast was equally distinguished—Leon Quartermaine, Frederick Lloyd, Martita Hunt, Clare Harris, Ivor Barnard, George Devine. Komis brought us a new translation which he had made himself with a friend in Paris and designed his own beautiful and impressive scenery for the play.

The revival was a really big success, though most people thought my own performance the least satisfactory in an almost perfect *ensemble* (the same success, and similar criticisms of my Vershinin, were to greet my revival of *Three Sisters* in 1938).

Now that I am considered to be a 'star', people cannot understand that I should sometimes play what may appear to be rather unsuitable parts in which I do not shine above the rest of the cast. But, as a matter of fact, I have been extremely gratified to find that it has sometimes been possible for me to make experiments in character work and to contribute in a supporting part without spoiling the balance of a fine team. I think it is fatal for a leading actor to appear in nothing but 'show' parts in which he can display his mannerisms and give an exhibition of virtuosity.

It was enormously interesting to work again in *The Seagull* and to

[1] D. W. Griffith's film, *Orphans of the Storm*.

see how differently the parts came out with a different cast. I remembered vividly all the performances when I had played Konstantin at the Little. Peggy was exquisitely eager and womanly in the first three acts, but could not efface for me entirely the vivid impression made by Valerie Taylor in the final scene of the earlier production when she returns to Sorin's house after Trigórin has deserted her. Nothing could have been more different from Miriam Lewes's striking performance than the brilliantly poised, temperamental Arcádina of Edith Evans. Miriam played the part as a tragic actress. She stalked on to the stage in the first act, angry and sullen, looking rather barbaric in appearance, dressed in a strange picture frock and pacing the stage like a tigress, violent in her rages and moody and self-accusing in her griefs. Edith, on the other hand, dressed the part like a Parisian, with a high, elegant coiffure, sweeping fashionable dresses, hats and scarves and parasols. On her entrance she was all smiles and graciousness, but one could see from the angle of her head, as she sat with her back to the audience watching Konstantin's play, that underneath all the sweetness she was a selfish woman in a bad temper. Her performance was full of the most subtle touches of comedy alternating with passages of romantic nostalgia, as when she listened to the music across the lake in the first act. In the scenes with Konstantin and Trigórin, in the third, she had sudden outbursts of tenderness followed by a show of violent possessiveness and self-justification. Her entrances and exits were superb, and I shall never forget the way she pointed the only moment when Arcádina and Nina are seen on the stage together in the second part of the play, just before Trigórin decides to run off with Nina. He is sitting at the lunch-table, and Nina runs off the stage when she hears Arcádina coming. The dialogue runs:

ARCÁDINA (*to* SORIN). Stay at home, old man. At your age you should not go gadding about. (*To* TRIGÓRIN.)
Who was that went out just now? Nina?

TRIGÓRIN. Yes.

ARCÁDINA. Pardon, we interrupted you. I believe I've packed everything. I'm worn out.

Her scornful look after the retreating figure, the weary harassed manner in which she sank into a chair, suggested all that had happened to Arcádina since the second act—her fear of losing her lover, her jealousy of the young girl, her weariness with the details of running a house and packing to leave it, her perfunctory affection for her old brother, her longing for attention and flattery, her dislike of being middle-aged.

Komis's garden for the first two acts made a lovely and romantic background, with its paths and pillars, banks of flowers and rustic bridge. I was surprised, however, to find him putting both acts into the same setting, as we had done at Barnes in the earlier production, with a neat little stage built for Konstantin's play, and a curtain drawn on strings to conceal it.

Chekhov's stage directions are—Act I: A part of the park on Sorin's estate. Act II: Croquet lawn of Sorin's house. In Stanislavsky's book there is a fine description of the setting for the first act at the Moscow Art Theatre. Remembering this, I always imagined the scene taking place in a damp and gloomy corner of the park, with wet leaves underfoot and slimy, overgrown foliage. Beyond the trees, a magnificent view of the lake, and, hiding it at first, a great flapping sheet hung between two trees. Here Arcádina must sit shivering in her thin shoes and evening dress while Konstantin declaims his prologue, and then the sheet falls, disclosing the placid lake and the figure of Nina, dressed strangely in some kind of modernistic costume, raised, perhaps, above the level of the onlookers on a clumsily contrived platform of planks and barrels. This is Konstantin's new theatre, so different from the conventional indoor theatre which he despises, the place where he can make love to Nina and lose himself in his romantic dreams.

In the second act there should surely be a great contrast—the croquet lawn with its neat beds of geraniums, hoops, mallets, deck-chairs and cushions, Arcádina's bourgeoise worldly atmosphere. Here she is mistress in her own domain, laughing at the slovenly Masha and making scenes with her servants. Here Konstantin is ill at ease and out of place with his old suit and his gun and his dead seagull, while Trigórin, strolling on the lawn with his stick and notebook, is in his element, master of the situation, easily able to impress Nina with his suave talk of the beautiful view over the lake and the anguish he suffers in the achievement of his successes as an author.

Apart from this purely personal feeling with regard to the scenery of the first two acts, I thought Komis's production magnificent. There was so much to admire—the double room, half library, half dining-room, seen from opposite viewpoints in the third and fourth acts, was so rich in atmosphere that one felt one knew the whole of the rest of the house. Then there was his masterly control of tone and pace, the groupings, especially in the first act of the play, and in the last, when the party sat round playing Loto, the handling of the whole contrapuntal scheme of the characters.

I conceived the part of Trigórin, with Komis's help, as a vain, attractive man, sincere in his insincerity, but not a first-rate writer by any means, really attracted by Nina in a weak kind of way, but not the professional seducer at all. In the last act Komis saw him as a tragic figure, aware of the disaster he has brought about, sorry for Konstantin (whose talent he recognizes as more important than his own), rather ashamed of his own return to Arcádina, and genuinely moved and horrified by the death of her son at the end of the play.

Sometimes I thought I conveyed this well, but many people disagreed with my performance, and complained that I was not enough the genius, that I was too smartly dressed, and that I was not passionate enough in the scenes with Nina. But Trigórin himself complains of his facile talent, says that he cannot write really first-class stuff. His innate weakness is shown in the two scenes with Nina at the beginning and end of the third act, and by his passive attitude in the scene with Arcádina which comes between. The difficulty, as always in a play, is to know how much of the real truth Trigórin reveals in his speeches about himself. Surely if Chekhov had meant the man to be a genius he would not have drawn the clear distinction and contrast between the two pairs of characters, Nina and Konstantin, both potentially brilliant but unsuccessful, and Trigórin and Arcádina, both successful but intrinsically second-rate. And what could be more second-rate than the existence of Trigórin, trailing like a tame cat at his mistress's heels—'Again there will be railway carriages, mutton chops, conversations——!'

The atmosphere behind the scenes in a theatre varies curiously according to the mood of the play which is being performed there. In *Romeo* we were always visiting one another or joking in Edith's dressing-room. Edith herself would sit in the middle of her sofa, dressed up in her voluminous padded garments as the Nurse, wondering perhaps, what sort of madhouse this was in which she had suddenly found herself. In *The Seagull* the atmosphere was entirely changed. The wings were dark in two acts of the play, and in the gloom Edith would sail gaily by in her lovely Edwardian creations, whilst most of the rest of us sat about in groups whispering furtively. In the last act, with the wind and rain 'effects' whistling all around us, we were often subdued into complete silence, while Peggy, with a shawl over her head, slipped noiselessly to her place in the corner, where she would sit alone all through the act working herself up for her entrance in the big hysterical scene at the end of the play.

The weeks flew by, and before I could have believed it possible, it was time for me to leave the cast to go abroad for my holiday. I had had a very successful year, and for the first time I was able to rent a villa in the South of France, with a swimming-pool in the garden, and enough rooms for me to be able to invite five or six guests to stay. This holiday promised to be far more exciting than my previous visits to the Riviera, when I had lived in small hotels and counted my money every day for fear it would run out too soon.

Still, even with such a grand holiday in view, it was sad leaving the New after four years. It was the end of a big chapter in my career. There were friendly faces everywhere among the staff and in the front of the house; many of my best friends were in the company. It seemed almost flying in the face of providence to leave the play while it was still playing to capacity.

The following day I went to France by car. For three weeks I was utterly content, lying in the sun, bathing, and eating enormous and delicious meals cooked by a treasure of a cook, an elderly peasant woman, stout, with a fine face, wearing espadrilles on her bare feet. Every evening she set off to her house half a mile up the mountain at the back of the villa. Away she would trudge about ten o'clock of an evening, undismayed by the prospect of her steep climb in the dark, carrying a big lighted lantern, and looking for all the world like Juliet's Nurse on her way to visit Friar Laurence. After she had gone we would leave our dinner-table on the verandah and motor to the coast, where we would gamble and dance till the small hours. Coming back from the casino early one morning, I found myself, for the first time for many weeks, thinking of the theatre. I had secretly been dreading having to begin work again in the autumn, and the prospect of packing, sailing alone, and facing a new company and a strange audience in America had depressed me very much. Now I knew that this phase had passed, and that I was anxious to get back to work again. My holiday was over.

We motored slowly back through France. When I arrived in London, my new cabin trunks had already been delivered at my flat, and there were only two more hectic days left before I must sail. Peggy Ashcroft gave a farewell party for me at her house. My friends, the people with whom I had worked so happily in the theatre during the past few years, were there to say good-bye. I experienced my usual feeling of despair. I was certain that *Hamlet* would be a failure, and wished with all my heart that I had never agreed to go.

Next morning, at Waterloo, there were more farewells, Mr Tilden[1] (among the passengers), a belated photographer (who had *not* come to photograph me, as it turned out), and a film-star, who almost missed the train (and the photographer), making a terrific entrance on to the platform at the last minute with orchids, a coloured maid, and a large retinue of admiring 'fans'.

We arrived at Southampton in the dark, and chugged our way out on a huge tender to the *Normandie*, which was lying far out at sea, a mass of twinkling lights. My cabin was filled with flowers and telegrams, books and presents, and I felt very important but extremely lonely as the liveried page-boys dumped the last of my luggage and I felt the ship begin to move.

I was determined not to think of *Hamlet* till I arrived. The boat was immensely impressive. There was a theatre, a cinema, and a glass 'sun lounge' with an aviary of singing birds which were only removed, rather ominously, when it was going to be rough. The film star continued to make wonderful entrances, arriving every night for dinner, in a succession of terrific gowns just as everyone else was drinking coffee.

The voyage was soon over. I rushed to the upper deck to see the famous view which had impressed me so much eight years before. It was equally impressive now, but I got very tired of looking at it when the ship slowed down and took nearly six hours moving gradually up the Hudson River towards the dock. It was very hot. The pressmen had boarded our ship at Quarantine, and Phil Baker, the well-known American radio star, whom I had met during the voyage, came to find me. He took me off to be interviewed in a small cabin, where a number of ladies and gentlemen were gathered with drinks and note-books and cigarettes. I felt rather like a criminal at a 'line-up' before the police. I was sure that

[1] Bill Tilden, the well-known champion tennis-player.

no one would be able to pronounce or spell my name properly or would know who I was or why I was coming to America. But I found everyone surprisingly amiable, I was asked no embarrassingly personal questions, and, when I read the interview in the newspapers next day, I was delighted to find them completely accurate.

Guthrie and his manager were on the dock to meet me and we drove to the McClintics' house in Beekman Place, where I had been invited to stay. The sounds and smells of New York came rushing back to me and I was surprised to find how familiar it all seemed—Third Avenue, with its clanking elevated railway and the iron pillars in the middle of the road, with the taxis swerving in and out between them, the long straight Avenues with their vistas of brilliant lights, the brick-fronted houses with steps and iron railings leading to the front doors, the little canopies outside the hotels and restaurants, and the restless shifting mass of foreign-looking faces in the crowded streets.

Guthrie's house was on the East River, and one of the oldest in New York. He lived there for many years. It had the atmosphere of a house in Chelsea, with panelled rooms, and bow windows looking out over a charming little garden. Beyond the garden wall I could see the lights of the boats going up and down, and a vague mass of buildings huddled on the other side of the river. It was wonderfully quiet and restful there having dinner out of doors, with candles on the table and deliciously strange iced food and drink. The stage manager was there to meet me, and after dinner Judith Anderson arrived, straight from the hairdresser, who had dyed and waved her hair in an elaborate new style for Gertrude. I stared at her and said, with my usual tact: 'Why not wear a wig? It looks better, and it's so much less trouble.' After we had dined we went out again in the car and drove through Broadway and Times Square. I dimly remembered some of the buildings and tried to recall the lay-out of the theatre streets. Guthrie pointed out the Empire, where we should play. We called on Jo Mielziner, who was working at the designs for the scenery in a studio twenty-three storeys up. Later we drove back to Beekman Place where I was shown into Katharine Cornell's bedroom. Miss Cornell, I hasten to add, was still on holiday. By this time I was very tired. I fell asleep at last, thinking it must surely bring me luck to spend my first night in America in Katharine Cornell's bed.

A week went by. I was measured for costumes, interviewed

every day by pressmen and, oddly, I thought, by several of the leading dramatic critics. I searched for a hotel to stay at when I should leave Guthrie's hospitable roof. I went to the theatres in the evening. Maurice Evans telephoned me, and we dined together, and went to see *On Your Toes*. It was a perfect evening, and a wonderful production—the kind of thing at which the Americans excel, and which we do not do nearly so well in England. Jeanne de Casalis was with us too. (She had come over to produce her play *St. Helena*, in which Maurice was to play Napoleon.) She was as enthusiastic as we were, praising Mielziner's scenery, the choreography of Balanchine, and the brilliant performances of Luella Gear, Tamara Geva and Ray Bolger.

Another night I saw *Dead End*, with its wonderful realistic setting of a waterfront slum by Norman Bel-Geddes, and its fine cast of child actors, climbing and diving in and out of the river, which appeared to flow (with most realistic splashings and gurglings) between the front of the stage and the first row of the stalls. I saw Fannie Brice in a lavish but rather disappointing revue, and I discovered several restaurants which I remembered before as 'speakeasies'. On my first Sunday night I climbed the palatial stairs of Radio City Music Hall, gazed upon the mighty orchestra which rose like a phoenix from below the floor, gasped at the elaborate convolutions of the stage performance, with its acrobats and jugglers, at the 'Rockettes', a troupe of chorus girls who step-danced in such incredibly perfect unity that one quite longed for one of them to slip or make a mistake, and finally enjoyed the comparatively normal pleasure of watching Fred Astaire in *Swing Time*.

Next day I bought the records from this film and others from *On Your Toes*, and I can never hear any of these tunes now without being suddenly transported back to my sitting-room in the Hotel Gotham, with the skyscrapers outside the window, the cactus plants on the mantelpiece, and the portable gramophone grinding away in the overheated atmosphere. The music was a pleasant relaxation during the long evenings when Harry Andrews and I stayed in the hotel, trying to work at the scenes between Hamlet and Horatio. Harry and Malcolm Keen, who was to play the King, were the only other English actors in the company.

The first rehearsal drew nearer. The heat was terrific. Every day I shed more clothes. After a week I was walking, rather timidly, down Fifth Avenue in the sleeveless shirt and linen trousers I had worn in the South of France. Wearing these clothes in London I should have been stared at in the streets, but in New York everyone seemed too busy to take much interest in anyone else. Judith and I went to be photographed at three different photographers one boiling afternoon, she in scarlet velvet, I in black with my high white collar, cloak and sword. The car could not draw up at the door in the crowded street, and we braved the throng and rushed across Park Avenue in all our finery. No one even looked round.

The first reading took place in the bar downstairs at the Martin Beck Theatre. Judith and Lillian wore hats with enormous brims, and bent over their books, hardly murmuring their lines above a whisper. Flashlights clicked, interviewers came and went, Guthrie perched on chairs with his hat tilted on the back of his head, and everyone was frantically nervous and drank a great deal of water from the filter in the corner, varied with occasional draughts of iced tomato juice produced by Guthrie from a thermos.

For a fortnight we read and re-read the play, then we rose shakily to our feet and began to rehearse. I enjoyed these first few days immensely. I was fresh from my holiday, found I knew every line of my part without the book, though I had not looked at it for two years, and acted my very best. If only it had not been quite so hot! Katharine Cornell returned from her holiday, and one day she emerged suddenly from the back of the dress-circle, where she had been hidden, watching the rehearsal without any of us knowing she was there. I had met her some years before in England, and again I was enchanted by her natural beauty and graciousness, and by the warmth of her affectionate, enthusiastic welcome. She took me to see the Lunts in *Idiot's Delight* and Helen Hayes in *Victoria Regina*, two evenings in the theatre that were unforgettable.

The days were passing quickly. A week before we were due to open in Toronto I was wounded in the arm rehearsing the fight. I fence abominably. In London I had nearly cut Benvolio's eye out at a rehearsal, and in *Romeo* I so badly wounded the actor who played Tybalt that he had to leave the cast for a week. In New York our instructor rashly allowed us to rehearse with real Elizabethan swords sharpened on both edges. This time I was the injured party. I was removed to a neighbouring surgery where I was given gas while several stitches were put in my arm. I was worried lest I should not be well in time for the opening performance.

A few nights later, when I had recovered, Alexander Woollcott came to a rehearsal. We acted the closet scene for him, and he appeared to be very much impressed, but made one or two good critical comments, and told me that I must pronounce 'satyr' 'sater' or nobody would understand me in America.

We arrived in Toronto at a skyscraper of a hotel amid very low-storied buildings. The town looked to me as if cowboys might appear in the main square at any moment (in the best silent-film manner), shoot off a bunch of revolvers in the air, and ride away again in a cloud of dust. The theatre was large and shabby, with looking-glasses all along the back of the pit in which I saw myself reflected six times over as I spoke my first soliloquy. Guthrie sent out for felt and had them covered up. We had two dress-rehearsals in one day and opened the following night.

We played in Toronto for a week with apparent success. In between performances I read or slept in the hotel, emerging only to eat. Radio sets blared from every bedroom as I walked along the corridors. After a long journey we arrived at Rochester in time to open on the Monday night. The hotel was packed with a Masonic Congress. The theatre was huge, built as part of a big college institute. We dressed in a large communal room, with a few small dressing-rooms partitioned off. There was a yawning orchestra-pit between the stage and the front row of the stalls, with a Wurlitzer organ lying like a mastodon in the middle of it.

I caught a heavy cold. We acted only two performances, Monday night and Tuesday afternoon—an extraordinary feat of engineering and efficiency on the part of the stage staff and electricians, for we were due to dress-rehearse on Wednesday night in New York, and open on the Thursday.

We left on Tuesday night for the journey back. I lay in my berth exhausted but sleepless, trying to forget my cold and concentrate on *Gone With the Wind*. There were negro porters and a sleeping-car with flapping curtains and beds one above the other. As a good film-fan I should like to have taken stock of every detail, and at any other time I should have been fascinated by a night journey in America. But I had frightful claustrophobia, and found I could not open a window in the air-conditioned train.

We arrived in New York early in the morning. I got a taxi and drove to a small flat which I had rented where I went to bed for the day. My cold was better but I did not play at the dress rehearsal. The next day dawned. Somehow I got through the morning and the afternoon. I attempted to eat some food, walked about the streets, went to a cinema for an hour or so, and tried not to remember the ordeal that was to come. About six o'clock I could bear it no longer and went to the theatre. My room was packed with telegrams, a huge pile from England and another from generous Americans, many of them famous actors and actresses whom I had never even met. Guthrie came into my room and told me that the theatre was packed with celebrities—it was the first fashionable opening of the season. Lillian Gish brought in a Hawaiian 'lei' of white carnations, and hung it round my neck for a minute for luck. I made up slowly, and put on my costume. It was curtain time. The first scene came to an end, and I walked blindly to my place in the darkness. The lights rose on the second scene. There was a roar of applause from the audience, a warm, reassuring burst of welcome that brought a big lump into my throat. I gulped it down, took a deep breath, and steadied myself to begin to speak.

The cue came at last, 'But now, my cousin Hamlet, and my son—' and I heard my voice, far away in the distance, beginning the familiar words:

> 'A little more than kin, and less than kind.'
> 'How is it that the clouds still hang on you?'
> 'Not so, my lord; I am too much i' the sun . . .'

I have three besetting sins, both on and off the stage—impetuosity, self-consciousness, and a lack of interest in anything not immediately concerned with myself or with the theatre. All three of these qualities are abundantly evident to me in reading over this book.

No doubt it would have been better to have written in some detail of the technical difficulties and problems of the craft of acting. But it is not easy to describe how actors go about their business. Perhaps it is more seemly that these mysteries should remain a secret. No one can understand the technical side of the theatre until he himself comes to practise it; and in spite of imploring letters from inquisitive enthusiasts, we actors do not encourage members of the public to watch us at our rehearsals.

Of all the arts, I think acting must be the least concrete, the most solitary. One gains experience continually, both at rehearsals and in performance, from the presence of a large assembly of people one's fellow-players and the audience in front. These are essential to the development of one's performance. They are the living canvas upon which one hopes to paint the finished portrait. These audiences, with their shifting variations of quality, are the only means by which an actor may gauge his acting. With their assistance he may hope to improve a performance, keep it flexible and fresh, and develop new subtleties as the days go by. He learns to listen, to watch (without appearing to do so), to respond, to guide them in certain passages and be guided by them in others—a never-ending test of watchfulness and flexibility.

But the struggles and agonies of the actor as he winds his way through this labyrinthine process every night upon the stage are of very little interest to anyone except himself. No one cares, or is even aware, that he works for many months to correct some physical trick, or fights against his vocal mannerisms, or experiments with pauses, emphases, timing, processes of thought. No one knows if he is suffering in his heart while he plays an emotional scene, or if he is merely adding up his household bills, considering what he will order for dinner, or regretting what he ate for lunch. Last night's audience, which he cursed for its unresponsiveness, may have enjoyed his performance every whit as much as tonight's, with which he seems to feel the most cordial and personal sympathy.

Actors talk unceasingly among themselves of all the varying feelings which assail them during the exercise of their craft; but the experience of each one is different, and nothing really matters except the actual momentary contact between actor and audience which draws the performance through its appointed action from beginning to end. At the close of each performance the play is set aside, for all the world like a Punch and Judy show or the toy theatre of one's childhood; and each time it is taken up again it seems, even in a long run, comparatively fresh, waiting to be fashioned anew before every different audience. This continual destruction and repetition make the actor's work fascinating, though it must always be ephemeral and often monotonous. The unending conflict in the player's mind as he tries to judge the standard of his work, wondering whether to trust in himself, in critics, in friends or in strangers, all this is bound to make it a disheartening and unsatisfactory business.

I have frequently envied painters, writers, critics. I have thought how happy they must be to do their work in private, at home, unkempt and unobserved, able to destroy or renew or improve their creations at will, to judge them objectively in their unfinished state, to watch their gradual development, and to admire their past achievements ranged in their bookshelves or hung upon their walls. I have often wondered how these artists would face the routine of the actor, which demands not only that he shall create a fine piece of work but that he shall repeat it with unfaltering love and care for perhaps three hundred performances on end. I have often wished I were able to rise in the middle of the night, switch on the light, and examine some previous performance of mine calmly and dispassionately as I looked at it standing on the mantelpiece.

In writing this book I have experienced for the first time some few of the trials and anxieties of authorship, but now that I have finished it I feel little urge to penetrate deeper into the mysteries of the writer's craft. I am happier to return to the theatre, where nothing tangible remains to reproach me for bad work or carelessness, and where there is always tomorrow's audience and tomorrow's inspiration which may yet, I hope, surprise me into doing my very best.

SUPPLEMENT TO FIRST AND SECOND EDITIONS: 1937–1952

My two seasons at the Old Vic in 1929–30 had given me confidence in myself and a new respect for integrity and teamwork. The untiring example set by Lillian Baylis was never more modestly and faithfully followed in that theatre than by Harcourt Williams, whose simplicity and singleness of mind enabled him to guide us all in the way we should go, despite severe limitations of time and money. Trained by Benson and coached by Ellen Terry, he combined the new ideals of Poel, Craig and Granville-Barker with the best traditions of the theatre that preceded them—the theatre of Irving, Tree and Alexander—and so linked in his work the most valuable lessons of both generations. I had the inestimable opportunity of justifying his belief in me as an actor, and, after a little while, he began to encourage me to contribute ideas to the productions. We collaborated in the original Sunday-night performances of *Richard of Bordeaux*, and from that time onwards I began to work at directing with even greater enthusiasm than at acting.

The character parts which I played in my Old Vic seasons—Macbeth, Hotspur, Antony, Malvolio, Prospero and Lear—were very valuable exercises, for they enabled me to practise a considerable amount of impersonation and also developed my vocal range. I was thus, on the whole, better equipped for a variety of different kinds of work after I left the Vic, though the highly-strung, neurotic rôles for which I was still being cast at this time brought me more noticeably before the public during the next ten years. I was fortunate in appearing in several plays in which there were very good parts of this kind. Hamlet and young Schindler in *Musical Chairs* were basically not so very dissimilar, and in the latter play I was able to use my experience in Chekhov to some advantage.

In playing these very tense emotional parts, however I worked under an almost unbearable physical strain, trying to project myself with a nervous realism that exhausted me continually, especially in long runs. *Richard of Bordeaux* might seem, on first reading, to be simply another variation on the same theme, but actually it was not so. The lightness of the style, the economy of dialogue, the ageing and development of the character of Richard from scene to scene, and, above all, the humour of the part, made it infinitely easier, more attractive and more rewarding to the actor than Shakespeare's Richard, who carries such a load of exquisite (but utterly humourless) cadenzas in a stream of unrelieved self-pitying monotony. In *Richard of Bordeaux*, too, I began to gain confidence in my abilities for casting, directing other players, and generally ordering the stage. The arrangement of scene changes, grouping and lighting delighted me, and I was fortunate besides in finding an admirable cast of actors and actresses to work on such an original and charming play, which needed an acting style combining the best qualities of romantic melodrama and modern comedy. The productions of *Hamlet* and *Romeo and Juliet* which followed not only gave me further opportunities of testing my powers as actor-director, but also brought me into contact with many who were—or have since become—outstanding players: notably Edith Evans, Peggy Ashcroft, Gwen Ffrangcon Davies, Léon Quartermaine, Laurence Olivier, Ralph Richardson and Alec Guinness. I was also engaged to direct plays (in which I did not act myself) by Somerset Maugham, Rodney Ackland, Emlyn Williams and others, and I experimented for the first time in modern realistic work. *The Old Ladies*, with Mary Jerrold, Jean Cadell and Edith Evans, was, I think, my best production at the time in this new field.

Although I did not satisfy the critics greatly either as Mercutio, as Noah (in Obey's play), as the schoolmaster in *The Maitlands* of Ronald Mackenzie, or as Trigórin in *The Seagull*, yet these were all experiments somewhat away from my usual run of parts, and I learnt much from playing them. For I foresaw the time not far distant when it would be necessary to find a new line for myself, since I seemed to have already exploited to the full the pangs of hysterical youth. On my return to London in 1937 (after I had acted Hamlet for six months in New York) I had proof that these instincts of mine were not at fault, for I unwisely chose to reappear as a romantic half-mad princeling—the lost Dauphin of the Temple

—in a play specially written for me by Emlyn Williams and directed jointly by us both. It proved a failure, though in manuscript it had seemed to provide us both with excellent parts and a number of effective scenes and situations. The withdrawal of this play after such a short time decided me to back my own judgement and go into management for a year with four classic revivals.

This season in management was a financial success, although the four productions had each of them to be paid for in advance before I knew whether the current play would show a profit. It is interesting to examine the budget of this season, only fifteen years ago. The most expensive production cost £2,200 (*Three Sisters*), the least expensive £1,700, and of the four plays presented only the Chekhov was a very great success. Each play only ran from eight to ten weeks and yet the final results were on the credit side. Such a programme today would be out of the question. It is impossible to stage a costume play in 1952 for less than £10,000, and, in addition to this sum, overheads would be four or five times greater than in 1937.

I was tired at the end of this energetic period, in which I had acted four big parts and directed two of the plays myself, as well as undertaking the extra burden of management—so, when I was offered a large salary to act in *Dear Octopus* (with Marie Tempest) I accepted the part, being also anxious for once to appear in modern clothes, though the character was not a very interesting one. The play opened on the night of the Munich pact, and, despite the anxieties of the time, was a huge success. I had arranged to leave the cast after nine months, and was rehearsing the part of Maxim de Winter in *Rebecca* (played eventually by the late Owen Nares) on the morning war was declared. The theatres in London closed and the play was shelved. Meanwhile I hastily got together a revival of *The Importance of Being Earnest* (which I had given for charity matinées a few months earlier), and this production toured successfully and afterwards played to full houses in London. I then returned for a short season to the Old Vic, playing King Lear and Prospero, rehearsing the former part for ten days with Granville-Barker who came over from Paris to help us. This was my only practical experience of the work of this great director, though we met and corresponded occasionally for some ten years before this time. His example was so powerful that I unhesitatingly consider him to have been the strongest influence I have known in the theatre, and his absence from it for the last twenty-five years of his life the most tragic loss our stage has suffered. As we laboured at the production of *Lear* during those fateful spring days of 1940, with Granville-Barker's masterly hand to guide us, the news-posters outside the Old Vic announced the fall of France. The fine company was disbanded soon after, and the Vic was closed. Shortly after the theatre was badly bombed and did not reopen till 1950.

The War years passed slowly, with endless difficulties of organization, makeshifts and emergency measures, but I was fortunate indeed in the quality of the artists who continued to appear with me and the standard of production maintained by H. M. Tennent, under whose management I worked from 1939 until 1950. Barrie's *Dear Brutus* and *Macbeth* were, I feel, more to my credit as productions than for the performances I gave in them, yet both plays ran for nearly a year in London and on tour. The choice of Congreve's *Love for Love* in 1943 was a fortunate one, and it was played continuously for more than a year. Rex Whistler, whose exquisite décor for this production was almost the last work he gave to the theatre he served so brilliantly, was killed in action in France during the run of the play—an irreparable loss.

Hoping to exploit the talents of the fine company working with me in *Love for Love*, I tried another experiment of four plays (in repertory, with a change of programme from night to night) in 1944 at the Haymarket Theatre. The choice of plays was perhaps not altogether happy, though *The Duchess of Malfi* was, I think, a bold experiment; although, ironically, I was rather against it at first, it was certainly the most interesting production. But somehow I lacked the necessary enthusiasm and inspiration to make the season a real success. I even found little pleasure in my favourite part of Hamlet—feeling confused and uncertain after so many previous productions with different directors. However, I left shortly after this on a tour of the Far East, when I acted *Hamlet* and Coward's *Blithe Spirit* to troops in India, Ceylon, Singapore and Egypt, and returned in 1946 to play Raskolnikov in Rodney Ackland's version of *Crime and Punishment* with Edith Evans. In this Anthony Quayle made a success as director, and, as he had acted in my companies before the War, we renewed a happy association which was to lead to my season at Stratford-on-Avon in 1950, where he had become director of the Memorial Theatre.

At the beginning of 1947 I took *The Importance of Being Earnest* and

Love for Love to New York for a limited season. The first play was enormously successful, the second less so. I remained in New York for another six months to work with American companies for the first time, when I directed *Medea* for Judith Anderson, and played the ungrateful part of Jason for the first eight weeks of the run. Thanks to Miss Anderson's performance the play was a great hit, though my work in it was not much liked, and when I directed it again in England it failed.

Crime and Punishment, which I persuaded my American management to put on for me after I left *Medea*, with Komisarjevsky directing, was also a failure in New York. On my return to London I did not act for eight months—the first time in my career that I have ever had such a long period of inactivity. My luck seemed to be out for the time being, for I chose to reappear in a revival of St. John Hankin's *Return of the Prodigal*, with décor by Cecil Beaton and a fine cast headed by Sybil Thorndike. But this proved a disappointment—to the critics, the public, and, I need hardly add, to the cast and management as well.

The Lady's Not For Burning had already been commissioned and put on by Alec Clunes at the Arts Theatre while I was in America. I did not see the production, nor had I read the notices; but hearing from many sources of the quality of the play, I was lucky enough to obtain a chance to read it, and was immediately charmed and fascinated by it. It was bought for me by H. M. Tennent, but the production was delayed by the commitments of Pamela Brown (who was acting elsewhere), since the author and I both thought her engagement essential to the success of the play. This venture, which triumphed equally in London and New York, gave me enormous satisfaction. The work of Oliver Messel, who designed the décor, and the acting of a most happily chosen cast, gave me the opportunity of working, both as director and actor, in a new and exciting medium, and I shall always be proud of the result. I regained some lost prestige, and recovered confidence and enthusiasm. This was further enhanced by my work with Peter Brook in *Measure for Measure*, the play with which I opened at Stratford in 1950. Here too I played Cassius for the first time, as well as Lear (my third attempt, with intervals of ten years between each production), and revived my happy associations with Peggy Ashcroft, Gwen Ffrangcon Davies and Léon Quartermaine. While playing the Fry play the year before, I had also directed Anthony Quayle and Diana Wynyard in *Much Ado About Nothing* at the Stratford Theatre, and this production I repeated there in the 1950 season, with Peggy Ashcroft as Beatrice and myself as Benedick.

After a six-month season in America of *The Lady's Not For Burning*, I returned to play Leontes in *The Winter's Tale* with Diana Wynyard and Flora Robson at the Phoenix Theatre, and this production (by Peter Brook), followed by my own *Much Ado About Nothing*, broke records for both these plays in London.

Since 1933, when I first directed a play in which I was acting myself (*Richard of Bordeaux*), I have been repeatedly advised by many people to avoid the heavy responsibility of combining the task of actor and producer. Yet, whenever I have undertaken the double burden, provided there has been plenty of time to work at the production (both in rehearsal and on tour) before coming in to London, I have found the result to be reasonably successful. The actors in these productions of mine have shown great patience and restraint—for I work very broadly at first, suggesting and inventing business and movement of all kinds (from which I trust them to select to their advantage), and experimenting and changing continually from one day to another. My own performance is at first necessarily tentative and lacking in concentrated sureness of attack, for my mind in the first few weeks is busy with details of lighting, movement, and the performances of my fellow players. Yet from these muddled and clumsy sketches I have achieved a number of productions of considerable style and finish, and I have found that so long as the preliminary work on a play from the practical point of view—that is, the planning of the scenery, costumes, music and the technical details of presentation—has been thoroughly and efficiently carried out beforehand, it is permissible to shape the acting and movement (with many false starts, corrections and revisions) as the potential abilities of the cast and the holding power of the play itself develop in rehearsal and performance.

I have noticed, in books written by actors and actresses about themselves, that the later chapters are inclined to deteriorate into a bald list of plays and parts, and consequently lack interest for the reader. This is hardly to be wondered at. A professional critic can write more or less objectively about the contemporary theatre. Indeed, it is his business to do so. The professional player cannot. He can look back on the early years of his career with some measure of detachment, but he cannot write with any sort of discrimination about the people with whom he is working every day. Some of them are more, some less successful than himself. To praise or criticize one's contemporaries is an impertinence, and one can neither see one's own work nor judge it with any kind of impartiality.

The theatre in London, as everywhere else, has changed enormously in the fifty-odd years during which I have worked in it. But changes, though far-reaching, are subtle and gradual, the trend of things difficult to summarize in a few sentences. Owing to various circumstances, some of chance and some of choice, I believe I have had some influence in reviving the popularity of the classics. This has been of value, I think, at a time when a dearth of contemporary playwrights would have otherwise given the best players of our time a very limited field in which to display their talents, and deprived the public of seeing them in the great parts which have always been the test of the leading actors and actresses of past generations. Working in my early days in many classic revivals, in repertory and at the Old Vic, I acquired a taste for Shakespeare, Congreve, Wilde and Chekhov (though not for Ibsen or Shaw), and dreamed of ways to stage them, and I determined then that if I ever reached the position in which I had the power to decide what plays I would direct and act in, then certain plays of those authors would be my first consideration.

Between 1930 and 1944 I achieved my ambition: besides creating three or four fine parts in plays by modern authors, I took part as actor and director in revivals—most of them successful—of nine or ten of my favourite classical plays. But by the close of the Second World War I had reached the end of this list, compiled so many years before, and I found myself tired, empty of ideas, less adventurous, more apprehensive of choosing badly.

Abroad, when actors have achieved a successful classical performance, they seldom play it for a long run, but alternate it with several other parts, gradually creating a repertoire of half a dozen contrasting plays, which they are able to repeat over a number of years, and which continue to stand them in good stead for foreign tours and revivals until they are too old to play them any longer. At the end of the last century Irving had created such a repertoire and continued playing it (until his stores were burnt), and even in my own time, as I have said elsewhere, Fred Terry and Martin Harvey still toured the provinces with their successes of thirty years before.

To my mind, the economic conditions of today make such a programme, though superficially an easy and attractive one for a leading actor, most difficult, if not impossible. I am not prepared to revive old successes without an equally good company and very full and careful rehearsals. Often one needs to take more pains than before. The excitement of the first conception, evolving slowly, and gradually coming to completion, with everyone concerned contributing their enthusiasm, is hard to recapture with a set prompt book. Preconceived results are death to spontaneity and inspiration. It is very hard to cast a number of plays adequately from the same company of actors without several parts being miscast. Deliberate compromise is far more damaging in the theatre than the compromise of emergency, which may justify itself at a critical moment in a new production but seems wilfully perverse when the impulse is no longer the original one. One must move on, find a new line, tackle different problems, act in the plays of new authors, beware of repeating one's effects, resist the temptation to imitate one's youthful performances without the youthful instinct which gave them vividness and life.

Ours is a paradoxical profession. On the one hand I enjoy the punctual routine of a successful run, the security of a steady salary, the nightly exercise and experiment of my craft. On the other I love the unexpected, the manuscript that appears suddenly out of the blue and sets my imagination racing off in a new direction, the making of plans far ahead, casting, discussing possible schemes of production with designers and musicians, the uncertainty of the future.

In some ways it might be pleasant to become an actor-manager, to be host in one's own theatre, with a permanent company and a settled policy—some ideal five-year plan of classic repertory alternating with modern work—and of course I have often hoped for this. But the financial organization of such a scheme is an added burden. I have no talent for it, and in actual practice I dread the responsibility of committing myself for more than a few months ahead, lest my own enthusiasm may wane before I have completed my task, and so bring the whole project to disaster. I do not believe in commissioning authors to write plays to measure for me, even if there were authors available and willing to do so. If a new play I have read appeals to me as a play, I like to direct it, or act a part in it if I think there is one that will suit me. There are many players with whom I enjoy directing and acting, but I think we work better together if we are not together for too long. I have no 'theory' of production or acting, but I believe a certain kind of play needs a certain kind of playing which rarely suits the capacities of a group of actors, however talented, who have just been playing a different kind of play. Besides, one cannot expect young players who make conspicuous successes in smaller parts not to become restive and move on to more ambitious work. The cinema, radio and television continually rob the theatre of writers as well as actors. The overheads and production expenses mount with terrifying and increasing regularity, while the money taken at the box-office cannot exceed the existing capacity of the theatres. One's duty to a new author and to the management obliges one to contract oneself to appear in a successful play for six or eight months at least, in order to repay its initial cost and make a profit. One may therefore be bound by success to a long period of comparatively monotonous security, or alternatively find oneself completely at a loss for a new play. After acting in the great classics it is more than ever difficult to find the suitable modern part in which one may display some range. One may disappoint the public and do the author no good service by appearing in an unsuitable modern play. It is tempting to fall back on old successes, but I do not believe this is the way to develop one's powers.

I hope in the years to come to make some more interesting experiments as a director, to work with designers and actors that I admire, to discover new talent, and to act myself when I can find a part. The line of my career has developed luckily for me hitherto, but I do not think I have ever been able to see clearly the way that I was going. Perhaps I should have had a duller time if I had planned more practically, though perhaps, on the other hand, I might have worked to a more constructive pattern, building a company or making a more definite contribution in a single direction. But the child in me (as I believe in many actors) still longs for great days, unlooked-for surprises, sudden and unexpected developments. Without the stimulus of such uncertainties I believe I should find the theatre a dull and drab professional business, instead of the magical absorbing hobby that, to my own continual amazement, it still remains for me today.

JOHN GIELGUD

Chronological Table of Parts and Productions

1921			
Nov	Old Vic	*Henry V*	Herald
1922			
Mar	Old Vic	*Peer Gynt*	Walk on
Mar	Old Vic	*King Lear*	Walk on
Apr	Old Vic	*Wat Tyler*	Walk on
Sept	Tour	*The Wheel*	Lieut. Manners, A.S.M. and understudy
1923			
May	Regent	*The Insect Play*	White Butterfly
June	Regent	*Robert E. Lee*	Aide de Camp, understudy
Dec	Comedy	*Charley's Aunt*	Charley
1924			
Jan	Oxford Playhouse	*Captain Brassbound's Conversion*	Johnson
Jan	Oxford Playhouse	*Love for Love*	Valentine
Feb	Oxford Playhouse	*Mr Pim Passes By*	Brian Strange
Feb	Oxford Playhouse	*She Stoops to Conquer*	Young Marlow
Feb	Oxford Playhouse	*Monna Vanna*	Prinzevalle
Feb	RADA Theatre	*Romeo and Juliet*	Paris
May	Regent	*Romeo and Juliet*	Romeo
Oct	RADA Players	*The Return Half*	John Sherry

Oct	Oxford Playhouse	*Candida*	Marchbanks
Oct	Oxford Playhouse	*Deirdre of the Sorrows*	Naisi
Nov	Oxford Playhouse	*A Collection will be Made*	Paul Roget
Nov	Oxford Playhouse	*Everybody's Husband*	A Domino
Nov	Oxford Playhouse	*The Cradle Song*	Antonio
Nov	Oxford Playhouse	*John Gabriel Borkman*	Erhart
Nov	Oxford Playhouse	*His Widow's Husband*	Zurita
Dec	Oxford Playhouse	*Madame Pepita*	Augusto
Dec	Film	*Who is the Man?*	Daniel
1925			
Jan	Oxford Playhouse	*A Collection will be Made*	Paul Roget
Jan	Oxford Playhouse	*Smith*	Algernon
Jan	Oxford Playhouse	*The Cherry Orchard*	Trofimov
Feb	Royalty	*The Vortex*	Understudy
Mar	Comedy	*The Vortex*	Understudy; 16 and 17 Mar & 21 Apr Nicky Lancaster
Apr	RADA Players (special perf.)	*The Nature of the Evidence*	The lover
May	The Little	*The Vortex*	Understudy
May	Aldwych (special perf.)	*The Orphan*	Castalio
May	Lyric, Hammersmith	*The Cherry Orchard*	Trofimov
May	Royalty	*The Cherry Orchard*	Trofimov
June	The Little	*The Vortex*	Nicky Lancaster
Aug	Oxford Playhouse	*The Lady from the Sea*	A Stranger
Aug	Oxford Playhouse	*The Man with a Flower in his Mouth*	Title Part
Sept	Apollo (special perf.)	*Two Gentlemen of Verona*	Valentine
Oct	The Little	*The Seagull*	Konstantin
Oct	New, Oxford (special perf.)	*Dr Faustus*	Good Angel
Dec	Prince's (special perf.)	*L'Ecole des Cocottes*	Robert
Dec	The Little	*Gloriana*	Sir John Harington
1926			
Jan	Savoy (matinées)	*The Tempest*	Ferdinand

Jan	RADA Players (special perf.)	*Sons and Fathers*	Richard Southern
Feb	Barnes Theatre	*Three Sisters*	Tuzenbach
Feb	Barnes Theatre	*Katerina*	Georg
June	Court	*Hamlet*	Rosencrantz
July	Garrick (special perf.)	*The Lady of the Camellias*	Armand
July	Court (300 Club)	*Confession*	Wilfred Marlay
Oct	New	*The Constant Nymph*	Lewis Dodd
1927			
Apr	Apollo (special perf.)	*Othello*	Cassio
June	Strand (special perf.)	*The Great God Brown*	Dion Anthony
Aug	Tour	*The Constant Nymph*	Lewis Dodd
1928			
Jan	Majestic, New York	*The Patriot*	The Tsarevich
Mar	Wyndham's (matinées)	*Ghosts*	Oswald
Apr	Arts	*Ghosts*	Oswald
June	Arts (matinées)	*Prejudice*	Jacob Slovak
June	Globe	*Holding out the Apple*	Dr Gerald Marlowe
Aug	Shaftesbury	*The Skull*	Captain Allenby
Oct	Court	*The Lady from Alfaqueque*	Felipe Rivas
Oct	Court	*Fortunato*	Alberto
Nov	Strand	*Out of the Sea*	John Martin
1929			
Jan	Arts	*The Seagull*	Konstantin
Feb	Little	*Red Dust*	Fedor
	Film	*The Clue of the New Pin*	
Mar	Prince of Wales (special perf.)	*Hunter's Moon*	Paul de Tressailles
Apr	Palace (special perf.)	*Shall We Show the Ladies?*	Captain Jennings
Apr	Garrick	*The Lady with the Lamp*	Henry Tremayne
June	Arts	*Red Sunday*	Bronstein (Trotsky)
Sept	Old Vic	*Romeo and Juliet*	Romeo
Oct	Old Vic	*Merchant of Venice*	Antonio
Oct	Old Vic	*The Imaginary Invalid*	Cléante

Nov	Old Vic	*Richard II*	Richard II
Dec	Old Vic	*A Midsummer Night's Dream*	Oberon
Dec	Prince of Wales (special perf.)	*Duaumont: or the Return of the Soldier Ulysses*	Prologue

1930

Jan	Old Vic	*Julius Caesar*	Mark Antony
Feb	Old Vic	*As You Like It*	Orlando
Feb	Old Vic	*Androcles and the Lion*	The Emperor
Mar	Old Vic	*Macbeth*	Macbeth
Apr	Old Vic	*The Man with the Flower in his Mouth*	Title Part
Apr	Old Vic	*Hamlet*	Hamlet
June	Queen's	*Hamlet*	Hamlet
July	Lyric, Hammersmith	*Importance of Being Earnest*	John Worthing
Sept	Old Vic	*Henry IV, Part I*	Hotspur
Oct	Old Vic	*The Tempest*	Prospero
Oct	Old Vic	*The Jealous Wife*	Lord Trinket
Nov	Old Vic	*Antony and Cleopatra*	Antony

1931

Jan	Sadler's Wells	*Twelfth Night*	Malvolio
Feb	Old Vic	*Arms and the Man*	Sergius
Mar	Old Vic	*Much Ado about Nothing*	Benedick
Apr	Old Vic	*King Lear*	Lear
May	His Majesty's	*The Good Companions*	Inigo Jollifant
Nov	Arts (special perf.)	*Musical Chairs*	Joseph Schindler

1932

Feb	OUDS	*Romeo and Juliet*	Director
Apr	Criterion	*Musical Chairs*	Joseph Schindler
May	Film	*Insult*	
June	Arts (special perf.)	*Richard of Bordeaux*	Richard (and director)
Sept	St Martin's	*Strange Orchestra*	Director
Oct	Film	*The Good Companions*	Inigo Jollifant
Dec	Old Vic	*Merchant of Venice*	Director

1933			
Feb	New	*Richard of Bordeaux*	Richard (and director)
Sept	Wyndham's	*Sheppey*	Director
1934			
Jan	Shaftesbury	*Spring, 1600*	Director
Apr	Tour	*Richard of Bordeaux*	
June	New	*Queen of Scots*	Director
July	Wyndham's	*The Maitlands*	Roger Maitland
Nov	New	*Hamlet*	Hamlet (and director)
1935			
Apr	New	*The Old Ladies*	Director
Apr	Tour	*Hamlet*	
July	New	*Noah*	Noah
Oct	New	*Romeo and Juliet*	Mercutio (and director)
Nov	Film	*The Secret Agent*	
Nov	New	*Romeo and Juliet*	Romeo
1936			
Feb	OUDS	*Richard II*	Director
Apr	Tour	*Romeo and Juliet*	
May	New	*The Seagull*	Trigorin
Sept	Alexandra, Toronto	*Hamlet*	Hamlet
Oct	St James's, New York	*Hamlet*	Hamlet
1937			
Feb	Tour	*Hamlet*	Hamlet
Apr	Tour	*He was Born Gay*	Mason, Producer
May	Queen's	*He was Born Gay*	Mason, Producer
Sept	Queen's	*Richard II*	Richard II (and director)
Nov	Queen's	*The School for Scandal*	Joseph Surface
1938			
Jan	Queen's	*Three Sisters*	Vershinin
Apr	Queen's	*Merchant of Venice*	Shylock (and director)
May	Ambassador's	*Spring Meeting*	Director
Aug	Tour	*Dear Octopus*	Nicholas

Sept	Queen's	*Dear Octopus*	Nicholas
1939			
Jan	Globe	*Importance of Being Earnest*	John Worthing (and director)
Apr	Globe (special perf.)	*Scandal in Assyria*	Director
May	Globe	*Rhondda Roundabout*	Director
June	Lyceum	*Hamlet*	Hamlet (and director)
July	Elsinore	*Hamlet*	Hamlet (and director)
Aug	Globe	*Importance of Being Earnest*	John Worthing (and director)
Sept	Tour	*Importance of Being Earnest*	John Worthing (and director)
1940			
Jan	Globe	*Importance of Being Earnest*	John Worthing (and director)
Mar	Haymarket	*The Beggar's Opera*	Director
Apr	Old Vic	*King Lear*	Lear
May	Old Vic	*The Tempest*	Prospero
July	ENSA and Tour	*Fumed Oak*	Henry Crow
		Hard Luck Story	Old Actor
		Hands across the Sea	Peter Gilpin
Oct	Film	*The Prime Minister*	Disraeli
1941			
Jan	Globe	*Dear Brutus*	Dearth (and director)
May	Tour	*Dear Brutus*	Dearth (and director)
Nov	Apollo	*Ducks and Drakes*	Director
1942			
Jan	Tour	*Macbeth*	Macbeth (and director)
July	Piccadilly	*Macbeth*	
Oct	Phoenix	*Importance of Being Earnest*	John Worthing (and director)
Dec	Gibraltar	ENSA Tour	
1943			
Jan	Haymarket	*Doctor's Dilemma*	Louis Dubedat

Mar	Tour	*Love for Love*	Valentine (and director)
Apr	Phoenix and Haymarket	*Love for Love*	Valentine (and director)
Oct	Westminster	*Landslide*	Director

1944

Jan	Apollo	*Cradle Song*	Director
May	Lyric	*Crisis in Heaven*	Director
June	Phoenix	*Last of Summer*	Director
July	Tour	*Hamlet*	Hamlet
Aug	Tour	*Love for Love*	Valentine (and director)
Sept	Tour	*The Circle*	Arnold Champion-Cheney
Oct	Haymarket	Repertoire Season (*Hamlet, Love for Love, The Circle*)	

1945

Jan	Haymarket	*A Midsummer Night's Dream*	Oberon
Apr	Haymarket	*Duchess of Malfi*	Ferdinand
Aug	Haymarket	*Lady Windermere's Fan*	Director
Oct	ENSA Tour of Far East	*Hamlet*	Hamlet (and director)
		Blithe Spirit	Charles

1946

Apr	Haymarket	*Importance of Being Earnest*	John Worthing (and director)
May	Tour	*Crime and Punishment*	Raskolnikoff
June	New and Globe	*Crime and Punishment*	Raskolnikoff

1947

Jan	Tour of Canada and US	*Importance of Being Earnest*	John Worthing (and director)
Mar	Royale Theatre, New York	*Importance of Being Earnest*	John Worthing (and director)
May	Tour of US	*Love for Love*	Valentine (and director)

Oct	National Theatre, N.Y.	*Medea*	Jason (and director)
Dec	National Theatre, N.Y.	*Crime and Punishment*	Raskolnikoff

1948

July	Haymarket	*The Glass Menagerie*	Director
Aug	Edinburgh Festival	*Medea*	Director
Sept	Globe	*Medea*	Director
Nov	Globe	*Return of the Prodigal*	Eustace

1949

Feb	Haymarket	*The Heiress*	Director
Mar	Tour	*The Lady's not for Burning*	Thomas Mendip (and director)
Apr	Stratford	*Much Ado about Nothing*	Director
May	Globe	*The Lady's not for Burning*	Thomas Mendip (and director)
Sept	Apollo	*Treasure Hunt*	Director

1950

Jan	Lyric, Hammersmith	*The Boy with a Cart* *Shall We Join the Ladies?*	Director
Mar	Stratford	*Measure for Measure*	Angelo
May	Stratford	*Julius Caesar*	Cassius
June	Stratford	*Much Ado about Nothing*	Benedick (and director)
July	Stratford	*King Lear*	Lear

1951

Jan	Royale, N.Y.	*The Lady's not for Burning*	Thomas Mendip (and director)
June	Brighton	*The Winter's Tale*	Leontes
Aug	Edinburgh Festival	*The Winter's Tale*	Leontes
Sept	Phoenix	*The Winter's Tale*	Leontes

1952			
Jan	Phoenix	*Much Ado about Nothing*	Benedick (and director)
	Stratford	*Macbeth*	Director
Aug	Film	*Julius Caesar*	Cassius
Dec	Lyric, Hammersmith	*Richard II*	Director
1953			
Feb	Lyric, Hammersmith	*The Way of the World*	Mirabell (and director)
May	Lyric, Hammersmith	*Venice Preserv'd*	Jaffier (and director)
July	Bulawayo	*Richard II*	Richard II (and director)
Oct	Tour	*A Day by the Sea*	Julian Anson
Nov	Haymarket	*A Day by the Sea*	Julian Anson
Dec	Brighton	*Charley's Aunt*	Director
1954			
Feb	New	*Charley's Aunt*	Director
May	Lyric, Hammersmith	*The Cherry Orchard*	Director
1955			
Apr	Stratford	*Twelfth Night*	Director
June	Brighton	*King Lear*	Lear
June	European Tour	*King Lear*	Lear
July	Palace	*Much Ado about Nothing*	Benedick (and director)
July	Palace	*King Lear*	Lear
Aug	Film	*Round the World in Eighty Days*	Foster
Sept	European Tour	*King Lear* and *Much Ado*	
Dec	Film	*Richard III*	Clarence
1956			
Apr	Haymarket	*The Chalk Garden*	Director
	Film	*The Barretts of Wimpole Street*	Mr Barrett
Sept	Tour	*Nude with Violin*	Sebastian (and director)

Nov	Globe	*Nude with Violin*	Sebastian (and co-director)
	Film	*St Joan*	Warwick
1957			
June	Covent Garden	*The Trojans*	Director
Aug	Stratford	*The Tempest*	Prospero
Sept	Edinburgh Festival	*The Ages of Man*	
Sept	Tour	*The Ages of Man*	
Dec	Drury Lane	*The Tempest*	Prospero
1958			
Jan	Brighton	*The Potting Shed*	James Callifer
Feb	Globe	*The Potting Shed*	James Callifer
Apr	Globe	*Variation on a Theme*	Director
May	Old Vic	*Henry VIII*	Wolsey
June	Cambridge	*Five Finger Exercise*	Director
Sept	Tour of Canada and US	*The Ages of Man*	
Dec	46th Street Theatre, N.Y.	*The Ages of Man*	
1959			
Mar	TV	*A Day by the Sea*	Julian Anson
Apr	CBS TV	*The Browning Version*	Andrew Crocker Harris
May	Tour	*The Complaisant Lover*	Director
June	Globe	*The Complaisant Lover*	
July	Queen's	*The Ages of Man*	
Sept	US Tour	*Much Ado about Nothing*	Director
Dec	Music Box, New York	*Five Finger Exercise*	Director
1960			
Sept	Phoenix	*The Last Joke*	Prince Ferdinand Cavanati

1961			
Feb	Covent Garden	*A Midsummer Night's Dream*	Director
Mar	ANTA Theatre, New York	*Big Fish, Little Fish*	Director
June	Globe	*Dazzling Prospect*	Director
Oct	Stratford	*Othello*	Othello
Dec	Aldwych	*The Cherry Orchard*	Gaev
1962			
Apr	Haymarket	*The School for Scandal*	Director
Oct	Haymarket	*The School for Scandal*	Joseph Surface (and director)
Dec	Majestic, New York	*The School for Scandal*	Joseph Surface (and director)
1963			
Jan	Majestic, New York	*The Ages of Man*	
June	Tour	*The Ides of March*	Caesar (and co-director)
Aug	Haymarket	*The Ides of March*	Caesar (and co-director)
Aug	TV	*The Rehearsal*	The Count
Sept	Film	*Becket*	Louis VII
1964			
Apr	Lunt-Fontanne, New York	*Hamlet*	Director
May	World Tour	*The Ages of Man*	
Aug	Film	*The Loved One*	Sir Francis Hinsley
Oct	Film	*Chimes at Midnight*	Henry IV
Dec	Billy Rose, New York	*Tiny Alice*	Julian
1965			
Aug	Tour	*Ivanov*	Ivanov (and director)
Sept	Phoenix	*Ivanov*	Ivanov (and director)
1966			
Mar	US Tour	*Ivanov*	Ivanov (and director)
May	Shubert Theatre, N.Y.	*Ivanov*	Ivanov (and director)

July	US TV	*The Love Song of Barney Kempinski*	
Aug	BBC TV	*Alice in Wonderland*	Mock Turtle
Aug	BBC TV	*The Mayfly and the Frog*	Gabriel Kantara
1967			
Jan	US Tour	*The Ages of Man*	
Feb	Film	*Assignment to Kill*	
Mar	BBC TV	*From Chekhov with Love*	Chekhov
Apr	Film	*Mr Sebastian*	Head of British Intelligence
Apr	Film	*The Charge of the Light Brigade*	Lord Raglan
Oct	Tour	*Half Way Up The Tree*	Director
Nov	Queen's	*Half Way Up The Tree*	Director
Nov	Old Vic (NT)	*Tartuffe*	Orgon
1968			
Jan	Film	*The Shoes of the Fisherman*	The Pope
Feb	BBC TV	*St Joan*	Inquisitor
Mar	Old Vic (NT)	*Oedipus*	Oedipus
Apr	Film	*Oh! What a Lovely War*	Count Berchtold
Aug	Coliseum	*Don Giovanni*	Director
Oct	Apollo	*40 Years On*	Headmaster
1969			
Apr	BBC TV	*In Good King Charles's Golden Days*	King Charles
Apr	BBC TV	*Conversation at Night*	The Writer
June	Film	*Julius Caesar*	Caesar
Oct	Film	*Eagle in a Cage*	Lord Sissal
1970			
Jan	Lyric	*The Battle of Shrivings*	Sir Gideon Petrie
Apr	BBC TV	*Hassan*	The Caliph
May	ATV	*Hamlet*	Ghost

June	Royal Court	*Home*	Harry
Nov	Morosco, New York	*Home*	Harry
1971			
July	Chichester	*Caesar and Cleopatra*	Caesar
1972			
Mar	Royal Court	*Veterans*	Sir Geoffrey Kendle
Mar	Film	*Lost Horizon*	Chang
Aug	Queen's	*Private Lives*	Director
1973			
July	Albery	*The Constant Wife*	Director
Sept	Film	*Eleven Harrowhouse*	Meecham
Oct	ATV	*Edward VII*	Disraeli
1974			
Jan	Film	*Gold*	Farrell
Mar	Old Vic (NT)	*The Tempest*	Prospero
Apr	Film	*Murder on the Orient Express*	Beddoes
July	Film	*The Life of Galileo*	Cardinal
Aug	Royal Court	*Bingo*	Shakespeare
Sept	US	*Private Lives*	Director
Nov	Royal, York	*Paradise Lost*	Milton
Dec	US	*The Constant Wife*	Director
1975			
June	Albery	*The Gay Lord Quex*	Director
July	Old Vic (NT)	*No Man's Land*	Spooner
Oct	Film	*Aces High*	Headmaster
1976			
Jan	Film	*Caesar and Cleopatra*	Caesar
Apr	National Theatre (Lyttelton)	*No Man's Land*	Spooner
Apr	Film	*Joseph Andrews*	Doctor
May	Film	*Providence*	Clive
July	Film	*A Portrait of the Artist as a Young Man*	Preacher

Aug	Film	*Caligua*	Nerva
Nov	Longacre, New York	*No Man's Land*	Spooner
1977			
Mar	National Theatre (Olivier)	*Julius Caesar*	Caesar
Apr	National Theatre (Olivier)	*Volpone*	Sir Politic Would-Be
Nov	Granada TV	*No Man's Land*	Spooner
Nov	National Theatre (Cottesloe)	*Half-Life*	Sir Noel Cunliffe
Dec	BBC Radio	*Romeo and Juliet*	Chorus
1978			
Jan	BBC TV	*Richard II*	John of Gaunt
Feb	BBC TV	*The Cherry Orchard*	Gaev
Mar	Duke of York's	*Half-Life*	Sir Noel Cunliffe
June	Film	*Les Misérables*	Valjean's father
Sept	TV	*The Dame of Sark*	Butler
Sept	Records	*The Ages of Man*	
1979			
May	Film	*The Conductor*	Title role
May	Film	*Omar Mukhtar*	Sheikh
June	Film	*The Human Factor*	Brigadier Tomlinson
Sept	Film	*The Elephant Man*	Carr Gomm
Oct	Anglia TV	*The Parson's Pleasure*	Clergyman
Dec	Film	*Sphinx*	Abdu
1980			
Feb	Granada TV	*Brideshead Revisited*	Edward Ryder
	Film	*The Formula*	Dr Esau
Apr	Film	*Chariots of Fire*	Master of Trinity
May	Film	*Priest of Love*	Herbert G. Muskett
June	Film	*Arthur*	Hobson
Sept	LWTV	*Seven Dials Mystery*	Marquis of Caterham
1981			
Jan	Film	*Wagner*	Counsellor to King Ludwig

Apr	Film	*Marco Polo*	Doge
July	BBC TV	*The Critic*	Lord Burleigh
Oct	Film	*Hunchback of Notre Dame*	Torturer
Nov	Film	*Inside the Third Reich*	Speer's Father
1982			
Mar	Film	*Buddenbrooks*	Narrator
July	Film	*The Wicked Lady*	Hogarth
July	Film	*The Vatican Pimpernel*	Pope Pacelli
Aug	Film	*Invitation to a Wedding*	Texan Evangelist
Nov	Film	*Scandalous*	Uncle Willie
1983			
Apr	HTV	*The Master of Ballantrae*	Lord Dumsdeer
Sept	Film	*The Shooting Party*	Cardew
1983			
	Thames TV	*Six Centuries of Verse*	
1984			
	Film	*Leave All Fair*	John Middleton Murry
	Film	*Plenty*	Leonard Darwin
	Yorkshire TV	*Romance on the Orient Express*	Charles Woodward
1986			
	ABC TV	*War and Remembrance*	Aaron Jastrow
	BBC Radio	*Gordon the Escapist*	
	BBC TV	*Quartermain's Terms*	Eddie Loomis
	HTV	*The Canterville Ghost*	Sir Simon du Canterville

INDEX